THE PROBLEM OF ICELANDIC SAGA ORIGINS

YALE GERMANIC STUDIES, I

KONSTANTIN REICHARDT, EDITOR

The Problem of Icelandic Saga Origins

A Historical Survey by
Theodore M. Andersson

New Haven and London, Yale University Press, 1964

Preface

The present study was undertaken several years ago for the purpose of providing the student of Germanic or medieval literature with a convenient synopsis of the controversy surrounding the origins of the Icelandic family sagas. In the meantime the need has become less acute. Marco Scovazzi's *La Saga di Hrafnkell e il Problema delle Saghe Islandesi* (1960) compiles much of the material reviewed in Chapters 3 and 4, in addition to some material not included here, and gives an abundance of key quotations. Paul Schach has provided a translation (with bibliographical preface and notes) of Peter Hallberg's introduction to the saga under the title *The Icelandic Saga* (1962) and has promised a review of research in Old Norse literature since 1930 to appear in a Modern Language Association handbook for students in medieval literature. Nonetheless it is hoped that this survey will still prove useful since, aside from the fact that Italian and English are not always interchangeable languages, it spans a longer period and is more synthetic in form than Scovazzi's book and more exclusively concerned with the central problem of origins than Hallberg's general essay. Unlike the latter it is not intended as an introduction to the saga but presupposes some familiarity with the sagas themselves and the reading of such books as Liestøl's *The Origin of the Icelandic Family Sagas* and Turville-Petre's *Origins of Icelandic Literature*. Especially Chapter 5 and Appendix 2 assume more than casual interest. At the same time the book is meant as an aid to the nonspecialist without a knowledge of the Scandinavian languages. All Scandinavian quotations in the text have therefore been translated and the original relegated to a foot-note if it was thought to serve some purpose. The bibliography, though it necessarily includes Scandinavian titles, is likewise conceived as an initial guide to the most important literature.

In its original form this book was submitted to Yale University as a doctoral thesis in 1960. Chapters 1 to 3 have been somewhat expanded; Chapter 5 is a reorganized and abbreviated summary of the conclusions arrived at in the dissertation; Chapter 4 and Appendix 2 are virtually unchanged.

The thesis was proposed and directed by Professor Konstantin Reichardt, to whose learning and long-standing kindness I am greatly indebted. It is also a pleasure to acknowledge the good advice of my colleague, Joachim Bumke. Most particularly I wish to thank my wife, Ellen, who survived many hours of typing and painstaking editing with unruffled spirits.

T. M. A.

Cambridge, Massachusetts
October 1963

Contents

I

From Humanism to the Enlightenment

A survey of modern saga scholarship might properly begin with P. E. Müller's commanding synthesis in the year 1813, but such a point of departure would have the disadvantage of suggesting that Bishop Müller's work broke new ground, when in fact it was only a rejoinder in a long-standing debate. What Müller undertook was not a pioneering enterprise but a systematic defense of the sagas against certain German scholars who had issued a blanket challenge to their historicity. The ideas from which he molded his influential theory were in some cases the legacy of many decades and can be retraced to precursors as early as the seventeenth century. For the sake of completeness and in order to clarify Müller's antecedents it is therefore well to review these early contributors, even though their work is only of antiquarian interest. A dipping into the prehistory of saga research finds special justification in that, unlike most prehistories, it is not a bottomless well and can be plumbed accurately. Saga study began in the early seventeenth century, when, after a prolonged eclipse, Norse literature was rediscovered and scrutinized for the first time by an alien generation.

The fact that early research was inspired by the national historiography which swept northern Europe in the wake of Italian humanism throws much light on the whole evolution of saga studies. The movement was particularly topical in Scandinavia, where a lively historical feud between Denmark and Sweden focused interest on national achievements. The controversy was precipitated by Albert

I

Krantz's *Chronica Regnorum Aquilonarium* (completed and available in 1504, printed in 1546), which portrayed the relative glories of the two realms in a manner not flattering to Swedish national pride. In rebuttal Johannes Magnus composed his *Historia de Omnibus Gothorum Sueonumque Regibus* (completed in 1540, printed in 1554), in which he far outstripped the claims of Gothic ancestry advanced in the previous century and constructed for Sweden a prehistory which brooked no rival. Denmark, relegated by Johannes Magnus to the position of a satellite nation set up in favor of a Swedish prince (Saxo's eponymous King Dan!), found herself constrained, under royal auspices, to reply with a *Refutatio Calumniarum Johannis Magni*.[1] Thus the stage was set for a new interest in national antiquities and a revival of Norse studies. The disputants soon cast about for undiscovered and decisive evidence with which to argue their past pre-eminence and found a very promising source of such evidence in the sagas. The old codices, dispersed in Iceland and nearly forgotten in the rest of Scandinavia, were gathered to satisfy a historical craving. This meant that the interpretation of the newly acquired manuscripts was subject to a historical bias that was all-exclusive and from which scholars were unable to free themselves for three hundred years. The value of the sagas as cultural documents was ignored until the advent of a new historical orientation in the eighteenth century, and the literary aspects went unheeded until the Norse renascence began to open the eyes of writers to Old Norse literature as form and mythology. These viewpoints, so familiar to us, were entirely unknown to the scholars of the seventeenth century, who studied the sagas and conjectured on their genesis only in the light of the historical issue.

Knowledge of the Norse classics seems never to have died out entirely in Norway, from whence it had penetrated to Sweden during the Middle Ages. As early as the first half of the fourteenth century a genealogical extract of the *Historia Norvegiae* was known and amalgamated with a list of Sweden's Christian kings to form a royal line of descent reaching back into the heathen period.[2] In the fifteenth century a few Norwegian and Icelandic manuscripts entered Sweden via

1. On the growth of national history in Scandinavia see Carl S. Petersen, *Den Danske Litteratur fra Folkevandringstiden indtil Holberg* (København, 1929), pp. 380–89; Johan Nordström, *De Yverbornes Ö* (Stockholm, 1934), pp. 91–154; Gustav Löw, *Sveriges Forntid i Svensk Historieskrivning* (Stockholm, 1908–10), *1*, 50–90; Curt Weibull, "Die Auswanderung der Goten aus Schweden," *Göteborgs Kgl. Vet.– och Vitterhetssamhälles Handlingar*, 6. följden, ser. A, 6 (1958), 5.

2. Vilhelm Gödel, *Fornnorsk-Isländsk Litteratur i Sverige* (Stockholm, 1897), pp. 13–14.

the monasterial route from Bergen to Vadstena and regenerated the work of the chroniclers.[3]

This early stream did not reach Denmark, which felt that its past was vouchsafed by Saxo and which appears to have lost sight of the West Norse sources entirely during the Middle Ages. When the anti-quarian movement began to stir, it was Saxo's praise of the Ice-landers which first directed the attention of Danish scholars to the saga island. Christiern Pedersen interlarded his translation of Saxo (early sixteenth century) with supplementary material from sources which have been identified as *Heimskringla* and the longer *Óláfs saga Tryggvasonar*.[4] It would appear however that Pedersen had no manu-scripts in his own possession but obtained his extracts from some acquaintances in Norway. This assumption might explain the con-fusion which led Pedersen to ascribe the writings to Bishop Ísleifr and "an old Norwegian priest named Ari."[5] Pedersen's work was not known until 1570 when the historian Vedel had recourse to it, but in the meantime (1548) two Danish scholars, Kristian Morsing and Hans Svaning, commissioned the Norwegian Laurents Hanssön to trans-late *Heimskringla* and received at least a partial manuscript from him. About the same time a second translation was executed by Mattis Störssön. Both these works circulated in manuscript until the latter was published by Jens Mortensen in 1594.[6]

Denmark had no real notion of the wealth of literature secreted in Iceland until contact was established with the learned Arngrímur Jónsson.[7] As a young man of twenty-four Arngrímur arrived in Copen-hagen (1592) for the purpose of placing a *Brevis Commentarius de Islandia,* in which he combatted the prevalent superstitions about Ice-land and sought to promote a more accurate understanding of his

3. On Norse literature in fifteenth-century Sweden see Gödel, pp. 15–55. He mentions still extant MSS of *Þiðreks saga, Barlaams saga,* an *Óláfs saga,* the *Hirðskrá* and younger Gulaþing law plus the lost originals to Swedish chronicles and lost codices of *Trójumanna saga* and *Thomas saga* (p. 37). About the particular influence of *Þiðreks saga* on Swedish history writing see pp. 50–53.

4. Gödel, p. 58.

5. Ibid.

6. Ibid., pp. 59–63.

7. The study of this chapter in Norse literature has been greatly facilitated by Jakob Benediktsson's handsome edition of Arngrímur's works in the *Bibliotheca Arnamag-næana,* vols. 9–12 (1950–57). The discovery of Old Icelandic literature is described by Kristian Kaalund, "Den nordiske (norrøne) oldlitteraturs samling og bevaring," *Katalog over de Oldnorsk-Islandske Håndskrifter i det Store Kgl. Bibl. og i Universitetsbibl.* (København, 1900), pp. III–LXV, and briefly by Halldór Hermannsson, "Icelandic Manuscripts," *Islandica, 19* (1929). The matter has also been dealt with from alternate viewpoints in the various scholarly briefs submitted in the controversy over ownership of the Icelandic manuscripts.

country. He succeeded not only in finding a publisher for his apologia but also in contacting the foremost historians of the realm: Arild Huitfeldt, Niels Krag, and Jon Jacobsen Venusin. These men encouraged Arngrímur's historical bent and, when he returned to Iceland, he became the mediator of Icelandic sources.[8] His colleagues in Denmark regarded Iceland as an untapped reservoir of Norse history which would serve to supplement Saxo. Their hopes and expectations are expressed in a letter addressed to Arngrímur Jónsson by Niels Krag: "Please procure for us clear and reliable documents about Danish, Norwegian, Swedish, and most particularly about your own affairs. We entertain the hope of finding nowhere more dependable and truthful matter than among you, because of what Saxo wrote concerning you." [9] Arngrímur responded by sending extracts from Icelandic manuscripts, which subsidized the interest of a generation of Danish historians.[10] At the same time he continued to study and publish works on his own initiative, delving into various aspects of Icelandic history. As Jakob Benediktsson has shown, his treatment of the sources was characterized by the humanistic veneration of the written word.[11] "Even the most extravagant exaggerations and fantastic tales are accepted by him in good faith. But in this AJ shared not only the absolute trust of many foreign humanists in the written word, but also his countrymen's unshakable conviction of the truthfulness and historical authenticity of the Icelandic sagas, a conviction which, we may note in passing, has been held since by many people with better opportunities than AJ to acquire a critical sense." [12] Arngrímur justified his confidence in the sources by paraphrasing the preface to *Heimskringla*.[13] Where the Icelandic account differed from Saxo, he already stood firmly on the ground of the "Icelandic hypothesis." [14]

The first generations of Danish historians were dependent on their Icelandic sourcemen. Not even Ole Worm progressed beyond the rudiments of Old Norse and together with Stephanius frequently complained about the lack of linguistic aids, which hampered his interpretation of the new manuscripts.[15] Under these circumstances the

---

8. *Bib. Arn.*, *12*, 12.
9. *Bib. Arn.*, *11*, 102.
10. See *Ole Worm's Correspondence with Icelanders*, ed. Jakob Benediktsson, in *Bib. Arn.*, 7 (Hafniæ, 1948), "Introduction," xiii.
11. *Bib. Arn.*, *12*, 45–61.
12. Ibid., 52.
13. *Bib. Arn.*, *9*, 169, and *12*, 59.
14. *Bib. Arn.*, *12*, 58–59.
15. *Bib. Arn.*, *7*, xviii.

assimilation of sources necessary for an overall perspective progressed slowly. When Arngrímur Jónsson died in 1648, Ole Worm turned to the bishop of Skálholt, Brynjólfr Sveinsson, later the donator of the codex containing the Elder Edda. At the same time the royal historiographers employed Icelandic amanuenses in Copenhagen to translate the material as it arrived from Iceland. The most celebrated of these amanuenses were Thormod Torfaeus (Þormóður Torfason, 1636–1719) and Árni Magnússon (1663–1730), men of very different character and men whose contributions to Old Norse studies have been differently assessed by posterity.

Thormod Torfaeus came to Copenhagen in 1654 and devoted himself to a theological course of study.[16] After a brief interlude in Iceland and Norway he returned to Copenhagen and was appointed royal translator of Norse literature by Frederick III. Following a trip to Iceland in 1662 in quest of parchments he composed his first work, *Series Dynastarum Regum Daniae* (not published until 1702). In this work Torfaeus advanced the so-called "Icelandic hypothesis," a theory which championed the validity of the Icelandic historical sources to the detriment of Saxo. In conversation the young scholar was apparently able to reconcile the monarch to his heretical viewpoint and others were not slow to follow.

Torfaeus led a restless existence. Persistently in financial straits and embroiled in litigation, he emulated his literary traditions to the extent of one, possibly two, slayings. In 1682 his career at least was given a firm course when he was appointed Royal Norwegian Historian. During his remaining years of health he was occupied with a number of historical enterprises, chiefly the final edition of *Series* and his vast compilation of Icelandic sources in *Historia Rerum Norvegicarum*.

According to later lights Torfaeus' was an uncritical mind, eager to believe in the historical reliability of what he found on Icelandic parchment, but tireless in compiling his material. His *Historia Rerum Norvegicarum* is a paraphrase interspersed with direct quotations from manuscripts of very unequal value. Not only bona fide history, but also family sagas and even legendary sagas found their way undiluted into his presentation. It has been pointed out that Torfaeus himself was of a superstitious and credulous nature. His letters are replete with references to dreams and omens and testify to the readiness with which he sought out and lent ear to the genuine traditions

16. On Torfaeus see Halldór Hermannsson, "Þormóður Torfason," *Skírnir, 128* (1954), 65–94, where the older literature is listed.

which he believed to be concealed in the tales told him by the elders in the Norwegian *bygder*. Nevertheless he made an effort, probably under the urging of his younger countryman Árni Magnússon, to justify his critical standpoint.[17] The extent of Árni's contribution cannot be ascertained, but it is certain that he was Torfaeus' constant guide among the perils and pitfalls of Islandica. He once unwittingly characterized the relationship between the two men with the phlegmatic words: "It is the way of the world that some people put errors into circulation while others try then to eradicate these same errors. This keeps everyone busy."[18]

The critical essay, chapter 6 of *Series*, entitled "De Historiarum Islandicarum Fundamentis ac Auctoritate," seems characteristically to have cost Torfaeus particular effort,[19] but once formulated his vindication of the tradition on which the Icelandic sources built became canonical. He distinguishes carefully between contemporary and non-contemporary sources. The reliability of the first is beyond question and the reliability of the latter is capable of substantiation on several counts.

1. Place names: "A great many names of provinces, mountains, rivers, lakes, bays, islands, farms and other places in Scandinavia can be enumerated; from these we learn something of the origins of the names and the reasons behind them."[20]

2. The Icelandic historians had pictorial records, such as the shields decorated with mythological stories in the possession of Einarr skálaglamm (*Egils saga,* chap. 78) and Saxo's Hamlet or the wall ornaments at Hjarðarholt (*Laxdœla saga,* chap. 29).

3. There were runic records carved on wood such as those referred to in *Egils saga* (chap. 78) and *Grettis saga* (chap. 62).

4. Finally there was a rich fund of oral tradition: "People retained lays and stories by memory far better than now, and these were the most excellent epitomes of all ancient history. The Norwegians knew these very ancient matters by heart and, leaving their country, brought them along to Iceland, where they taught them to their descendants."[21]

Torfaeus attached particular importance to scaldic poetry and quoted

---

17. On the importance of Árni's cooperation see Carl S. Petersen, *Den Danske Litteratur*, p. 797, and *Árni Magnússon, Levned og Skrifter*, ed. Finnur Jónsson (København, 1930), *1*, 40–43.

18. *Levned og Skrifter, 1*, 24; Jón Helgason, *Handritaspjall* (Reykjavík, 1958), p. 113.

19. *Árni Magnússon, Brevveksling med Torfaeus*, ed. Kr. Kaalund (København, 1916), p. XVI.

20. Thormod Torfaeus, *Series Dynastarum et Regum Daniae* (Hafniae, 1702), p. 50.

21. Ibid., p. 53.

Snorri to support its value. He reasoned that in addition to the poetry itself there must have been a stock of tradition which enabled audiences to interpret the stanzas, which were "frequently so obscure, that without an interpreter they could hardly be understood by the listeners." [22] And he continues:

> But a fuller knowledge of events was necessary for the proper exposition of history. This was provided to the writers by accounts not written but transmitted orally from parents and grandparents; sons and grandsons retained them by memory and passed them on in the same way to their descendants, until finally they reached those who rescued them from oblivion with the aid of letters. Verelius is also of this opinion when he writes in his notes to *Gautreks saga ok Hrólfs* that our ancestors were not sparing in their praise of their heroes and kings and that neither at their assemblies nor on any other occasion for recreation did they cultivate other pastimes more eagerly than the reciting of their deeds; and he adds that these stories were handed down from their ancestors and were later consigned to writing.[23]

This passage is worth quoting at length to emphasize that formal oral tradition was not a hypothesis first formulated in the nineteenth century. Torfaeus ends by stressing the far-reaching travels of Icelanders, such as Halldórr Snorrason, who were able to supplement their domestic traditions with foreign sources. He concludes that the Icelandic historians "are not to be repudiated" and affixes a eulogy to the veracity which Theodricus Monachus praised in the men of Thule.

The "Prolegomena" to *Historia Rerum Norvegicarum* also contain a brief criticism of the sources, but this appears to be the work of Þorleifur Halldórsson after a stroke had disabled Torfaeus in 1706.[24] The demonstration is restricted to a review of the reliable sourcemen available to Icelandic historians, done after the manner of Snorri.

Árni Magnússon, sixteenth in line of descent from Snorri, was a man of a different stamp. His fame rests on the unparalleled library of manuscripts which he was able to amass during a lifetime of avid collecting. He wrote little but adhered to a healthy scepticism, which, as we saw, exercised a salutary influence on less critical contemporaries.

22. Ibid., p. 56.
23. Ibid., pp. 56–57.
24. Hermannsson, "Þormóður Torfason," p. 90.

Like Torfaeus, Árni Magnússon came to Copenhagen to complete his theological training. Subsequently he was attached to the antiquarian Thomas Bartholin and was ultimately appointed professor in 1694.

Whereas Torfaeus was willing to extend the reliability of an Ari or a Snorri to cover much of what he read in Icelandic sources, Árni Magnússon drew a sharp line between old and young documents, historical and legendary sagas. In a letter of 1690 he asks Torfaeus to be critical in his use of *Friðþjófs saga* and *Qrvar-Odds saga* in his book on the Orkneys: ". . . I would be very grateful to you if you would eliminate or designate as fabulous that awful story from *Friðþjófs saga* about Angantýr and Herrauðr[?], and likewise from *Qrvar-Odds saga;* indeed that spoils the whole book, which is otherwise splendid. We know for a fact that those are not Anglo-Saxon names, but rather the fiction of Icelanders, and very late fiction at that." [25] Torfaeus is as usual loath to relinquish his material and replies:

> I will take this matter under consideration and first write to Magister Iver, the dean in Sogn, and inquire about the places referred to there, such as Baldurshagi and other places, about the two barrows of Beli and Þorsteinn, to determine whether there is not some tradition among posterity about this; otherwise I see nothing fabulous in *Friðþjófs saga,* and their children and grandchildren are mentioned at length in *Gautreks saga,* and King Víkarr is very well known to Saxo and previous centuries, furthermore all their genealogies are correct. . . .[26]

One of the best accounts of Árni's critical reserve is found in a letter of September 1690:

> I have a very low opinion of *Hrólfs saga Gautrekssonar, Bósa saga, Þorsteins saga Víkingssonar, Hervarar saga, Sturlaugs saga starfsama,* and such. This is chiefly because I nowhere find the names and deeds, which they contain, referred to by trustworthy men, as is the case with most of our other sagas; that leads me to think that they were probably written in the fourteenth century, and if this is so, then it is clear what trust we can place in them [since it is hardly conceivable] that their authors should know something which Snorri, Ari fróði, etc. never heard of; the

25. *Árni Magnússon, Brevveksling med Torfaeus,* p. 33.
26. Ibid., p. 49.

diction is also such that it cannot be old. And that they were known in the time of Saxo and other ancients seems to me to be of little importance; there are plenty of such traditions in Iceland, about Gullbrá, who was supposed to live in Dalasýsla when Unnr came there, about Jóra in Jórukleif and such, that everyone believes in Iceland, while it is proven by others that they are untrue; and even if they did exist, I regard the genealogies as wrong and the events as invented. Snorri and other old authorities rejected them because they had no certain evidence about them, but those who came later wanted to write something too, as one can see from *Flateyjarbók,* which is full of nonsense, false traditions, and exaggerations; for example *Flateyjarbók* has a long tale about Þorleifr Jarlscald's enmity toward Hákon Jarl and quotes verses which he allegedly composed to mock Hákon. These are the greatest falsehoods, Þorleifr was Hákon's scald and follower as one can see in Skáldatal appended to Snorri Sturluson. . . .[27]

It is clear from these pronouncements that Árni brought to bear not only a sceptical turn of mind but also some philological precepts and an unusual standard of source criticism. He had freed himself from the practice of guaranteeing the validity of anonymous sagas by attributing them to known historians[28] and was perhaps the first to oppose the belief that Sæmundr was the author of the *Elder Edda.*[29]

It is not surprising that a man of such acid temperament took a dim view of some of the symptoms which characterized the Nordic revival in neighboring Sweden, where the saga fever raged from 1650 on.[30] Until that time there had been little interest or activity. Johannes Messenius (ca. 1579–1636) had used "Jens Mortensen's" *Heimskringla* and *Óláfs saga ins helga.*[31] The antiquarian Johannes Bureus (1568–1652) and a relative Laurentius Bureus (1623 or 1624– 65) had concerned themselves with sagas and translated portions still

27. Ibid., p. 66. For further references see pp. 224, 234, 239, 305, and 327.
28. See *Levned og Skrifter, 1,* 112, and Carl S. Petersen, *Den Danske Litteratur* p. 789.
29. *Levned og Skrifter, 1,* 108.
30. There is a diary of Olof Celsius reporting a conversation in which Árni Magnússon had sharply criticized Rudbeck's *Atlantica,* especially its blind faith in the legendary sagas: "Dhe Isländska Sagorna vare intet att bygga uppå. Isländarnas lärda seculum har varit circa an. Chr. 1000, då dhe skrefvo sant. Men seculo 1200 och 1300 togo dhe mehr och mehr af sedan dhe blefvo oroade af krijg. Når dhe intet hade mehra sant att skrifva, hade ey heller connoissance med andra folck, begynte dhe att fingera sådana atopa, som aldrig kunna skee, alt om Krigzhandlingar, gifftermåhl, frijeri och sådant mehra" (*Levned og Skrifter, 1,* 158). His letters speak the same language. See *Brevveksling med Torfaeus,* pp. 179 f., 306, 318. See also *Levned og Skrifter, 1,* 26.
31. Gödel, p. 216 and Löw, *1,* 108–28.

preserved in manuscript, but they published nothing.[32] Only in Kristina's culturally animated and book conscious Sweden did the revival begin. The collecting of manuscripts and the organization of antiquarian studies owed much to the personal initiative of the queen's sometime favorite Magnus Gabriel de la Gardie.[33] In 1652 he was able to take advantage of Danish inertia and possess himself of Stephanius' considerable library. The collection contained a number of valuable Icelandic codices, which De La Gardie later donated to the library at Uppsala and which now form the nucleus of Uppsala's Old Norse inventory. Less significant windfalls came into Swedish hands in 1658. During Charles X's lightning conquest of Denmark in that year the illustrious traitor Korfitz Ulfeldt seized and transported Jørgen Seefeldt's library as war booty. The following summer a young Icelander, Jónas Rugman, was apprehended by the Swedish fleet while bound for Copenhagen. In his possession were a few Icelandic manuscripts, some of which were of particular interest to Swedish historians, for example *Hervarar saga* and *Bósa saga*. Rugman was presently set to translating Old Norse texts. In 1662 the whole enterprise was centralized under the direction of Olof Verelius, who was appointed to a professorship in antiquities.[34] Five years later the movement acquired new impetus through the founding of the Antikvitetskollegium.

32. Gödel, pp. 217–41.

33. Ibid., pp. 82–83. On the assembling of Icelandic manuscripts in Sweden see, in addition to Gödel, Henrik Schück, *Kgl. Vitterhets Historie och Antikvitets Akademien: Dess Förhistoria och Historia* (Stockholm, 1932–44) *1; 3,* 45–118. For a short account Gun Nilsson. "Den Isländska Litteraturen i Stormaktstidens Sverige," *Scripta Islandica, 5* (1954), 19–41.

34. What was expected of Verelius and his study of the sagas is seen clearly in a letter addressed by Rudbeck to Magnus Gabriel de la Gardie in support of Verelius' installation as University Librarian. The letter is analogous to the one from Niels Krag to Arngrímur Jónsson quoted above (p. 4): "Ty E. H. Excellens wäl weet, att nu stå wåra literæ i Antiqviteterna på högsta trawet, om Swerige wil wisa sigh hafva warit det gamla hyperboreorum land som alla älsta Grekiska poeter oc Historici wetta at tala om, ok om dät Scytiska språket är det älsta, ok om alt detta skal ske, moste dett af åtskillige gamla monumenter mera ok mera bekräftas, ok att literæ oc scientiæ hooss wåra fäder för i flor hafva warit, än hooss andra folk i wärden. Ok sosom detta antiqvitatis studium wil hafva en godh tidh ok mycken lessningh, wilket inthet är allom gifvit, ingen ok gärna på sigh tager, emedan dät inthet är de pane lucrando, ty seer man huru mekta få personer i från de elsta tider in til denna dagh hafva lagt sig på det studium. Wij hafva inthet för Cristi tidh mera än den enda Diodorum Siculum. Ty sosom iagh seker är att ingen efter Verelium kommer som wil den mödan på sig taga, ok dät förståndet hafver som han, ok den Lecturam uthi wårt gamla språk ok handlingar, så lära alla de edla clenodier blifva med honom begrafne, som E. H. Excell. hafver til större delen hijt skenkt, som en kunna komma genom honom i liuset, som är Edda, Gretla, Troiomanna Saga, Olofs Tryggesons, Skaldekonsten, ok många flera. . . . Iagh slepper E. H. Excellens inthet för än E. Excellens welsignar wåra Antiqviteter genom Verelium" (in Johan Nordström, *De Yverbornes Ö,* pp. 134–35).

Moreso than in Denmark, the rise of antiquarian interest in Sweden was the corollary of a political development. The rediscovery of ancient Sweden coincided with the rise of contemporary Sweden as a European power. A belt of provinces had been thrown around the Baltic and during the Thirty Years' War Sweden became a force to be reckoned with. Her newly awakened national consciousness was a factor in the search for a glorious past, a past which the Icelandic sagas promised to illuminate. Johan Nordström has shown how Verelius used his sagas to confirm and buttress the historical speculations of his predecessors, who, motivated by national pride, identified Scandinavia as the home of the fabled Hyperboreans.[35] This serves to explain the eccentric selection of texts which he set about editing. Aside from *Óláfs saga Tryggvasonar* the first works to appear were *Hrólfs saga Gautrekssonar* and *Herrauðs saga oك Bósa,* fictional sagas from a late date but ones which were partly set in Sweden and were believed to shed light on its early history. Verelius and his followers had a blind faith in the authenticity of the Icelandic accounts. Where excessive demands were made on their credulity, they resorted to rationalization. Thus Verelius justifies the superstitious content by urging the reader to bear in mind "what horrendous sorcery prevailed here during the heathen period, so that one did not find it odd or astonishing when someone made himself invisible or changed his shape. . . . One should therefore not regard this saga as untrue when it tells of such things." [36] In general the reliability of the material was ascribed to an unbroken tradition, the current belief being that the ancient "Goths" who helped to colonize Iceland had transported their sagas with them and had maintained them just as they had existed in Sweden. Peringskiöld writes in this vein in his preface to *Heimskringla* (1697): "Thus the Swedes and Norwegians who emigrated to Iceland brought with them both our ancient language and sagas, both of which they have

35. *De Yverbornes Ö,* pp. 131–32: "Det är i Verelius' noter till hans bekanta editioner av Gautreks och Rolfs saga och av Hervararsaga, som detta lärjungeskap tydligast framträder. I flera av de omfångrikaste och i samtidens ögon förvisso mest fängslande av dessa begagnas hyperboréerlegenden till förklaring och belysning av sagornas uppgifter. . . . I bägge sagorna finner han anledningar att med en viss utförlighet anföra de skäl, som visa, att Sverige måste vara hyperboréernas land. Då det i Gautrekssagan berättas om ättestupan Gillingshammer i Västergötland, därifrån de gamla kasta sig utför och glada och lustiga 'fara till Odens,' finner Verelius trovärdigheten härav bestyrkt genom de liknande uppgifter om hyperboréernas självmord, som vi finna t. ex. hos Plinius, och söker i detta sammanhang genom en analys av Diodorus Siculus' geografiska bestämningar å ådagalägga, att dessa uppgifter måste avse förhållanden hos våra förfäder."

36. *Herrauds och Bosa Saga* (Upsaliae, 1666), in the dedication to Magnus Gabriel de la Gardie.

preserved until this very day, in the same pronunciation and dialect which is found on our ancient stones and native sagas written down of old." [37]

The historical intoxication brought about by the discovery of the sagas culminated in the imposing scheme set forth in Olof Rudbeck's *Atlantica* (1679–1702). This work was the fruition of Sweden's national precocity: "In a certain sense Johannes Magnus created Sweden's greatness; conversely Sweden's greatness created the *Atlantica*." [38] Rudbeck undertook with the ingenious but undisciplined use of biblical, classical, and Icelandic materials to equate Sweden with Plato's Atlantis, establish her as the cradle of history, and reveal the true grandeur of her antiquity.[39] The work is dedicated to Verelius and is rooted in the Icelandic revival. Rudbeck's antiquarian studies were in fact galvanized by what he believed to be classical echoes in the geography of *Hervarar saga*.[40]

We have seen Verelius' rationalization of the oral tradition behind the sagas in the quotation from Torfaeus (p. 7). Rudbeck goes into more detail.[41] He argues that oral tradition is the primary source on which the earliest writings are based. We know that Moses was one of the first to write, but even he must have acquired his information about the period from the Deluge to his own time through tradition. Similarly the Greeks and Romans composed their annals from the accounts of elders. This is clear from the frequent references to living traditions found in Herodotus, the father of all historians. Such traditions can be found among the populace of Sweden, who can neither read nor write, but whose tales correspond tolerably well to the reports of foreign writers. Elsewhere Rudbeck expresses the opinion that nowhere are traditions so well preserved among the people as in Sweden, for the (Tacitean) reason that as she is untouched by foreign rule or intercourse so her traditions are necessarily unadulterated. In dealing with the written sagas Rudbeck is not without his own standard of criticism. He states that the older the written saga is, the more value it has as a source, since, just as rumor grows, sagas can in the course of time be altered by envy, hypocrisy, or by a scribe's inaccuracy. A saga can never be corrected by a younger saga but only by contem-

37. Gödel, p. 250: Árni Magnússon protested against this belief, which apparently originated in Reenhjelm's saga editions. See below, p. 36.
38. Löw, *1*, 139.
39. In general see Löw, *1*, 139–60, and Nordström, *De Yverbornes Ö*.
40. Löw, *1*, 140, and *De Yverbornes Ö*, pp. 136–37.
41. *Atlantica* (Uppsala, 1937–50), *1*, 7–14.

porary writings. He disagrees, however, with those people who regard mythological traditions as false, since they are no more false than current history described in metaphorical guise. He also disagrees with those who doubt even the unambiguous sagas because there are discrepancies among them. Rudbeck regards such documents as complementary, not contradictory. Though the four Gospels all tell the truth, they are not identical in words and details. To be sure, there are few native Swedish sagas, but should one not attach particular importance to the reports of foreigners, since these are free of patriotic distortion?

Having once been cast into the stream of historiography the sagas were obliged to float with the current. They were the exclusive property of the historians and together with other source material shared in the evolution of historical thinking in the eighteenth century. Historiography evolved on the one hand toward a stricter source criticism represented notably by Hans Gram in Denmark and Sven Lagerbring in Sweden, and on the other hand toward a general scepticism engendered by the Enlightenment. Symptomatic of the more mundane spirit was Ludvig Holberg's appointment to the chair vacated by Árni Magnússon's death in 1730.[42]

Latter-day Rudbeckianism survived as late as the middle of the eighteenth century in figures such as Biörner and Göransson.[43] The latter persisted in assigning anonymous works to known authorities and went so far as to define the meaning of the word saga as "history."[44] But at this juncture Rudbeckianism had outlived the conditions which fostered it and gradually dissolved. There was a slump in antiquarian enthusiasm and inactivity in the archives.[45] Jacob Wilde (1679-1755) put his pen in the service of reason and made some modest advances in the direction of critical history in his *Sueciae*

42. Holberg vented his views in a grandiloquent parody of Rudbeck's etymologizing ("Epistel 193").

43. Löw, *1*, 160–74.

44. Johan Göransson, *Svea Rikes Konungars Historia ok Ättartal* (Stockholm, 1749), "Inledning" (unpaginated): "Ingen må läta detta goda ordet Saga giöra saken misstänkt, som skulle Saga, Sägn ok Sögn, eller dikt vara alt et. Så tänka de, som uti vårt gamla språk ok Historia ingen insigt hafva. Saga, af Sägia, betyder just det samma hos de gamla Göter, som Historia hos oss, af Historien, besöka, på minnet lägga." Göransson reasoned that *Hervarar saga* begins where Snorri leaves off, "hvaraf man lätteligen kunde sluta, Sturlesson vara jemväl hennes uphofsman." By a similar sleight of hand he ascribes *Fundinn Nóregr* to Ari.

45. Henrik Schück has described the decay into which the Antikvitetsarkiv had fallen before 1750 in *Ett Porträtt från Frihetstiden, Carl Reinhold Berch* (Stockholm, 1923), pp. 126 ff., and Finnur Jónsson has described the slumber of the Arnamagnæanske Legat through much of the eighteenth century in *Árni Magnússon, Levned og Skrifter*, *1*, 197–218.

Historia Pragmatica (1731).[46] Olof Dalin, who embodied the spirit
of the reaction in Sweden as Holberg did in Denmark, gave a whimsi-
cal paraphrase of *Ragnars saga loðbrókar* in *Then Swänska Argus,* using it not for patriotic history but as a vehicle for a parody of man-
ners.[47] The antiquarian pedants were discredited by his merciless
lampoon *Herr Arngrim Berserks Förträffelige Tankar öfver et Fynd
i Jorden Intet Långt från Stockholm* (1739), in which the learned
Arngrim proves with the help of Icelandic sagas that an artifact is
not, as commonly believed, a copper kettle, but rather a "Gothic" hel-
met, worn in fact by one of Hrólfr kraki's warriors.[48] In the introduction to his *Svea Rikes Historia* Dalin gives a judicious if traditional
estimate of the sagas: "I find to be sure that they are not without their
errors and vagaries, any more than Sturluson himself, who requires
correction here and there; but their simplicity and naïveté speak in
their defense." [49] Rudbeck is dismissed politely: "One cannot read
Rudbeck's ingenious *Atlantica* without admiration for the author's
genius. But to accord it historical certainty is not possible; for where
Plato's Atlantis lay, whether in ancient Scythia or in the Promised
Land, or in this philosopher's brain, or whether it drowned already
in the Deluge, is and will always remain an unresolved matter. . . ." [50]
Even the nation's stronghold of antiquarianism succumbed to this
spirit when in 1750 the Antikvitetsarkiv came under the administra-
tion of Carl Reinhold Berch, a sceptic who did not share his predecessors' pious regard for the sagas' historicity.[51]

In Denmark the changing attitude was proclaimed by the great
vulgarizer of Norse antiquities, Paul Henri Mallet, who broke the

46. Löw, 2, 3–18. Pragmatic or not, Wilde's history retained an inordinate respect
for oral tradition (Löw, 2, 8). See also Ludvig Stavenow, "Den Moderna Vetenskapens
Genombrot i Svensk Historieskrifning," *Göteborgs Högskolas Årsskrift,* 19 (1913), 7.
47. See Martin Lamm, *Olof Dalin, En Litteraturhistorisk Undersökning af Hans
Verk* (Uppsala, 1908), p. 235.
48. Ibid., pp. 345–57, on Dalin's war against the antiquarians. Cf. Holberg's "Epistel
194": "Og hvad vinder man ved, efter langsom Søgen at have fundet afbrudte Knap-
penaale, eller andet af samme Værdie udi en Møding?"
49. "Företal."
50. Ibid.: Dalin's enlightenment thus permitted him to reject Rudbeck's Biblico-Platonic
prelude, but it did not prevent him from peopling the first millennium of Swedish history
with saga royalty.
51. See Henrik Schück, *Ett Porträtt,* p. 132: "Några äro såsom Sturleson goda
historier, skrivarten mer eller mindre poetisk, och värda att läsas [a first glimmer of
literary appreciation?]; andra återigen eländiga utdrag av vad gamla främmande
skribenter långt bättre utfört; om Trojanska kriget, Martyrerna, Vilhelm Conquestor
etc., lönandes det icke mödan at lasta sig med elaka kopior, när man haver tillgång till
goda original. Eller äro de uppdiktade till att giva hjältemod igenom några chimerique
kämpars till eftersyn framsatta exempel, ofta ock allenast munkarnes parodier över
hedendomens vantro."

historical bias more decisively than anyone else. In his *Introduction à l'histoire de Dannemarc* (1755) he initiated a program of cultural history which had European repercussions.[52] In his judgment of the sagas he spoke with the prudence of the French Enlightenment and is worth quoting as a representative example of how common sense was substituted for close-work.

En effet, quoique les Annales des Islandois soient sans contredit les seuls monumens que nous puissions consulter avec quelque confiance sur ces tems reculés, quoique les raisons que Torfaeus allégue en leur faveur, soient de quelque poids, bien des gens auront de la peine à se persuader qu'on puisse en tirer des con-noissances assez sures & assez détaillées, pour en former le tissu d'une histoire complette & solide. Car 1° les Islandois nous ont laissé un grand nombre d'ouvrages dans lesquels il paroit que leur goût les portoit au merveilleux, à l'allégorie, & même à ce genre de fiction qui consiste à orner de fables une narration dont le fonds est vrai. Torfaeus avoue lui même qu'il y en a plusieurs dans lesquelles il est très difficile de dèmêler le mensonge d'avec la vérité & qu'on n'en trouve presque aucune ou la fiction n'entre pour quelque chose. Il est bien à craindre, qu'en suivant de pareils guides on ne s'égare quelque fois. 2° Ces annales ne sont pas d'une grande antiquité; nous n'en avons aucune qui ait été établi dans le Nord, & depuis Odin, ou depuis le commencement des tems Historiques, jusqu'au premier Islandais qui a écrit une histoire, il s'est écoulé environ onze siecles. Si les Auteurs de ces annales n'ont trouvé aucun mémoire écrit avant eux, come il y a bien lieu de le croire, leurs narrations ne sont donc fondées que sur des traditions, des inscriptions, & des Poésies. Mais ajoutera-t-on beaucoup de foi à des traditions qui ont dû embrasser tant de siécles, se conserver chez des hommes credules & peu éclairés? Nous voyons de nos jours, que parmi le peuple un fils se souvient de son pére, fait quelque chose de son ayeul, & ne songe jamais à ce qui est au dela. Les hommes ne s'occupent guéres que dans

52. See Anton Blanck, *Den Nordiska Renässansen i Sjuttonhundratalets Litteratur* (Stockholm, 1911), pp. 40–55. It is interesting to note that Berch anticipated this program in 1750: "Även uti de onyttigaste sagor finnas understundom märkvärdiga ställen, som lära oss de gamles meningar i religion och sedoläran, deras allmänna levnadssätt, beskrivningen om byggningar, gevär och annan redskap, jämväl åtskilligt i gamla geografien och orternas förra namn m.m., vilket allt, när det under sina kapitel excerperas, kan med tiden bringas till et långt pålitligare corpus om svenska antik-viteterna, än vad man emellertid under en blind iver för sitt fädernesland bygger på gissningar" (in Henrik Schück, *Ett Porträtt*, p. 132).

une longue oisiveté des choses qui ne sont plus sous leurs yeux. Quant aux inscriptions nous avons deja vû de quel secours elles pouvoient être; ajoutons qu'il n'y en a qu'un petit nombre qui ayent été écrites avant la conversion du Nord au Christianisme, & que come cela sera prouvé dans la suite, l'on faisoit peu d'usage des lettres avant ce tems là. Enfin pour ce qui s'agit des hymnes qu'on apprenoit par cœur, on ne peut nier, que les Auteurs dont nous parlons, n'en ayent pû tirer diverses lumieres sur l'histoire des tems peu éloignez des leurs. Mais est-il probable qu'on eut retenu soigneusement beaucoup de Poésies composées, sept, huit, ou neuf siécles auparavant? Y trouvoit-on beaucoup d'exactitude & de clarté? Les Poétes avoient-ils dans ce tems là cette précision, & suivoient-ils cet ordre que l'histoire demande? 3° Si les Annalistes Islandois n'ont pû savoir avec certitude ce qui s'étoit passé longtems avant eux en Islande & en Norvége, leur autorité n'est elle pas encore plus foible pour ce qui concerne un Etat éloigné come la Dannemarc, qui n'avoit pas alors sans doute avec ces parties du Nord les mêmes liaisons qu'il a eues depuis? On sent aisément, que presque tout ce qu'ils ont pû en savoir, se bornoit à des bruits populaires, & à quelques hymnes qui de loin en loin se répandoient en Islande, par le moyen de quelque Scalde Islandois qui retournoit dans sa patrie.[53]

Scepticism had progressed so far that Sven Lagerbring felt called upon to issue a defense of the sagas. In a disputation from the year 1763 he gives a point by point refutation of Mallet.[54] He agrees with Mallet's objection that sagas have a penchant for the supernatural, allegory, and fiction, but adds that not all the sagas are similarly constituted. Snorri, Ari, and *Fundinn Nóregr* are largely free of such ornament. Furthermore, what seems incredible is often true, and what seems probable is often untrue. When improbable matters are scattered in history, they deface it just as wounds and welts deface a body, without however reducing it to nothing. Nor are such improbabilities restricted to Icelandic literature alone. They are rampant in the historians of antiquity, of the Middle Ages, and even of the most recent times, though they do not cast doubt on the major events of history. To Mallet's objection that the sources are all recent and date from after the Christianization of Iceland Lagerbring replies by emphasizing

53. *Introduction á l'histoire de Dannemarc* (Copenhague, 1755), pp. 31–34.
54. Johan A. Stechau, *De Fide Historica Monumentorum Islandicorum* (Londini Gothorum, 1763). A disputation by Lagerbring.

the quality and repute of the first authorities (Sæmundr, Ísleifr, Ari, Snorri) and assuming that such eminent men must have had a basis for explaining the interval between Odin and their own time, especially since the times were distinguished not by vague and dubious but by exact accounts. There was probably even written material prior to Ari, and the fact that inscriptions could be of use to the historian is apparent from the inscription passages in *Egils saga* and *Laxdœla saga* cited by Torfaeus. To Mallet's statement that traditions are ephemeral and that among common people memories are short except in times of protracted idleness, he counters that the peasants of today can hardly be compared to the illustrious men of the ancient North. Among the peasants memories may die, but kings are well remembered, to wit Gustaf Vasa among the Dalecarlians. Monuments such as the barrows of Uppsala serve as a constant reminder. Nor did the early Scandinavians lack leisure when the winter suspension of activities allowed them to relax at the hearth. The life of traditions in the old days can therefore not be calculated on the basis of modern standards. Mallet had expressed doubt that the poems of the Norsemen could be retained accurately for seven, eight, or nine centuries. Lagerbring again rejects any analogy with contemporary popular songs. The songs of old were (with an allusion to Tacitus) "the only order of annals and erudition," the vessel of the highest matter both secular and religious, so that no one could doubt that they were granted long life, unlike our "cantilenae," which are condemned to extinction. Snorri knew the poems of Harald Fairhair's scalds 380 years later, and the poetry of Starkaðr, dated by Dalin to the fifth century, could be read in *Hrólfs saga Gautrekssonar*. To be sure most of this poetry was retained by memory, but in view of Þorgerðr's runic inscribing of her father's verses (*Egils saga*), it is doubtful that nothing was preserved in writing. Concerning the reliability of the poems, Snorri tells us that learned men regarded them as true. *Ynglingatal* bears witness to the organization and care with which they were composed and at a much earlier period Jordanes referred to Gothic poems of an almost historic nature, thus testifying to the esteem in which the scalds of antiquity were held. On the score of the uncertainty which the Icelanders might have about their own and Norwegian history, Lagerbring cites Ari's record of Iceland's settlement and the frequenting of Norwegian courts by Icelandic scalds. Against the supposition that Icelandic ignorance of Denmark must have been proportionately greater because of the lack of ties, he contends that scalds visited Danish and Swedish as well as Norwegian courts. In such cases their historical authority was enhanced by the fact that they were neutral and, concluding with a modest flight of rhetoric, "procul ab invidia, procul ab assentatione, spe liberi ac timore vacui, soli veritati suas lucubrationes dedicare potuerunt." [55]

This is substantially the argument which Lagerbring used in his critical introduction to *Svea Rikes Historia* (1769). Despite his reputation as a pioneering historian it is apparent that, here at least, he is moving in the old circles. His authorities are Snorri and Torfaeus, and there are even echoes from Rudbeck.

Denmark's most prolific historian P. F. Suhm, one of the first to employ the Norse background as a literary vehicle, never arrived at such a clearly defined approach to the sources.[56] After the customary eulogy of Snorri's trustworthiness he passes curiously mild judgment on the fabulous sagas. One is reminded of Torfaeus' unwillingness to relinquish a source once he had discovered it. Suhm grants that most of the sagas published in Sweden "are so constituted as to contain controversial things compared to the trustworthy reports of other historians, and they are furthermore full of tales. . . ." [57] He suspects them of being young and of borrowing either from Saxo or from a common source, "namely the people's uncertain tradition, and their own vigorous imagination." [58] After stressing their value as cultural documents he goes on to say that they should not be entirely dismissed as history, "for from *Fundinn Nóregr* we learn a great deal concerning Norway's oldest history, and in *Volsunga saga* and *Alfs saga* there are preserved the most splendid verses. On the other hand I do not see how one can build any historical truth on such sagas as *Samsons saga fagra, Illuga saga Gríðarfóstra, Hálfdanar saga Brönufóstra* and others." [59]

On the whole it is remarkable how little progress was made in understanding the formation of the sagas during the reign of reason. Criticism was either historically oriented without superseding Torfaeus or it adhered to Mallet's common-sense line. The first incisive criticism

55. Ibid., p. 25.
56. See Ellen Jørgensen, *Historieforskning og Historieskrivning i Danmark Indtil Aar 1800* (København, 1931), p. 218, and C. Paludan-Müller, "Dansk Historiografi i det 18de Aarhundrede," *Historisk Tidskrift*, 5. Række, 4 (1883–84), 185–86.
57. Peter F. Suhm, *Samlede Skrifter, 9,* "Tanker om de Vanskeligheder som Møde ved at Skrive den Gamle Danske og Norske Historie" (København, 1792), 77.
58. Ibid.
59. Ibid.

came from Germany, where Schlözer, Adelung, and Rühs propounded a much more uncompromising scepticism.[60]

Schlözer gave exhilaratingly fresh if ruthless expression to his opinion. He was one of the first categorically to reject *Fundinn Nóregr,* to which, as we have seen, both Lagerbring and Suhm clung. He adopted a distinction between what he called "Annalen" on the one hand and "Sagen" on the other, "die der Barbarey, der Nachahmung, dem Muthwillen, und folglich ganz andern Quellen ihr Daseyn zu verdanken haben."[61] He theorized that the saga genre was a Provençal import negotiated by traveling Icelanders. "Island wimmelte von Sagnmadir [sic], Sagenmännern, oder wie sie in der Provenzal-Sprache heissen, von Contadores, Cantores, Iuglares, Truanes und Bufones, welche aus den verworfensten historischen Büchern der Ausländer den Stoff erborgten, und daraus mit dem rohen Witz, der allein einem noch ungebildeten Volke gefallen konnte, Sagen verfertigten. . . ."[62]

Schlözer's pupil Friedrich Rühs, a more thorough connoisseur of Norse literature, also detected a strong poetic strain in the sagas, but he was content to explain it as a native hazard. Everything concerning the period to Harald Fairhair's reign he counted a late fiction without basis in tradition, thus departing radically from the hedging of a Dalin or a Lagerbring.[63] But even the more recent history was problemati-

60. The historicity of the sagas had already been summarily judged by Leibniz. Some of his pronouncements are collected in the notes of Louis Davillé's *Leibniz historien: Essai sur l'activité et la méthode historiques de Leibniz* (Paris, 1909), pp. 522–30. These views were known in Scandinavia. See the "Företal" to Olof Dalin's *Svea Rikes Historia* and Lagerbring's *De Fide Historica Monumentorum Islandicorum,* p. 4. On the ensuing debate see Bengt Henningsson, *Geijer som Historiker* (Uppsala, 1961), pp. 216–24.

61. August L. Schlözer, *Allgemeine Nordische Geschichte* (Halle, 1771), p. 216.

62. Ibid., p. 217. In his introduction to the Arnamagnaean edition of *Gunnlaugs saga,* Jón Eiríksson opposed Schlözer's views (see Finnur Jónsson, *Árni Magnússon, Levned og Skrifter, 1,* 205). Schlözer had renewed his harsh criticism of the sagas and especially the *Edda* in *Isländische Litteratur und Geschichte* (Göttingen und Gotha, 1773). It was this work which drew Jón Eiríksson's retort, couched in rhetorical dignity and rather vacuous from the point of view of method. On Adelung see Karl-Ernst Sickel, *Johann Christoph Adelung: Seine Persönlichkeit und Seine Geschichtsauffassung* (Diss. Leipzig, 1933): " 'Vor dem Gebrauch der Schrift findet keine Geschichte statt.' Die Sagen erscheinen ihm auch deshalb unglaubwürdig, da sie nur einzelne Abenteuer und Fehden enthalten und die grossen historischen Ereignisse wie die Wanderungen der germanischen Völker, die Normannenzüge oder die Einführung des Christentums übergehen. Die isländischen Sagen sind ausgesonnen, um die Langeweile zu vertreiben. Sie sollten für Neuheit und Abwechslung sorgen, sind aber 'so plump und abgeschmackt, dass auch die eifrigsten Verehrer der Sagen sie verachten' " (pp. 127–28). Sickel gives his source as: "Über die nordische Litteratur, Geschichte und Mythologie," *Erholungen,* hrsg. von W. G. Becker (1797), 2, 86–124. This volume is not available to me.

63. See Ludvig Stavenow, "Friedrich Rühs' Betydelse för Svensk Historieskrifning," *Nordisk Tidskrift* (1918), p. 319.

cal. Like Mallet, Rühs pointed out that written records were of late date in Iceland and that without their support history in any true sense of the word was hardly thinkable. The judgment he passed on tradition is important not only because it was the burr under Müller's saddle, but because it is prophetic of more recent criticism.

> Wir wollen den Werth der Tradition nicht ganz und gar, und unbedingt verwerfen; allein sie ist immer äusserst unzuverlässig, weil uns nichts ihre Reinheit und ihren Ursprung verbürgt und aufklärt; sie ist unaufhörlichen Beimischungen und Umstaltungen ausgesetzt, unzählige Beispiele beweisen, dass selbst Ansichten und Meinungen in einer spätern Zeit sich unter das Volk verbreiten, die sich erhalten und nach mehrern Jahren als Traditionen, als Volkssagen erscheinen; es fehlen alle Kriterien zur Prüfung, und endlich findet sie nur zu bald ihre Gränze; keine Tradition dauert ohne durch die Schrift aufgefasst zu seyn, mehrere Jahrhunderte. Alle Geschichte, die nur die Tradition als ihre Quelle angiebt, ist daher ihrer Natur nach äusserst schwankend, ungewiss und verdächtig. Nicht viel wird gewonnen, wenn man sie durch Gesänge gebunden ansieht; erstlich ist es durch die Betrachtung aller ächten Volkspoesie unwiderleglich klar, dass Lieder und Gesänge eben so schnell und unmittelbar als sie hervorgebracht werden, auch untergehn, dass sie nie eine lange Zeit fortdauern, denn wie die Volkspoesie sich ewig neu erzeugt, so werden die alten Geburten stets durch neue verdrängt. Zweitens die Annahme, dass neben den Gesängen noch eine erklärende Tradition fortläuft, ist an sich nicht nur sehr unnatürlich, sondern wird auch auf keine Weise empirisch bestätigt; der umgekehrte Fall hingegen lässt sich viel öftrer nachweisen, dass zur Erklärung eines Gedichts eine Geschichte späterhin ersonnen ward, um den Zusammenhang herzustellen. Drittens, wer bürgt uns dafür, dass ein gegebnes Gedicht einen wirklichen Gegenstand besingt, dass es nicht etwa eine blosse Dichtung enthält? Lässt sich wohl überhaupt ein historischer Stoff poetisch und treu behandeln? Viertens die isländischen Gedichte sind zu jung, um für die Zeiten zu beweisen, die man durch sie aufklären will; besonders ist das Alter und die Entstehung der eigentlich historischen Gesänge sehr problematisch. . . .[64]

64. Friedrich Rühs, *Die Edda* (Berlin, 1812), pp. 281–82.

Rühs was perhaps the first to maintain that the sagas of the Icelanders were not primarily intended to inform but to entertain. Stories
were gathered uncritically and means of making them diverting were
in no wise shunned. Even the revered Snorri does not come off with
a clean slate: ". . . auch Snorri war zufrieden, wenn er eine Tradition
vor sich fand, die ihm nur wegen ihres Alters, wegen des Ansehens
desjenigen, der sie ihm mittheilte, oder aus andern Gründen einige
Autorität zu haben schien, er hielt sich berechtigt, sie aufzunehmen,
ohne über ihre Beschaffenheit sehr bekümmert zu seyn." [65] Fictions and
foreign motifs are the rule not the exception, also in the family sagas:
"Die Spuren der Erdichtung sind bei andern Stücken, wie z.B. in
Egilssaga, in Niala u.A. vielleicht weniger auffallend, aber man lese
diese Geschichten, und man wird überzeugt seyn, dass sie eben so gut
Romane sind als die Sagen von Amleth, von Herraud und Bosi, und
unzählige andre. . . ." [66]

This is the stage at which saga criticism had arrived around 1800.
A long period of extreme credulity was superseded by an equally
strong expression of disbelief. It is the task of the next chapter to show
how the proponents of saga antiquity and historicity in Scandinavia
consolidated their position before again being challenged from Germany.

65. Ibid., p. 284.
66. Ibid., p. 287.

2

The Romantic Era

With somewhat disparate success Peter Erasmus Müller (1776–1834) divided his time between theology and the study of old Scandinavian literature. Shortly after his death it was noted that: "In the field of national literature he is a sure and steadfast Peter, in the field of theology a subtle and inadequate Erasmus."[1] Appointed Professor of Theology in 1810 and Bishop of Zealand in 1830, Müller created little enthusiasm in the lecture hall and less in the pulpit. Unlike his richly talented brother in orders and fellow antiquarian N. F. S. Grundtvig he kindled no spark in his audience. But though Grundtvig's advocacy of northern antiquities loomed large on the national scene, he left no mark on the scholarly world. In Müller's case it was precisely the un-Grundtvigian qualities of skeletal logic and dry presentation which enabled him to establish the foundation for nineteenth-century saga research.

Müller made his scholarly debut with a study of the gold horns of Gallehus crowned by Videnskabernes Selskab in 1805. This was followed by works on Icelandic language, mythology, historiography, and literature and by important source studies of Snorri and Saxo. Those works which touch on his view of saga origins are *Über den Ursprung und Verfall der Isländischen Historiographie* (1813)[2] and his three-volume *Sagabibliothek* (1817–20).

1. Johannes C. H. R. Steenstrup, *Historieskrivning i Danmark i det Nittende Aarhundrede* (København, 1889), p. 128.
2. Danish in *Nordisk Tidskrift for Oldkyndighed, 1* (1832).

The first is a direct answer to Friedrich Rühs's attack on the genuineness of the sagas.[3] His reply goes beyond the usual conjuring of
Snorri's reliability and the cataloguing of sourcemen coupled with an
encomium of their capacious memories. Müller was the first to see
the problem in historic context. By applying the methods of cultural
history evolved during the eighteenth century, he tries to trace historiography as a necessary outgrowth of the specific cultural conditions
which separated Iceland from the rest of Scandinavia. The study is
divided into four sections, which give a genetic step-by-step review of
the rise and fall of Icelandic historiography:

    1. Wie die Begierde, von der alten Zeit zu erzählen, bey den
Isländern entstehen muste
    2. Auf welche Weise man in Island vielen historischen Stoff
gesammelt, und durch den mündlichen Vortrag bearbeitet hat
    3. Was die Isländer veranlasste, ihre Erzählungen nieder zu
schreiben, und wie sich die eigentliche Geschichtschreibung ent-
wickelte
    4. Warum die Isländer aufhörten, Geschichtschreiber zu seyn.

In the first section Müller shows how the sagas were rooted in the
manner of colonization and the nature of the colonists. The new
settlers were not a motley troop of vikings but established chieftains
with traditions and an inbred feeling of independence. "In Thrönde-
lagen ruhte Norwegens grösste Stärke; dort äussert sich der Geist des
Alterthums am kräftigsten. Die eigene Beschaffenheit jener Gegenden,
die grossen Meerbusen, und die vielen fruchtbaren Inseln hatten dort
vorzüglich das Bedürfnis der Unabhängigkeit tief einwurzeln lassen,
und brachten dort die häufigsten Auswanderungen der edelsten
Geschlechter hervor" (pp. 3–4). The social system which arose was
patterned after the one in Norway, but in the absence of a king it
allowed even a greater degree of independence. With the exception of
some slaves all the settlers were free and on an equal footing; the ac-
quisition of power depended on personal qualities and was contractual.
During the period of settlement internal peace was promoted by the
thin population and the vicissitudes of colonization. Collisions abroad

    3. Peter E. Müller, *Ueber den Ursprung und Verfall der Isländischen Historiographie*
(Kopenhagen, 1813), pp. X–XI: "Es konnte mir daher nicht anders als unangenehm
und unerwartet seyn, als Hr. Prof. Rühs, den ich als Schwedens Geschichtschreiber hoch
schätzte, in seiner Schrift: die Edda, nebst einer Einleitung über nordische Poesie und
Mythologie, den isländischen Berichten von dem Zustande des Nordens vor der Annahme
des Christenthums alle Glaubwürdigkeit absprach." Müller delivers a methodical rebuttal in an "Anhang" entitled "Ueber die Nationalität der altnordischen Gedichte, etc."

were prevented by Iceland's geographical situation and viking expeditions were impeded by the lack of appropriate timber for shipbuilding, the difficulty of assembling crews from a small population, and the distances to be sailed. Thus, on the one hand a period of unaccustomed peace emphasized and gave lustre to a martial past: "Ehedem an Kriegszüge gewöhnt, verweilten sie nun auf ihren Höfen, und theilten ihren Hausknechten das Tagwerk zu. Die natürliche Folge dieser veränderten Lage war, dass die Erinnerung oft in die verschwundene Zeit zurück gieng, deren Thaten um desto mehr hervor treten musten, da sie ein abgeschlossenes, der Gegenwart so ungleiches Ganze ausmachten" (p. 14). On the other hand, pride of birth brought about a consolidation of the traditions connected with Norway. "Schon die väterlichen Grabhügel und der Odelshof bezeugten die ruhmwürdige Geburt. Von allen diesen Herrlichkeiten konnte nur die Sage mit nach Island übergehn" (p. 15). These ancestral reminiscences were therefore cultivated with special fondness. "So muste sich eine zusammenhängende Darstellung der Begebenheiten ihrer Vorfahren von selber entwickeln" (p. 15).

In a digression aimed at the cultural arrogance of the Enlightenment, which had caused Mallet and others to doubt the capacity of the Old Norse language to preserve historical accounts, Müller focuses his attention on the refined idiom of the scalds. He argues that the striking discrepancy between the language of the scalds and that of the oldest sagas, especially in vocabulary, shows that there was a deep-rooted difference between prose and poetry and that the latter had a long development behind it. The extraordinary cultivation of language is explained as a reflex of a political system which attached great importance to parliamentary eloquence.

As among the Greeks and Goths the purpose of the poetry was to celebrate gods and heroes, but unlike Greek poetry the scaldic genius was episodic, not epic. Greek poetry set in at the close of a heroic age and sang the praises of the past; scaldic poetry flourished during a heroic age and, with the exception of the Æsir, Gjukungar, and Vǫlsungar, neglected mythical themes in favor of contemporary deeds. This choice of subject was detrimental to poetic imagination but enhanced historical accuracy.

Assuming that scaldic poems were vessels of history, Müller goes on to a more traditional account of how they were passed on from one generation to the next. They were either memorized (Battle of Stiklastaðir) or carved in runes (*Egils saga, Grettis saga*). Examples of the scalds' historic knowledge are cited and Snorri's arguments for their reliability are arrayed. But in addition to the professional scalds other people composed occasional stanzas which gave permanence to tradition. Müller admits that these conditions apply to other parts of Scandinavia, where they did not give rise to a historical literature. The difference lies in Iceland's peculiar political and social position. While in Norway memories of ninth-century events tended to be obscured by the rapid succession of new events, they were more easily retained in the political lull of tenth-, eleventh-, and twelfth-century Iceland. Again, many of the titled families who had stock in their ancestral annals succumbed during the Norwegian civil wars while their cousins in Iceland survived.

The first section of Müller's study was devoted to showing how the desire to tell of the past necessarily made itself felt among the Icelandic colonists. The second section shows how the desire was transmuted into history. "Vorzüglich waren es Sinn für Dichtkunst und Gefühl der Ehre, die, durch die Beschaffenheit des bürgerlichen Vereins genährt, solche Früchte hervor locken konnten" (p. 29). Events in Iceland during the period of feuding were commemorated in stanzas which dealt with a number of topics, but chiefly with history. "Selbst Klima und Lebensart konnten die von den Vätern ererbte, und durch den Freiheitsgeist genährte Neigung zur Dichtkunst unterhalten, weil sie den Bewohnern viele ledige Stunden und ein häufiges Zusammenleben gewährten" (pp. 33–34). Long winter evenings, assemblies, and games gave the poets an opportunity to unfold their poetic talents (but cf. p. 3). These meetings emphasized "das Leben als Männervergleich" in a free society where reputations were jealously guarded and closely followed by the rest of the nation. Thus talent for narrative combined with curiosity about contemporary events to produce stories. These developed from first-hand reports to artistically constructed sagas. "In den meisten Sagaen herrscht die Gesprächsform . . . Selbst unsere gemeinen Leute pflegen unwillkürlich ihre Berichte zu dialogisieren. Dadurch erhielt die Erzählung poetische Gestalt" (pp. 39–40). The dialogue could be fairly accurate in the early stages. "Allein je mehr der Erzähler es verstand, sich und Andern die Personen zu versinnlichen; je mehr er ihren Ton zu treffen wuste; um desto lebendiger ward auch die Erzählung und das Interesse, welches sie weckte. Wo man viel erzählt, und Erzählungen gern hört; wird sich das Talent, gut zu erzählen, bey dem Einzelnen leicht entwickeln" (p. 40). At this stage the sagas were essentially historical, but as the

25

interest in the stories as such increased, the content suffered neglect. "War es nun zu einer Kunst gediehen, gut zu erzählen, war sogar die Form der Erzählung ein Gegenstand allgemeiner Aufmerksamkeit worden; so muste der Uebergang zu dem Bestreben, die Einkleidung zur Hauptsache zu machen, und durch erdichtete Erzählungen zu unterhalten, bald und leicht geschehen" (p. 42). This shift of interest marked the vogue of the *fornaldarsǫgur* with their purely fabulous themes. Thus Müller saw in the development of Icelandic storytelling a cycle which progressed from mythical to historical to fictional matter.

The next question is why the Icelanders extended their historical interests to the affairs of other countries. The answer lies in the constant communication maintained between Iceland and the rest of the world, notably Norway. Scalds and sagamen especially were welcomed at foreign courts as stewards of ancient traditions preserved in their purest form in that part of the north which resisted absolutism and Christianity longest. When travelers returned from abroad, their accounts were eagerly awaited—"Insulaner beschuldigt man überhaupt der neugierde" (p. 57)—and were absorbed in the oral tradition of Iceland.

The third section is devoted to showing how history was written down once it had been gathered and formed orally. The thirteenth century had written sources at its disposal, among which the works of Sæmundr and Ari were prominent. These works were in the annalistic tradition of Europe and were chronologically weighted. Snorri's achievement was to weld the annalistic approach to the national art of storytelling, a task already broached by his predecessors, Eiríkr, Oddr, and Gunnlaugr. In general however the emphasis was not placed on the recorder but on the oral sources from which the historian drew his material. In the case of domestic history it was not even necessary to name these sources since the accounts were common knowledge. "Wer solch eine Erzählung aufschrieb, konnte nicht darauf verfallen, seinen Namen hinzu zu fügen, um sich auf diese Weise Schriftstellerehre zu erwerben. Denn er schrieb blos ab, was er von Andern gehört hatte. Der Vortrag war daher grösstentheils nicht sein, sondern des Zeitgeistes Erzeugnis. Hier entdecken wir die Ursache, warum die allermeisten Sagaen anonym sind" (p. 81).

The last section deals with the decline of Icelandic historiography, which is correlated to the political dissolution of Iceland during the Sturlung Age. As the power became concentrated in a few hands, public interest followed only the fates of the powerful families while the formerly prominent independent farmers sank into historic oblivion. This trend culminated in the subjugation by Norway in 1264. And as the interest in events at home decreased, the interest in foreign affairs began to ebb as well. Some of the same causes which had throttled historiography in Norway now led to the extinction of that art in Iceland.

The sagas had been edited only in fits and starts since the seventeenth century. During the eighteenth century no concerted effort had been made to publish the texts or translations and the Arnamagnaean Commission had been conspicuously inactive. As a result most of the sagas were not conveniently available. Müller's *Sagabibliothek* had the twofold function of making the contents accessible and providing a critical basis for their study.[4] The sagas are divided into three classes and each class is made to fill a volume. The first volume contains those sagas concerned with Iceland, the Orkneys, the Faroes, and Greenland; the second, mythical sagas about events antedating Iceland's settlement; the third, sagas dealing with the history which had transpired in Scandinavia since Iceland's settlement. The sagas in volumes one and two are arranged according to the date of the events described. Each summary of contents is followed by a brief consideration of the saga's reliability. In addition the first volume is prefaced with "General Comments on the Rules, According to which the Genuineness of the Icelandic Sagas Can Be Ascertained." Here Müller lays down rules for separating the old sagas from the young. He distinguishes between external and internal criteria of age.

EXTERNAL:
1. paleography
2. the manuscript material (vellum/paper)
3. the number of old vellums in which a saga appears
4. the availability of confirmation in other sagas
5. corroboration in bona fide historical sources (Ari, etc.)

INTERNAL:
1. absence of young loanwords
2. the use of simple syntax
3. the presence of genuine stanzas
4. the use of naïve diction (oral style)
   a. dialogue

4. Peter E. Müller, *Sagabibliothek* (Kjøbenhavn, 1817), *I*, IX.

    b. artless composition
    c. objectivity
    d. self-assurance on the part of the teller (protestations of
        truth are a certain sign of recent origins)
  5. general probability
  6. proximity of the events to the teller
  7. inclusion of straightforward matter unlikely to be invented
  8. exact topographic or genealogical information
  9. the recording of customs anterior to the time of writing
  10. lifelike characterization unlikely to be invented

On the other side of the ledger Müller lists three qualities which compromise a saga's historicity:

  1. The impossibility or improbability of the narrative matter betrays an unreliable saga. But the reader must be careful to distinguish between true and truthful (the author's veracity). A saga can be truthful without being true, i.e. historically unimpeachable. The supernatural is for example not untruthful. On the contrary, for the thirteenth century Icelander a saga stripped of the supernatural would have been untruthful. Nor does dialogue which is not strictly accurate compromise a saga's truthfulness.

  2. A saga is unhistorical when it conflicts with other reliable sources or has internal contradictions. There are, however, various grades of inaccuracy and minor errors do not jeopardize a saga.

  3. Anachronisms reveal fiction.

Müller was the first scholar since Torfaeus who familiarized himself with the total extent of Icelandic literature and tried to establish some order among the heterogeneous monuments. Torfaeus also distinguished between reliable and unreliable, and in some ways Müller's approach in *Sagabibliothek* is merely an extension and refinement of this categorization. What is new is the theory of origins developed in the essay of 1813.

Many of Müller's ideas were suggested by forerunners: the role of Iceland's aristocratic population in maintaining traditions (Lagerbring), her political isolation (an argument used by Rudbeck in favor of Sweden's pristine traditions), the value of monuments in keeping reminiscences alive (Torfaeus, Lagerbring), the historical burden of scaldic poetry (Arngrímur Jónsson, Torfaeus, etc.),[5] the

5. The notion that the scalds were the historians of the North recurs again and again even in fairly recent times (e.g. Gödel, pp. 8–9). The earliest occurrence of the idea I

preservation of records in runes (Torfaeus, etc.), the political lull and leisure available for historical pursuits (a loophole left by Mallet and seized on by Lagerbring), the gradual development of artistic stories (a tempering of Rühs's insight), Icelandic knowledge of foreign affairs because of their traffic abroad (Lagerbring), the justification of the supernatural (Verelius), the distinction in degrees of inaccuracy (Lagerbring), etc. But Müller went beyond a persuasive synthesis of these old ideas; he was the first to view the sagas not only as history but in history, not as a record of events but as a cultural manifestation. The theory was constructed from the new thinking of the eigtheenth century. Beginning in France an environmental view of human activity had gradually gained currency and was successively adapted to various fields. Montesquieu had revivified a classical idea and explained various forms of government against the background of geography and climate and Voltaire's history had emphasized the part played by climate, religion, and government in the shaping of events. The climatological doctrines found their most elaborate Scandinavian exposition in the works of the Swede J. F. Neikter, whose series *De Efficacia Climatum ad Variam Gentium Indolem Precipue Ingenia et Mores* appeared in sixteen parts from 1777 to 1797.[6] Winckelmann applied this thinking to the history of art and interpreted Grecian art in relation to Greek culture, customs, institutions, and climate. His programmatic statement is reminiscent of Müller's title: "Die Geschichte der Kunst soll den Ursprung, das Wachstum, die Veränderung und den Fall derselben, nebst dem verschiedenen Style der Völker, Zeiten, so viel möglich ist beweisen." [7] This opened the way for literary history in the same spirit; Mme. de Staël's *De la Littérature considérée dans ses rapports avec les institutions sociales* (1800) considered literature as a product of environment. One of the recurring themes in this cultural history was the positive role of freedom.[8] It was abetted by the admiration of English constitutional government, which was correlated to Germanic freedom, by the Rousseauistic idealization of free, primitive man, and on the economic side, by the physiocratic doctrines. These ideas were alive in Denmark as elsewhere. Justus Möser's Dan-

find in a passage from Arngrímur Jónsson, in which he speaks of Þjóðólfr ór Hvini and Eyvindr Skáldaspillir: "Illi igitur duo rythmistae antiquissimi sunt historiarum Norvegicarum authores" ("Supplementum Historiae Norvagicae," *Bib. Arn.*, 9, 169). The idea originates in a liberal interpretation of the prologue to *Heimskringla*.

6. See Anton Blanck, *Den Nordiska Renässansen* (Stockholm, 1911), pp. 243–65.
7. Johann Winckelmann, *Sämtliche Werke* (Donauöschingen, 1825), 3, 9–10.
8. See Friedrich Meinecke, *Die Entstehung des Historismus*, (München, 1936), 2, 315, and Madame de Staël, *Œuvres Complètes* (Bruxelles, 1830), 4, 181–182.

ish counterpart, Tyge Rothe, idealized the free Norse farmer at a time when the first glimmer of Norwegian national consciousness was drawing attention to the traditions of independence among Norway's farmers and when rural reform and the welfare of Denmark's own farming class was the foremost political issue of the day.[9] The end of the eighteenth century also produced the first systematic efforts to understand the formation of ancient literatures. In 1795 F. A. Wolf's influential *Prolegomena ad Homerum* advanced the idea that the Homeric epics were the sum creation of successive rhapsodists. Similarly Niebuhr in his *Römische Geschichte* (1811–32) postulated lost Latin poems as the source of early Roman history and outlined the development of history through mythological, poetic, and contemporary stages. It was against this general background that Müller evolved his coherent theory of origins.

Müller has been accepted by later scholars as the initiator of the idea that the oral sagas existed in set form. It is uncertain how set he imagined the tradition to be. The statement that the wording was "grösstentheils" not the work of the scribe leaves a certain latitude of interpretation and the concept of "des Zeitgeistes Erzeugnis" is abundantly vague. In any case Müller certainly paved the way for the more drastic form of rigid tradition propounded by the national historians of Norway, P. A. Munch (1810–63) and R. Keyser (1803–64).

After the separation of Norway from Denmark in 1814 nationalism was on the rise in Norway.[10] Its positive manifestation was a revived interest in things Norwegian—language, literature, folklore, and antiquities. The negative manifestation was a revulsion against Denmark, whose culture was now felt to have been oppressively dominant during the long period of unification.[11] Thus we observe that the pan-Scandinavian movement, which issued chiefly from Denmark, was much slower in gaining a foothold in Norway than elsewhere. The young nation's fear of amalgamation prompted it to direct its energies inward during the first decades of the nineteenth century.

In the reviews and essays which Munch published in the 1830s and '40s the neglect of Norway's merits abroad, especially in Denmark, is a nagging theme. An undercurrent of resentment occasionally colors his

9. Edvard Holm, *Kampen om Landboreformerne i Danmark* (København, 1888), pp. 66–73, 136–38, 158–66.
10. In general see Oscar J. Falnes, *National Romanticism in Norway* (New York, 1933).
11. A convenient brief review of Munch's and Keyser's controversy with Denmark is Gustav Indrebø, "Den norske historiske skulen og Danmark," *Syn og Segn, 31* (1925), 337–51, 369–83, 437–46.

historical work. In conjunction with Keyser he had evolved a migration theory according to which the Germanic people entered Europe in two streams from Russia. The southern stream migrated south of the Baltic into Germany. The northern tribes entered Scandinavia via Finland and the Bay of Bothnia, settled Sweden and Norway, but collided with the Gothic peoples, the southern stream, in Denmark. The population of Denmark was therefore linguistically and ethnically mixed and the racial brotherhood on which the Scandinavianists based their call to unity was without historic foundation. The Danish brothers were in fact only half-brothers. On the other hand the purest descendants of the northmen who settled Scandinavia were the Norwegians and that language which most closely approached the prototype was Icelandic or some of the Norwegian dialects which had resisted the intrusion of Danish. From this point of view it could only be regarded as an injustice when Danish scholars spoke of an "old-nordisk" language and literature, thus arrogating to Denmark a share in a culture which did not properly belong to her. The alternate term "Islandsk" was no better since it evoked the false impression that Icelandic language and literature were independent of Norwegian. In reality the languages were indistinguishable and the literature was common, a product of constant interchange. "Concerning the kings' sagas, by their very nature they first came into being and were first told in Norway, even if they were later edited, not always correctly, by Icelandic scholars, who, after the decline of the language in the mother country, assumed the same relationship to her literature as the Alexandrian scholars had to Greek literature, without the latter's becoming Egyptian for that." [12] Underlying this statement is the theory of rigid tradition which is phrased clearly in the introduction to *Antiquités russes*. Here the saga is defined as ". . . un récit détaillé, exposé dans une forme déterminée et produit par la transmission orale. . . . Pour qu'elles [the sagas] pussent se transmettre de bouche en bouche sans laisser dehors des circonstances accessoires mais importantes, il fut nécessaire de les réduire bientôt en une certaine forme qui se maintenait ensuite constamment, en admettant des modifications non essentielles." [13] In other words the sagas originated in Norway, whence they were imported by the Icelanders.

This theory, which can only be gleaned from scattered references

12. Peter A. Munch, *Samlede Afhandlinger* (Christiania, 1874), 2, 116. Quoted from Munch's *Fornsvenskans och Fornnorskans Språkbyggnad*.

13. *Antiquités russes*, ed. C. C. Rafn (Copenhague, 1850), 1, 235.

in Munch's works, was fully developed and stated by Rudolf Keyser in his *Nordmændenes Videnskabelighed og Literatur i Middelalderen*, published posthumously in 1866.

Keyser begins his exposition with a "Historical Survey," in which he traces the general lines of literary development in a primitive culture. Even before the advent of writing a nation gradually reduces its legal, mythological, and literary traditions to some type of ordered form. Writing itself can be introduced at an early or late stage in this development. If it is introduced early, the borrower is likely to reflect the literary modes as well as the orthographic habits of the nation from which it learned the art of writing. Only if the native literature has reached a high degree of formation will the products of writing have a national stamp. A sign of this oral literature is that it is the anonymous property of the whole people. Those who commit it to writing act only as scribes and a considerable period of time elapses before literary activity passes into the hands of individuals. This is the pattern to which the early literature of the Norsemen adheres; it cannot be compared with that of the cultured peoples of antiquity or of modern times but must be taken for what it is, "for the intellectual stirring, and the product of this stirring, among a people, who during the greater part of the period described here is at the stage of intellectual development where oral tradition dominates the act of writing, where authorship can only be ascribed to individuals to a limited degree, where there can therefore be little question of the intellectual activity or intellectual creations of individual men."[14]

The initial organization of tradition occurred in verse.[15] Somewhat later prose accounts were developed to accompany and supplement the poems and these too acquired a set, circumscribed form. In Norway the rise of absolutism supplied the impetus and the focal point for the gathering and combining of the popular traditions, "which had already assumed such a set and rounded form that they only awaited men with sufficient practice in writing to record them easily in order to appear as literature."[16] Writing was learned from Anglo-Saxon clerics, and already in the middle of the eleventh century Magnus the Good ordered laws committed to parchment. However it was another full century before the constantly growing oral literature began to be set down. The written literature was "a faithful reflection of the oral tradi-

14. Rudolf Keyser, *Efterladte Skrifter, 1: Nordmændenes Videnskabelighed og Literatur i Middelalderen* (Christiania, 1866), 9.
15. See Anton Blanck, *Den Nordiska Renässansen*, pp. 48, 293, 298.
16. Keyser, p. 13.

tion, which it replaced. . . . The scribe as a rule used only his pen; thoughts and words belonged to the tradition." [17] This is what gives medieval Norwegian literature its unique character; it is not the work of individuals but the reflection of a whole people's thoughts and feelings. Individuality expressed itself only in scaldic verse and the more learned current of historical investigation. However, the strength of the scalds lay chiefly in their formal artistry and the learned historians achieved their reputations more as critical sifters than as authors. Not until most of the oral literature had been written down did the written word begin to replace the spoken word and to undermine the use of memory. The Norwegian translations of foreign literature marked the emancipation of the individual writer from the popular spirit on which he had theretofore been dependent. This outline of Keyser's theory plainly amounts to a fairly orthodox adaptation of the romantic theory of literary origins to fit Norwegian conditions.

In dealing with the relationship of Norwegian and Icelandic literature Keyser, like Munch, concedes no distinction. The Icelanders colonized their new homes from Norway and established a state which was politically independent until the thirteenth century. "But despite this political independence, which lasted several centuries, Iceland's inhabitants never ceased to regard themselves as Norwegians." [18] Though Iceland evolved her own political form, the same cannot be said of her cultural development, the basis for which was brought from Norway and the unfolding of which was conditioned by constant contact with and emulation of Norwegian models. "The Icelandic sagaman in Norway told to a large extent of Norwegian events only what he had learned either first-hand or second-hand through Norwegian tradition, without reserving for himself any credit other than the ability to retain and recite fluently what already in Norwegian tradition had assumed a more or less rigid form." [19] The specific deserts of the Icelanders lay merely in the preservation of a literature which would otherwise have been lost. Iceland can make no claim to an independent literature until about 1400, when the common language fell into disuse in Norway.

Scholars elsewhere in Scandinavia and beyond stood in the shadow of P. E. Müller and assumed a greater or lesser extent of set tradition

17. Ibid., p. 15. Cf. on rigid tradition Falnes, *National Romanticism in Norway*, esp. pp. 176–77. The prose tradition of the Norwegian folktales was also believed to be rigid (p. 257).

18. Keyser, p. 21.

19. Ibid., p. 23.

behind the sagas. In Sweden, Lindfors cited Bishop Magnus' recital of news at the Thing on his return from Norway as the typical point of departure for a saga. "Furthermore the oldest sagas show clear traces of their origin in oral traditions. This is evinced by their simple narrative style, without digressions or reflections, and their dialogue form, in which the author never asserts himself. Nor did he ever reveal his name, for he merely copied what he had heard from others and could therefore claim no honor for himself." [20] Similarly, Geijer, goaded by F. Rühs's sceptical *Geschichte Swedens* as Müller had been by Rühs's *Edda*,[21] argued that the sagas approached poetry in their strictness of form. "But the prose narratives must also in some way have been artistically elevated, and the oral tradition have acquired such a strict form that they were not so much composed as written down ready-made." [22]

In Germany Köppen put particular emphasis on the derivation of the sagas from poetry. He supposed that the confining staccato of the Norse meters obliged the Icelanders to supplement their poetry with prose accounts which allowed greater breadth of presentation. The mythical sagas "sind ja nichts andres als die prosaisch gehaltene Tradition, welche direct aus der Auflösung heidnischer Volkslieder hervorging." [23] The same applies to the historical and family sagas. "Quellen waren auch hier die Skaldenlieder, daneben aber auch die Stammbäume oder Langfedgatals, auf welche die Häuptlinge eben so eifrig hielten, als bei uns die Landjunker. Diese lieferten das Gerippe, jene das Fleisch, d.h. den Inhalt, den man nur der poetischen Sprache zu entkleiden brauchte, um ihn wirklich, factisch und historisch wiederherzustellen." [24] At the same time he embraces a very strict form of set tradition. He assumes that many sagas originated before

20. Anders O. Lindfors, *Inledning till Isländska Literaturen och dess Historia* (Lund, 1824), pp. 129–30.

21. L. Stavenow, "Friedrich Rühs' Betydelse för Svensk Historieskrifning," *Nordisk Tidskrift* (1918), p. 323: "Detta Geijers berömda verk [*Svea Rikes Häfder*] är egentligen ett knippe af speciella undersökningar, genom hvilka Geijer vill framvisa och bestämma dels värdet af de klassiska auktorernas uppgifter om norden, dels af den isländska historiska sagoskrifning (särskildt ynglingasagan) och häfda eddadiktningens folkliga och äkta nordiska ursprung samt allmän-skandinaviska karaktär. Detta sistnämnda är särskildt Geijers hufvudintresse. I hela arbetet för han en förtäckt, i dess hufvudkapitel, om den nordiska gudasagan, öppen polemik mot Rühs' idéer."

22. Erik G. Geijer, *Samlade Skrifter*, 2 (Stockholm, 1850), Part 1, p. 161. See also B. Henningsson, *Geijer som Historiker*, pp. 231–42.

23. C. F. Köppen, *Literarische Einleitung in die Nordische Mythologie* (Berlin, 1837), p. 93.

24. Ibid., p. 116. This fusion between the old idea that scalds were historians and the new romantic belief in the historical attributes of popular traditions was not uncommon. Cf. the references in note 15.

the twelfth century "und haben sich, ganz und fertig, wie wir sie haben, durch Generationen mündlich fortgepflanzt, ehe sie aufgezeichnet wurden."[25]

In the absence of evidence that epic poems ever existed Theodor Möbius rejects Köppen's derivation from verse and arrives at set form by a different route.[26] He believed that the sagas are accurate because of the striking correspondence to independent and reliable sources, but accuracy is only feasible under the assumption of set form. He argued that a stereotype form develops of itself when a story is repeated often enough.

Less doctrinaire is the account of saga origins given by Rosselet. He adheres to the assumption that the sagas were handed down from one generation to the next from the time of the events which they describe, but he stresses the fluidity of oral tradition and the role of the pen. "Der Historiker schreibt die Überlieferung nicht bloss auf, sondern benutzt sie, mündliche so gut wie schriftliche, als Quellen und verarbeitet sie."[27] He reckons the Icelandic family sagas among the half-historic accounts and harks back to Rühs in likening them to novels, though the word is probably meant more in a generic than in a genetic sense.

H. Wheaton's French handbook[28] emphasizes set form but is interesting for its folkloristic argument in so far as it draws attention to the ability of primitive peoples to retain quantities of verse and prose by memory. Homer and the Serbian rhapsodists are cited as analogies.

In Denmark, Müller's successor in the field of saga research was N. M. Petersen. Petersen departed significantly from the current hypothesis and assigned the saga writers a distinct contribution in the creation of the sagas as we have them. He too believed that the oral stories originated contemporaneous with the events, quickly solidified into sagas, and were learned verbatim by several generations of sagamen. But these oral stories must not be confused with the written sagas. In the introduction of his saga translations Petersen traces the development of the written sagas as a gradual progression from the annalistic notations to a fuller imitation (but not reproduction) of the oral stories.[29] In *Den Oldnordiske Literaturs Historie* there is a clearer

25. Ibid., p. 105.
26. Theodor Möbius, *Über die Ältere Isländische Saga* (Leipzig, 1852).
27. Emil Rosselet in Ersch und Gruber, *Allgemeine Encyklopedie*, 2. Section, XXXI Theil (Leipzig, 1855), p. 304.
28. Henry Wheaton, *De la Littérature scandinave* (Rouen, 1835). Cf. Adolph B. Benson, "Henry Wheaton's Writings on Scandinavia," *JEGP*, 29 (1930), esp. 557.
29. Niels M. Petersen, *Historiske Fortællinger om Islændernes Færd* (Kjøbenhavn,

picture of the transition from oral to written saga.[30] Petersen confesses that the direct recording of an oral saga is an attractive idea: "To write a saga would then be the easiest thing in the world. But when one looks more closely, one sees that this can really only apply to the actual kernel of the saga matter. The longer and better sagas all bear the obvious marks of editing."[31] The genealogies were probably not recited by the sagamen but were added at the time of writing. Some of the sagas show traces of being composites; the hand of the author can be detected in the somewhat primitive attempts at arranging the parts. Finally, the quotations from authorities such as Snorri and Ari cannot have belonged to the oral stage. For the historical sagas proper, matter was carefully gathered from heterogeneous sources and critically sifted before being written down.

The simultaneous appearance of Keyser's and Petersen's very different treatments of Old Norse literature was the immediate cause of a new phase in the controversy over origins. They touched off a scholarly feud which echoed in Scandinavia and Germany for three years. Even before 1866 voices had been raised in protest to the Norwegian expropriation of Old Norse literature in its entirety. In *Safn til Sögu Íslands,* I, Jón Þorkelsson published a study in which he acknowledged the accomplishments of Norwegian scholarship while expressing sober and documentary disapproval of the intransigeance with which it sought to make good Norway's deed to the older literature. "We are entirely cognizant of their merits, but we are unable to agree with all their judgments. We wish them to publish as much Norse literature as possible, whether it be Norwegian or Icelandic, but we do not want them to call Icelandic books Norwegian, which by the testimony of the old manuscripts were written on Iceland by Icelanders. . . ."[32]

1839), pp. 55–56: "Hvad man først opskrev var naturligvis enkelte Hovedbegivenheder og den Tid da de vare indtrufne; man havde derved et Slags kronologiske Fortegnelser, hvortil man kunde henføre de Begivenheder, der indeholdtes i en vel bekjendt Sang eller mundtlig Fortælling. Man opskrev vel ogsaa, ligesom man allerede under Hedenskabet havde gjort det med Runer, visse Hoveddele af Sangen, hvorved man kom Hukommelsen til Hjælp; og omdannede efterhaanden denne Sang til en Saga, der var kort og, ligesom Sangen, kun indeholdt Hovedstrøgene. Men jo mere øvet man blev i at bruge Pennen, desto hellere beklædte man denne Benrad med Kjød og Blod, for at den skrevne Saga kunde saa meget mere komme til at ligne de gamle, udførlige, de livfulde Islændere saa kjære, mundtlige Fortællinger."

30. N. M. Petersen, *Den Oldnordiske Literaturs Historie* (Kjøbenhavn, 1866). First printed in *Annaler for Nordisk Oldkyndighed,* 1861.

31. Ibid., pp. 199–200.

32. Jón Þorkelsson, "Um Fagrskinnu og Ólafs Sögu Helga," *Safn til Sögu Íslands* (1853), *1,* 137. Árni Magnússon had already protested against a similar expropriation by the Swedes in the seventeenth century: see *Levned og Skrifter,* 2, 109–10; cf. *1,* 104–05.

In 1865 Konrad Maurer had presented a paper later revised and published under the title *Ueber die Ausdrücke: Altnordische, Altnorwegische und Isländische Sprache* (München, 1867). The purpose of the book was to arrive at an adequate terminology, but, as Grundtvig pointed out,[33] the title is deceptive. In establishing his terms Maurer gave in fact a brief history of Norse prose literature supported by 182 pages of learned notes setting forth the priority of Iceland's claim to the great majority of Old Norse literature. He traced the growth of the Icelandic literary idiom from Ari on and stressed the unbroken tradition in Iceland contrasted to the linguistic diffusion which set in in Norway after 1300, when Swedish, then Danish, became the medium of communication in literary and official circles.

Keyser's book was therefore partially outdated when it appeared and it met with immediate and extensive criticism. Maurer published a sixty-three page review in the first number of *Zeitschrift für Deutsche Philologie*. His criticism was distinguished by a thorough treatment of the theoretical basis for Keyser's inflexible tradition.

Maurer believed in "massenhafte überlieferungen von mund zu mund"[34] and did not doubt that the form of the written saga was determined by the habits of oral storytelling, but he believed the tradition to be fluid and subject to the vagaries of time, memory, and personality. He found it inconceivable that sagas such as *Njáls saga, Laxdœla saga, Óláfs saga helga,* and *Óláfs saga Tryggvasonar* were ever told in the form in which they are preserved on parchment. Nor could he imagine the survival through centuries of a set tradition untouched by changes in conditions and tastes. He cited Snorri on the frailty of oral tradition and urged that the critical use of scaldic verse was a late development and not an age-old pillar of prose tradition. He reviewed the eclectic combination of sources and sourcemen which was the basis of *Íslendingabók* and later kings' sagas, showing that the gathering of isolated details from a few well qualified individuals spoke against the availability of full-blown historical accounts. He further drew attention to the illogicality of deriving an impulse to record traditions mechanically from Ari, the joiner and fitter par excellence. The references to saga telling are far from suggesting a set form. Halldórr Snorrason is given short shrift: ". . . wer wollte aber glauben, dass Halldórr, der uns überall als ein rauher kriegsmann derb-

33. Svend Grundtvig, "Om Nordens Gamle Literatur," *Historisk Tidskrift,* 3. Række, *5* (1867), 14, 16.
34. Konrad Maurer, "Die Norwegische Auffassung der Nordischen Literatur-Geschichte," *ZfdPh, 1* (1869), 53.

sten schlages geschildert wird, sich damit befasst habe, eine kunst-
gerecht stylisierte sage zusammenzusetzen, und diese dann jahr für
jahr am alldinge herzusagen, bis sie endlich Þorsteinn stück für
stück auswendig gelernt hatte?" [35] Nor does the anonymity of certain
works bespeak an anonymous origin. It is fortuitous, due to the author's modesty or to the repeated reworking of a text, which thereby
lost the mark of personal authorship. The chronological progression
from fragmentary to fuller accounts does not, as Keyser believed, reflect a gradual perfecting of the oral medium but simply a failing of
memory in proportion to the remoteness of events from the chronicler.

Maurer placed Keyser's national aspirations in as favorable a light
as possible, attributing the malproportions of his book in part to a
poetic vein. At the same time he reaffirmed Icelandic proprietorship
to the point of regarding the literary idiom in Norway as an Icelandic
import. He emphasized the ubiquitous Icelandic bias even in the Norwegian kings' sagas and the plain words of Theodricus Monachus
about his Icelandic sourcemen. What, he asked, would account for the
detailed interest in Icelandic affairs in the *Íslendinga sǫgur* proper if
these were to be counted a Norwegian product?

Much harsher criticism was forthcoming in Denmark, where there
appeared in *Historisk Tidskrift* a very lengthy comparative review
of Keyser's and Petersen's works by Svend Grundtvig. The review
was entitled "Oldnordisk Literaturhistorie," a choice of words which
indicates both the slant and the scope of the criticism. Grundtvig opposed vigorously what he felt to be Keyser's not only false but to some
extent falsified claim of Norwegian literary rights. On the one hand
he defended the Icelandic prerogatives, stressing the unanswered study
by Þorkelsson and discrediting in no uncertain terms the obscure
Þorgeirr afráðskollr, who Snorri tells us was, indirectly, one of Ari's
sourcemen, but whom Keyser conceived as the central figure in a
blossoming school of Norwegian historiography. On the other hand
Grundtvig polemicized for the term *oldnordisk,* which would vindicate the participation of Denmark and Sweden in the ancient Norse
mythological and heroic poetry, then believed to date from the Scandinavian Iron Age. Unlike Maurer, Grundtvig failed to enter into a
discussion of the theory of set tradition, though he stated his disbelief
in passing: ". . . although it is after all clear that long, carefully composed prose works could never be imagined to have passed for cen-

35. Ibid., p. 71.

turies unchanged from mouth to mouth like short, strictly formed, rimed poems. . . ."[36]

In part due to its tone Grundtvig's essay brought a storm of protest from the Norwegian press and aroused dissent even in Denmark, where the irrepressible Edwin Jessen countered with charges of Danish chauvinism and emphasized the German roots of heroic poetry. In reply Grundtvig took the floor in 1869 with another hundred page contribution to *Historisk Tidskrift*. He is visibly, if somewhat grudgingly, enlightened by Maurer's more fundamental discussion, which he reports in extenso without adding considerations of his own on oral tradition.

The final stage of the controversy was a conciliatory summary by Gustav Storm.[37] Storm acknowledged the correctness of Maurer's and Grundtvig's position in respect to the prose literature while taking definite exception to Grundtvig's view of Eddic poetry. He appraised Keyser's position in the development of northern research, pointing out that his theory was reasonable at the stage of ethnographic, linguistic, and literary studies attained when he wrote. His only precursor was Müller, whereas the mid-century research concerning the sources of the kings' sagas was unknown to him. His book therefore had the misfortune to appear at a time when it was already superannuated.

In the wake of this controversy appeared the first detailed investigation of an *Íslendinga saga*, Maurer's *Ueber die Hœnsa-Þóris Saga*.[38] Until this time the family sagas had for the most part been regarded as a phenomenon subsidiary to the kings' sagas and what was legislated for the latter was carried over without much ado to the former.

A paramount issue was dating. In *Ausdrücke,* Maurer had passed over the family sagas briefly, commenting on the extreme difficulty of determining their date of composition and suggesting that their age was commonly overestimated. Since the days of Müller the practice was to regard the sagas as a product of the twelfth century on the strength of a passage in *Sturlunga saga:* "Flestar allar sögur, þær er gjörzt höfðu á Íslandi, vóru ritaðar áðr Brandr biskup Sæmundarson andaðist; en þær sögur, er síðan hafa gjörzt, vóru lítt ritaðar, áðr Sturla skáld Þórðarson sagði fyrir Íslendingasögur." Müller took

36. Grundtvig, "Om Nordens Gamle Literatur," p. 552.
37. Gustav Storm, *Om den Gamle Norrøne Literatur* (Christiania, 1869).
38. Konrad Maurer, "Ueber die Hœnsa-Þóris Saga," *K. Bayer. Akad. d. Wiss., München, Philos.-Philol. Classe, Abhandl., 12* (1871), Part 2, pp. 157–216. Cf. Sigurður Nordal, *Hrafnkels Saga Freysgoða,* Eng. trans. R. G. Thomas (Cardiff, 1958), p. 65.

"flestar allar sögur" to apply to all Icelandic sagas, which had then to be dated before 1201, the date of Brandr's death. In his *Historie* Petersen contended that the passage had reference only to the written sagas incorporated in the Sturlunga complex.[39] To this Guðbrandr Vigfússon added a footnote in which he revealed that there was no basis at all for the early dating since the passage in question was corrupt. The correct reading, preserved in AM122B gives an entirely different meaning: "Flestar allar sögur, þær er gjörzt höfðu á Íslandi, áðr Brandr biskup Sæmundarson andaðist, vóru ritaðar. . . ."[40]

Armed with this correction and the experience gained in a close investigation of the kings' sagas, Maurer made a fresh start. The result of his analysis of *Hœnsa-Þóris saga* was, stated briefly, that the saga in its original form was written on the basis of oral traditions independent of Ari sometime between 1200 and 1245, since, as Maurer supposed, the written saga was used by Styrmir fróði in his *Landnáma.* Then early in the fourteenth century the saga was interpolated and clumsily cast in the form we now know.

Maurer's essay represented an extraordinary advance in saga research. It anticipated most of the techniques of present investigation, the studious comparison of a saga with the available written sources, especially *Landnáma,* the careful testing of the saga's internal logic and probability, the assumption of the reworker's if not the author's prerogative to innovate and speculate, the dating according to literary interrelationships. There is even a hint of the latter-day Icelandic typological dating when Maurer speaks of a "sehr gewandte Darstellung"[41] which forbids us to count the work among the first ungainly products of saga writing. With Maurer we enter the stage of research which does not have mere historic interest but brings us face to face with the issues still under debate.

39. N. M. Petersen, *Den Oldnordiske Literaturs Historie,* p. 236.
40. For the most recent discussion and some of the literature see Marco Scovazzi, *La Saga di Hrafnkell e il Problema delle Saghe Islandesi* (n.p., 1960), pp. 280–81. Scovazzi's translation and his reversion to the old interpretation on the basis of the new reading puzzle me. A concise summary of the problem and the apparently correct solution is provided by E. Ó. Sveinsson, *Dating the Icelandic Sagas* (London, 1958), pp. 42–47.
41. Maurer, "Ueber die Hœnsa-Þóris Saga," p. 54.

3

Modern Trends

In view of the proliferation of Norse studies over the last century a slightly different and more impressionistic approach to the modern era recommends itself. It becomes advisable to abandon a presentation by personality in order to review various trends of thought about the family sagas after they emerged as an object of study in their own right. The present chapter is concerned with the historicity of the sagas, the growth of literary analysis, the theory of Irish influence, the so-called *þáttr* theory, and the bearing of these theories and viewpoints on the question of origins.

Historicity

That the sagas were essentially historical was an assumption that had survived with only minor revisions since the discovery of the Icelandic codices. The kings' sagas, properly weighed and combined, were regarded by Munch and others as a sure foundation for the early sections of Scandinavian history, and the family sagas were felt to be, if anything, still more reliable, since they dealt with domestic affairs. It could surprise no one when in 1856 G. Vigfússon assembled a complete and allegedly historical chronology of the Saga Age by ingeniously comparing and dovetailing the testimony of the family sagas.[1] As we have seen, Möbius had at the same time turned Torfaeus'

1. Guðbrandur Vigfússon, "Um Tímatal í Íslendinga-Sögum," *Safn til Sögu Íslands,* *1* (1856).

old reasoning upside down by arguing that the undeniable historicity of the sagas was unthinkable without set form.[2]

When, therefore, Edwin Jessen assailed the credibility of *Egils saga*, his view was regarded as so heretical that, according to his own testimony, he was not given a voice in Denmark but was obliged to take refuge in a German journal.[3] By comparing *Egils saga* with foreign sources, especially Ohtere's voyage of discovery around 890 as reported in King Alfred's *Orosius*, Jessen arrived at a very negative estimate of the Icelandic source's trustworthiness. He found anachronisms in the presence of Kylfingar in Finnmark, the collection of a Lapptax, the use of the title *hertogi*, and the suspiciously intimate knowledge of Finnmark at a time when it was supposedly being explored for the first time by Ohtere. He pointed to the geographic ignorance reflected in Þórólfr's enormous grainbarn in Hálogoland, the converse failure to mention whaling and reindeer, the conflict between *Egils saga*'s Tönsberg and Ohtere's Skiringshal, two trading centers which were so close to one another that they could not have flourished simultaneously. He questioned the legal arrangement whereby Barðr made Þórólfr his universal heir to the exclusion of his own son and the chronological discrepancy between *Egils saga*'s dating of the Battle of Vínheiðr (according to Vigfússon) and the *Anglo-Saxon Chronicle*'s dating of the seemingly identical Battle of Brunanburh. Also chronologically dubious was the apparent naming of Guttormr's children, Ragnarr, Sigurðr, and Áslaug, after the legend of Ragnarr loðbrók, a legend which could not have been formed as early as the ninth century. Even some of the domestic tradition, notably Egill's youthful exploits, was palpably fictitious, and it was in itself suspicious that so much space was devoted to Egill's deeds abroad and so little to his activities in Iceland. As far as I can see, Jessen was the first to maintain that an accurate chronology, far from proving a historical tradition, revealed the conscious manipulation of an author.[4] He drew forth kinks in the chronology which led him to believe that the author had tried to impose an annalistic structure on a loose popular tradition. A sign of the underlying folktale was the werewolf motif. Jessen concluded that at least those portions of *Egils saga* which transpired

2. *Über die Ältere Isländische Saga*, pp. 5–6.
3. Edwin Jessen, "Glaubwürdigkeit der Egils-Saga und Anderer Isländer-Saga's," *Historische Zeitschrift*, 28 (1872), 61–100.
4. Ibid., p. 65. Cf. Björn M. Ólsen, "Um Íslendingasögur," *Safn til Sögu Íslands*, 6, Parts 5–7 (1937–39), 42–43; and Walter Baetke, "Über die Entstehung der Isländersagas," *Berichte über die Verhandl. der Sächs. Akad. der Wiss. zu Leipzig, Philol.-Hist. Kl.*, 102, Part 5 (1956), 32, and note 3.

abroad were wholly fictitious. There may have been a historical basis for the saga, but this basis had been transformed beyond recognition. "Einem Roman kann Geschichte irgendwie zu Grunde liegen: damit wird er nicht selbst zum geschichtlichen Bericht."[5]

An aspect of the saga touched on by Jessen and subsequently subjected to a particularly thorough study was the jurisprudential apparatus. The comparative material afforded by the Icelandic lawbooks was an instrument with which to measure the sagas' accuracy at least in this one area. The first investigations were spurred by the foremost authority on Norse law, Konrad Maurer, who set two of his students to the task of analysing *Njáls saga,* especially from a legal viewpoint. Lehmann, who bore the burden of the legal studies, observed a confusion of terminology, an unfamiliarity with the law of republican Iceland, and a mechanical dependence on the written lawbooks which led him to conclude that the author could not have lived during the period of Icelandic independence. He therefore dated *Njáls saga* a century later than was customary, to the last third or quarter of the thirteenth century, when the Icelandic institutions had been supplanted by the Norwegian crown. At first vigorously opposed by V. Finsen and F. Jónsson, who regarded the legal sections as part of the baggage of ancient tradition, the balance of Lehmann's thesis has gained substantial acceptance.[6]

Maurer himself made two smaller contributions to the study of saga jurisprudence.[7] In the first, Maurer's findings did not bear out Jessen's criticism but showed that in all essentials *Egils saga* gave an adequate account of ninth century procedures. The results for *Eyrbyggja saga* were similar. By tracing the evolution and specific departures of Icelandic law from the Norwegian prototypes Maurer demonstrated, for example, that the *dyradómr* in *Eyrbyggja saga* was probably a genuine remnant of Icelandic practice, though it appears nowhere in the codified law.

This line of inquiry was pursued exhaustively in two books by An-

5. Jessen, p. 99. Cf. Frederick York Powell, "Saga-Growth," *Folk-Lore,* 5 (1894), 97–106.
6. Karl Lehmann and Hans Schnorr von Carolsfeld, *Die Njáls-sage Insbesondere in Ihren Juristischen Bestandtheilen* (Berlin, 1883); Vilhjálmur Finsen, "Om den Oprindelige Ordning af Nogle af den Islandske Fristats Institutioner," *D. Kgl. Danske Vidensk. Selsk. Skr.,* 6. R. *Hist. og Phil. Afd.,* 2, Part 1 (1888); Finnur Jónsson, "Om Njála," *Aarbøger for Nordisk Oldkyndighed* (1904); E. Ó. Sveinsson, *Um Njálu* (Reykjavík, 1933), pp. 305–11.
7. Konrad Maurer, "Zwei Rechtsfälle in der Eigla," *Sitzungsberichte der Philos.-Philol. und der Hist. Cl. der K. Bayer. Akad. d. Wiss.* (1895); "Zwei Rechtsfälle aus der Eyrbyggja," *Sitzungsberichte,* etc. (1896).

dreas Heusler.[8] Heusler's thesis was that the *Íslendinga sǫgur* represented an independent legal source at once older and more oriented toward actual practice than the theoretical organ of Iceland's thirteenth-century legal academicians, the *Grágás*. However, one of the by-products of the first book was to show that almost all the deviations from *Grágás* practice were common to the family sagas and the contemporary *Sturlunga saga*. Since this correspondence tended to impugn the supposed age of the family sagas, Heusler emphasized in his second study the consistent differences between the two classes of sagas. He pointed out that *Sturlunga saga* shows greater complication in the transaction of settlements, more frequent mediation by a powerful *goði* or bishop, the introduction of the *trúnaðareiðr,* the practice of exempting certain persons from the conditions of a judgment prior to its pronouncement, the voluntary relinquishing of *sjálfdœmi,* an increase in broken agreements. But compared to the many cases in which *Sturlunga saga* and the family sagas go hand in hand these divergencies seem slight and circumstantial. In general, therefore, and despite the quick welcome given the new evidence by the advocates of saga historicity, Heusler's conclusions have not been incorporated into the body of accepted research. Nevertheless, it has not seemed unlikely, even to conservative scholars, that the sagas do preserve an occasional legal relic.[9]

Another discipline placed at the service of the sagas was archeology. As early as 1836 N. M. Petersen identified a woman's corpse recovered from a bog near Vejle as that of Queen Gunnhildr, whom King Harald Bluetooth is reputed in the sagas to have disposed of in a swamp. The merits of the identification were spiritedly debated with J. J. A. Worsaae. In Iceland digging began systematically, particularly under Sigurður Vigfússon, who undertook a long series of excursions and excavations in the '80s in an effort to verify saga topography and sites. The consensus among present scholars is that Vigfússon wielded a somewhat overzealous spade. Since his day excavations have been continued and carried out repeatedly, especially at Bergþórshváll, but the yield remains problematic. The scanty findings make it difficult to exclude the element of coincidence to the satisfaction of the sceptics.[10]

8. Andreas Heusler, *Das Strafrecht der Isländersagas* (Leipzig, 1911) and "Zum Isländischen Fehdewesen in der Sturlungazeit," *Abhandl. der K. Preus. Akad. d. Wiss.* (1912), No. 4.

9. Jón Helgason, *Norrøn Litteraturhistorie* (København, 1934), p. 128; Baetke, "Über die Entstehung," p. 35 and notes; E. Ó. Sveinsson, *Um Njálu,* pp. 201–05.

10. Niels M. Petersen, "Udsigt over den Norske Dronning Gunhildes Levned," *Annaler for Nordisk Oldkyndighed* (1836–37), 80–104; Jens J. A. Worsaae, "Hvorvidt Kan

In general the most emphatic and persistent advocate of saga reliability was Finnur Jónsson. "I will maintain and defend the sagas'
historical trustworthiness—no matter how 'grand' that may sound—
until I am forced to lay down my pen." [11] He stressed the many references to trustworthy sourcemen, believing that these reflected both the
sincerity—". . . the respect for his listeners and readers, we would say
for the public, the desire to narrate in such a way as to be believed . . ." [12]—and the considerable critical sense of the saga writers.
The tangible means of corroboration are divided into three categories:
1. comparison with foreign sources; 2. comparison with other Icelandic sources; 3. topographic and antiquarian verification. [13]

In direct opposition to Jessen, Finnur Jónsson argued a great degree
of correspondence between *Egils saga* and Ohtere's report and defended the former's over-all accountability. The chronological disloca-
tion of the Battle of Vínheiðr is explained as the result of a confusion
between this major encounter and a minor skirmish fought by King
Aðalsteinn ten years earlier. With reference to Maurer, emphasis is
placed on the preservation of ancient legal practices both in *Egils saga*
and in *Eyrbyggja saga*. Finnur Jónsson admitted to some uncertainty
on the part of the sagas about early Norwegian matters, e.g. the improbability of Ingibjǫrg's affair with Kjartan at the very time she was
being courted, and the curious legend of Gunnhildr Gormsdóttir's
Lappish parentage. On the other hand he urged the remarkable accuracy of some accounts as indicated, for example, by the identification of the King Gnúpa in the large *Óláfs saga Tryggvasonar* (chap.
63) with the Gnúpa mentioned in the Vedelspang inscriptions, [14] the
greater credibility of the Norse sources in making Rollo a Norwegian

---

Man Antage, at det i Haraldskiær-Mosen (1835) Opgravede Liig er den Norske Dronning Gunhildes?" *Historisk Tidskrift, 3* (1842), 249–92; N. M. Petersen, "Yderligere
Bemærkninger om Dronning Gunhilde," *Annaler for Nordisk Oldkyndighed* (1842–43),
263–326; e.g. S. Vigfússon, "Rannsókn um Vestfirði, Einkanlega í Samanbandi við
Gísla Sögu Súrssonar," *Árbók hins Íslenzka Fornleifafélags* (1883), pp. 1–70; "Rannsókn í Borgarfirði," *Árbók* (1884–85), pp. 61–138, and *Árbók* (1886), pp. 1–51;
"Rannsókn í Rangárþingi og Vestantil í Skaptafellsþingi, 1883 og 1885, Einkanlega
í Samanbandi við Njáls Sögu," *Árbók* (1887), pp. 1–37, and *Árbók* (1888–92), pp.
1–75; Sigurður Nordal, *Hrafnkels Saga Freysgoða,* pp. 20, 23; E. Ó. Sveinsson, *Fornrit,
12* (1954), v–lx; Walter Baetke, "Über die Entstehung," p. 27 n.
    11. Finnur Jónsson, *Norsk-Islandske Kultur- og Sprogforhold i 9. og 10. Århundrede*
(København, 1921), p. 141.
    12. Finnur Jónsson, *Den Oldnorske og Oldislandske Litteraturs Historie, 2,* 216.
    13. Ibid., 216–41.
    14. Ludvig F. A. Wimmer, *De Danske Runemindesmærker* (København, 1893), *1,*
66–72.

rather than a Dane as in Dudo,[15] and finally the good correspondence between the Icelandic accounts of the Battle of Clontarf and the Irish records.

Under the second heading special importance is attached to the alleged oral variants, notably those in *Glúms saga* and *Reykdœla saga*, which Finnur Jónsson believed to bespeak a highly stable tradition. His confidence in this tradition was such that in one case of conflicting reports he preferred *Reykdœla saga*'s version to the scaldic authority of *Íslendingadrápa*. Further evidence of stability he gleaned from the extensive genealogical agreement with *Landnáma*, which he regarded as an independent tradition not always superior to the sagas.

Under the third heading Jónsson stressed the topographical accuracy of the sagas, an accuracy which gained greatly in significance when it entailed sites in Norway and England, with which the saga writer was not likely to have had first-hand acquaintance and about which he must therefore have learned from tradition. S. Vigfússon's excavations are accepted with only mild reservation. Lastly Jónsson drew attention to the saga's famed realism, the absence of stereotypes and the high degree of individualization, which strongly suggest a firm basis in fact.

The reaction to Jónsson's faith in the sagas came from the professional historians, especially Lauritz Weibull. In a series of critical investigations Weibull urged a much stricter source criticism than that practiced by Munch and his successors.[16] He preached the absolute priority of the oldest sources, which meant for example that the West Norse sagas must bow to Adam of Bremen. He stressed the legendary accretions visible in the work of the Norse historians, citing the following utterance in regard to the practice of purging sources in order to reveal their historical kernel: "One could just as well, Seignobos once said, amputate the supernatural in a fairy tale, excise puss in boots and make the Marquis of Carabas into a historical personality." [17] Weibull's criticism extended even to scaldic verse, which he doubted was as impartial as Snorri and his modern followers believed. The rigorousness of his methodology went so far that he questioned the presence of Jomsvikings at Hjǫrungarvágr because the relevant stanza speaks only of vikings, not of Jomsvikings. To the essentially negative criteria with which Finnur Jónsson supported the reliability of the

---

15. Cf. Lauritz Weibull, "Rollo och Gånge-Rolf, en Sägenhistorisk Undersökning" (1911), *Nordisk Historia, 1* (Stockholm, 1948–49).

16. E.g. Lauritz Weibull, "Kritiska Undersökningar i Nordens Historia Omkring År 1000" (1911), *Nordisk Historia, 1,* 249–360; "Historisk-Kritisk Metod och Nordisk Medeltidsforskning," ibid., pp. 407–58.

17. Ibid., p. 412.

lausavísur,[18] Weibull opposed the demand that they give positive evidence of their genuineness. "What is necessary is not to prove that there is little or no reason to doubt the genuineness of the *lausavísur,* which are in themselves very dubious, but rather to prove that they really are genuine."[19]

The first and only scientific attempt to assess the historic content of the sagas was made by Knut Liestøl.[20] By applying the knowledge acquired in studying the mechanics of change in oral stories through comparison of Norwegian traditions with diplomatic records, Liestøl tried to arrive at an approximate proportion between history and fiction in the sagas. The presence of very considerable deformation is shown by:

1. The failure of the sources to agree on details (e.g. the name or genealogy of a person).

2. Conflicts between the prose and the imbedded verse.

3. Confusions, coalescings, transferences (there are for example two stanzas attributed to two different scalds).

4. Exaggerations and impossibilities.

5. A national bias in favor of the Icelanders.

6. The corruptions due to the artist's prerogative, especially in the matter of dialogue.

7. The presence of pure invention.

8. The late place name speculations.

9. Chronological errors.

10. The large part played by things supernatural.

As an illustration of the total effect produced by these deformations Liestøl noted the discrepancy between *Íslendingabók* and *Hœnsa-Þóris saga.*

The reasons for believing in a degree of historicity in the sagas despite the laws of change are:

1. The relatively few oral links needed to bridge the gap between event and saga (three links as the optimum, e.g. father > son > grandson).

2. The use of sourcemen.

3. The control exercised by the constant comparison of existing versions (W. Anderson's "Gesetz der Selbstberichtigung").

---

18. Finnur Jónsson, "Sagaernes Lausavísur," *Aarbøger for Nordisk Oldkyndighed* (1912).
19. Lauritz Weibull, *Nordisk Historia, 1,* 456.
20. Knut Liestøl, *Upphavet til den Islendske Ættesaga* (Oslo, 1929).

4. The stability of a tradition told often within a family.

5. The many references to saga telling, which suggest that the sagas were repeated frequently.

6. The preservative influence of place names.

7. The accurate description of Vínheiðr, which cannot be ascribed to the author's personal inspection of the site.

8. The pronounced feeling for genealogy unknown in later times.

9. The close agreement of oral variants.

10. The necessity of a prose commentary to accompany many of the stanzas.

11. Heusler's observation of legal relics.

12. The historical sense evident in the sagas' concern with old customs.

13. The relatively good chronology.

14. The survival of an interpretable Irish phrase in an Icelandic context.

15. The misinterpretation of old memories (Kinck).

16. The presence of supernumeraries, who could not be invented because they have no function, but some of whom are verified by *Landnáma*.

17. The disinterment of Svend Estridsen and the medical confirmation of his fabled lameness.

Liestøl concluded: "The family sagas have a historical basis, they were history from the beginning and were considered to be historical. But in their extant form they contain much that is unhistorical. . . . where there is no reason to believe that something is unhistorical, there is reason to believe that it is historical." [21]

Liestøl's criteria for the family saga's historicity have been sharply criticized by Baetke: [22]

1. The references to oral tradition ("menn segja," etc.) are formulaic and are consciously designed to vouch for the trustworthiness of the report. Where variants are cited, they seem to apply to very unimportant matters and are likewise a stylistic device.

2. The formal allusion to sources is almost exclusively restricted to the historical sagas. The only such references in the family sagas are to the building of churches (*Eyrbyggja saga* and *Bjarnar saga*) and have no bearing on the narrative. Liestøl's assumption that the saga

21. Ibid., pp. 229–30.
22. Walter Baetke, "Über die Entstehung," chap. 3.

writers only neglected to give their sources because the stories were so well known is wrong. There were no sourcemen.

3. Following Jessen and Björn M. Ólsen, Baetke maintains that good chronology betrays the calculating spirit of an author rather than reliable tradition. Similarly, accurate topography was within the author's ken and proves nothing about tradition.

4. Readers have been duped by the realistic tone and style of the sagas. These do not reflect an oral epic but are the natural idiom of the author.

5. Heusler's hypothesis that the sagas preserve early legal conditions has been disarmed by Lehmann, Schwerin, and Björn M. Ólsen.

6. The preservative value of familiar sites connected with saga events has been overestimated. Such memories are of short duration and can maintain only a single event, not the skein of a whole saga.

7. The same reservation applies to the *lausavísur,* which might preserve the memory of an event or situation but never a saga plot. The thirteenth-century author used them as pieces in his mosaic but was obliged to fill in and compose the gaps himself. This method is apparent from the conflicts between prose and verse in the sagas. Moreover the *lausavísur* do not deserve the same credence as the stanzas in the kings' sagas, which constituted a part of the official historical tradition. (Baetke believes in the necessity of distinguishing between loose family lore and the carefully guarded national traditions.)

8. One has gradually come to the realization that what seemed to be historical in other literatures—the French chansons de geste, the Arabic epics—is pure construction. The same realization for the Icelandic sagas is slow in coming because of the realistic content and oral style so unusual at such an early date.

The shades of opinion on historicity are many and have little more than the value of opinion.[23] The definition of a "reason to believe something is unhistorical" remains at all events a subjective matter and the calculation of a historical proportion in the absence of corroborative material is problematic as long as there is disagreement about the

23. Ibid., passim; Halvdan Koht, *The Old Norse Sagas* (New York, 1931), pp. 119–20; Rudolf Meissner, *Die Geschichte von den Leuten aus dem Lachswassertal,* in *Thule,* 4 (Jena, 1923), 12; Will. A. Craigie, *The Icelandic Sagas* (Cambridge, 1913), pp. 34–36; Eugen Mogk, *Geschichte der Norwegisch-Isländischen Literatur* in *Pauls Grundriss der Germanischen Philologie* (Strassburg, 1904), p. 740; Fredrik Paasche, *Norges og Islands Litteratur indtil Utgangen av Middelalderen* (Kristiania, 1924), pp. 314, 317.

growth and nature of the saga. Because of Liestøl's extensive treatment of the problem there has been a tendency to regard historicity as part and parcel of the freeprose doctrine. Despite Heusler's disavowal of the unhappy marriage—"Wo eine Prüfung nicht gelingt, also in 99 Fällen von 100, da bleibt uns nichts, als die Glaubwürdigkeit auf sich beruhen zu lassen." [24]—not all quarters have taken cognizance of the divorce.[25] There is however no logical connection or interdependence between the view that the sagas are documentary history and the theory of oral transmission. The only claim implicit in the freeprose theory is that the sagas were at one time history. Quite a different matter is Liestøl's postulate "the family sagas claim to be history." This is an aesthetic statement aimed at clarifying the relation of the saga writer to his material. That it is an axiom on which most scholars can agree is shown by Nordal's estimate of the history in *Njáls saga*. "Whether the oral traditions about Njáll have amounted to more or less, and whether the writer felt himself more or less dependent on or bound by them, it has certainly been of no small consequence for his handling of the story that Njáll was not his invention, but a historical person who had lived at a certain place and time and suffered a certain fate, and that the writer wanted his public to accept his Saga as history." [26]

The matter of historicity has now merged with the genetic problems of saga research and further endeavors in the field appear fruitless until agreement is reached in the question of origins. In the meantime one can only commend the tactful if captious solution proposed by Nordal: "And let us not either, in our gratitude to the authors, forget that we owe them the courtesy to detect rather too little than too much of what they themselves wanted to be hidden." [27]

Literary Analysis

The treatment of the sagas as history was hallowed by a long tradition. This was the earliest viewpoint and one which stubbornly maintained itself into this century, especially in the many works of Finnur Jónsson. The trend toward a literary approach, hinted at by Rühs,

24. Andreas Heusler, *Die Altgermanische Dichtung,* 2. Aufl. der neubearb. und verm. Ausg. (Potsdam, 1945), p. 213.
25. Peter Hallberg, *Den Isländska Sagan* (Stockholm, 1956), p. 43; Baetke, "Über die Entstehung," passim; Nordal, *The Historical Element in the Icelandic Family Sagas* (Glasgow, 1957), p. 13.
26. Nordal, *The Historical Element,* p. 25.
27. Ibid., p. 35.

developed haltingly and was usually on the defensive against the proponents of historicity; it required a strenuous effort even for the literary scholars to free themselves from the historical bias. Even now,
in the heyday of literary interpretation, it is remarkable how much of
the literary analysis is preoccupied with polemic against the his-
toricists, a polemic prompted either by a sense of insecurity or by a
sense of new-world discovery. But even if the literary terrain is still
far from being annexed, it is not entirely unexplored.

The earliest attempt was made by the Danish critic Carsten Hauch
in an essay which contains many good observations and good formulations and which remains readable today.[28] Hauch feels obliged to
begin by urging that despite their appearance of strict history (we
may note how appearances change) the sagas do have a poetic dimen-
sion. They stand halfway between the poetry of legend and the facts
of history, and it is as if these two were competing for Iceland's early
heroes. The fact is that history and poetry are not so distinct as one
could suppose; the dividing line is fluid and it is important not so
much to distinguish exactly between truth and fiction as to grasp the
poetry of the sagas. Hauch's analysis of *Njáls saga* shows how the plot
derives from the false auspices under which Gunnarr first acts; this
one moment of falseness precipitates the whole conflict, which, as
Hauch moralizes, is constructed on the wages of deceit. Here and
elsewhere Hauch perceives the artistic mind obeying the aesthetic
rule that the conclusion may only contain what is latent from the
outset.

Hauch was ahead of his time. The next step did not come until
twenty years later on the wave of Maurer's Old Norse studies. This
stage is represented by general characterizations of the family saga, a
brief one by Döring and a very full one by Heinzel.[29] Both are strong
in compilation and weak in evaluation. Döring sees in the sagas, because of their stereotype style, ". . . eine bestimmte Kunst, eine bestimmte Manier des Erzählens, ein stehender Geschmack."[30] But with
Maurer he believes in the author's independence in the selection and
arrangement of his material and the elaboration of the historical facts.
He then gives examples of description, of the dramatic technique, es-

28. Carsten Hauch, "Indledning til Forelæsninger over Njalssaga og Flere med den
Beslægtede Sagaer," *Afhandlinger og Æsthetiske Betragtninger* (Kjøbenhavn, 1855),
pp. 411–67.
29. Karl Bernhard Döring, *Bemerkungen über Stil und Typus der Isländischen Saga*
(Leipzig, 1877); Richard Heinzel, "Beschreibung der Isländischen Saga," *Sitzungsberichte
der K. Akad. der Wiss., Philos.-Hist. Cl.*, 97 (Wien, 1880), Heft 1, 107–308.
30. Döring, p. 8.

pecially the dialogue, of the use of stanzas, similes, proverbs, and syntax. All this material and more is provided by Heinzel in great detail. His monograph is especially useful for the extensive cataloguing of themes and parallels employed in the sagas. That the historical viewpoint is still fundamental is shown by his division of the material into "aus dem Leben" (historical) and "aus der Überlieferung" (literary). Today much of the former category would be assigned to the latter.

Some of the more prominent literary dimensions were subsequently treated in more specialized studies, in which inferences were drawn on the genesis of the sagas. We will see how Bååth regarded the use of fate as the connecting thread in the sagas and therefore as the decisive moment in the birth of the written saga as we know it.[31] Another device which has proved its fascination is the use of dreams in the sagas. It is interesting to observe how the various dream monographs vacillate between the historical and literary poles.[32] The problem for Henzen is to establish whether the dreams are real or unreal. He decides that they are to be regarded as an artistic device because of the regularity with which dream prophecies are borne out by later events, but one sees that this was no foregone conclusion for him and, having found his answer, he does not proceed to any literary evaluation of the dreams. Similarly Margarete Haeckel summons up all the learned apparatus to arrive at the conclusion that the function of the dream is an aesthetic one, since the feature of prophecy or revelation is common to all of them and serves to induce a tragic atmosphere. The line of inquiry is analogous in Kelchner's dissertation. Though she recognizes the literary aspects, especially in the more elaborate dreams, she attributes to them a modified reality because they emphasize fate and this-worldliness and are "a typical expression of heathenism" (p. 75). Their real substance is also vouched for by a couple of instances where dreams are connected with ritualistic practices.

The same tension is visible in a couple of dissertations about gesture

---

31. A. U. Bååth, *Studier öfver Kompositionen i Några Isländska Ättsagor* (Lund, 1885).

32. Wilhelm Henzen, *Über die Träume in der Altnordischen Sagalitteratur* (Leipzig, 1890); Margarete Haeckel, *Die Darstellung und Funktion des Traumes in der Isländischen Familiensaga* (Hamburg Diss., 1935); Georgia Dunham Kelchner, *Dreams in Old Norse Literature and Their Affinities in Folklore* (Cambridge, 1935). On dreams see also Walther Gehl, *Der Germanische Schicksalsglaube* (Berlin, 1939), pp. 155–63, and G. Turville-Petre, "Dreams in Icelandic Tradition," *Folklore, 69* (1958), 93–111, esp. 106–11.

in the sagas by Gödecke and Graf.[33] Both are borne up by the conviction that saga behavior mirrors Germanic reality. But both must temper their conviction with literary concessions. Gödecke analyzes the types of emotions which occur and shows how they are expressed either directly or indirectly by gesture, action, discourse, or dreams. He characterizes his results as a contribution to the stylistic description of the sagas, but maintains that the basis of the style is a selection from heroic reality. The style is ultimately true to life.

The years 1934–35 saw the almost simultaneous publication of three monographs on discourse in the sagas, a subject treated by Heusler for the *Edda* and made topical for the sagas by Liestøl.[34] Most exhaustive but purely descriptive is Netter's study; briefer, more readable, and more sensitive to saga style are Jeffrey's and Ludwig's. Jeffrey concludes that the discourse has a threefold function: "development of action, characterization, creation of atmosphere," which corresponds very well to what Ludwig found in his section on *Hœnsa-Þóris saga*.[35] Jeffrey was content with a purely literary analysis while Ludwig remained in the genetic tradition of studies and applied his observations to the problem of development. He distinguishes two styles of discourse, a more primitive objective-symptomatic style and a later subjective-contemplative style (the latter is also observed by Jeffrey, p. 85, but termed "rare"). He does not suggest that this observation can be used to determine the absolute chronology of the sagas but only to distinguish what is stylistically more archaic.

A more recent dissertation pursues a similar thesis. Sprenger seeks to distinguish two styles on the basis of the use of the historical present and the preterite in a number of sagas.[36] In the early sagas (*Heiðarvíga saga, Hœnsa-Þóris saga, Gísla saga*) the present predominates and accounts for the basic nucleus of the narrative, while the preterite is used for accent and heightening of effect. The author gives analogies

33. August Gödecke, *Die Darstellung der Gemütsbewegungen in der Isländischen Familiensaga* (Hamburg, 1933); Heinz J. Graf, *Untersuchungen zur Gebärde in der Íslendinga saga* (Bonn Diss., 1938).
34. Andreas Heusler, "Der Dialog in der Altgermanischen Erzählenden Dichtung," *ZfDA, 46* (1902), 189–284; Liestøl, *Upphavet,* chap. 3; Irmgard Netter, *Die Direkte Rede in den Isländersagas* (Leipzig, 1935); Margaret Jeffrey, *The Discourse in Seven Icelandic Sagas* (Bryn Mawr diss., 1933); Werner Ludwig, *Untersuchungen über den Entwicklungsgang und die Funktion des Dialogs in der Isländischen Saga* (Halle, 1934).
35. Jeffrey, p. 85; Ludwig, pp. 70 ff.
36. Ulrike Sprenger, *Praesens Historicum und Praeteritum in der Altisländischen Saga* (Basel, 1951).

from recent German folktale collections to show that this is oral style. The larger and later sagas (*Egils saga, Eyrbyggja saga, Njáls saga, Grettis saga*) have a predominance of preterite and use the historical present for accent (*Laxdæla saga* is intermediate). This style she attributes to probable influence from ecclesiastical history writing and regards as a literary overlay. The conclusion is that the distinction in the use of tenses shows a development from a freeprose to a book-prose manner of composition.

The study of literary dimensions in single sagas is the particular forte of the Icelanders and will be dealt with separately. But the idea did not originate with the first *Fornrit* editions. The justification of the literary approach had already been categorically pronounced not only by B. M. Ólsen but also on the Continent, where Bley's *Eigla-Studien* represented a surprisingly abrupt departure from the norm.[37] Written as a study of opposition to Maurer and Jónsson it makes no concessions to their historical orientation. Contrary to the former it seeks out literary perspectives in the juridical passages and contrary to the latter it analyzes the discrepancies between prose and verse in terms of the author's arbitrary and artistic use of Egill's poetry. The central chapter is programmatically entitled "Die Eigla is kein historisches, sondern ein poetisches Werk." Bley justifies his thesis by pointing out the saga's preoccupation with emotional factors rather than events, its use of poetic themes designed to arouse the reader's interest, the unified composition and strict pragmatism of the plot, the use of simplification, variation, parallelism, idealization, differentiated characterization, the absence of strict chronology, and the presence of strong improbabilities. Bley concludes that the primary aim of the author (whom he identifies as Snorri) was artistic, while history was only a secondary aim.

In the same year appeared another study of *Egils saga* by W. H. Vogt.[38] Operating like Bley on the supposition that the saga is the premeditated work of an author, Vogt tried to read the author's signature by applying literary criteria to separate his contribution from what was predetermined by the sources. To the author's sphere he assigns the arrangement of episodes, the use of fate, the use of race and character contrast in Kveldúlfr's family, and errors in chronology and pragmatism. Vogt demonstrates how the author is sometimes able to absorb and integrate into his scheme the episodic material available in written and oral tradition, while at other times he is not.

---

37. André Bley, *Eigla-Studien* (Gand, 1909).
38. W. H. Vogt, *Zur Komposition der Egils saga* (Görlitz, 1909).

Utilizing Olrik's epic laws he determines that the first part of the saga has synchronic narrative while the latter part has single-ply narrative, so that the author appears to have worked according to literary precepts in one section and according to folktale precepts in another.

The same principles are applied in a detailed essay on *Bjarnar saga*.[39] Vogt distinguishes between two groups of narrative matter, one characterized by visualness, brevity, unsophisticated tone, and one-ply narrative. The other group is less visual, more dependent on the conscious use of *lausavísur,* more inclined toward psychological effects, and apt to use two-ply narrative. This latter group is the work of the author, the product of a period in which literature was a matter of reading and writing.

Vogt's theory, which in general supposes that a writer found angular units of tradition in primitive style and fitted and molded them into an artistic narrative, found its most elaborate application in Prinz's monograph on *Gísla saga*.[40] Using Vogt's stylistic criteria Prinz separates from the saga a skeleton of original episodes which was at the disposal of the author. The latter's activity is then analyzed in terms of unity of episodes, insertion of stanzas, articulation of composition through the narrative and characterization, plot design, chronology, linking of use of repetition, parallelism, dramatization, and so forth.

This technique failed to catch on. More recent literary analyses have abandoned the attempt to distinguish traditional and literary layers. Whether or not the author may have had traditions to work with, the constitution of the saga is seen exclusively as a literary creation. There is thus a growth of literary appreciation which runs parallel to the dwindling of faith in the saga's historicity. The last hundred years have shown the gradual replacement of the historical viewpoint by an aesthetic viewpoint.[41] Throughout the nineteenth century the historical view was preponderant, but at the beginning of this century a kind of balance was achieved (Vogt, Liestøl), and today the historical content of the sagas is valued at not much above nil while their literary qualities enjoy a reputation in inverse proportion.

39. W. H. Vogt, "Die Bjarnar saga Hítdœlakappa," *ANF, 37* (1920), 27–79.
40. Reinhard Prinz, *Die Schöpfung der Gísla Saga Súrssonar* (Breslau, 1935). A more intelligent dissertation with a better sense for the saga's structure and artistry is Franz Seewald, *Die Gísla saga Súrssonar* (Göttingen, 1934).
41. The ultimate step has been taken in recent years by Baetke and his students. The most vivid example is Rolf Heller, "Die Literarische Darstellung der Frau in den Isländersagas," *Saga,* 2 (1958), which rejects completely any effort at documenting the character and condition of Norse women from the sagas and instead treats their various functions (rightly, I believe) as literary conventions. The older, historically oriented literature on saga women is cited on pp. 3–6.

The Irish Hypothesis

By the Irish hypothesis is meant a view, devised and debated during the first two decades of this century, according to which the roots of the Icelandic saga grew in the soil of Irish storytelling. The background of the idea was an increased awareness of the cultural currents which flowed between Scandinavia and the western and southern world during the Viking Age and before. The first impulse came, as so often, from Guðbrandur Vigfússon. In preparing his *Corpus Poeticum Boreale* (Vol. I, 1883) Vigfússon focused his attention on the material culture reflected in the *Elder Edda* and discovered a number of things which do not fit into our picture of the ancient north.[42] Ladies embroidering in a bower, men hawking and hunting with dogs, life in *salr* and *borg* suggested a height of medieval civilization unknown in Iceland and not attained in Norway until long after the Viking Age. The flora and fauna (hazel, oak, ash, willow, peat-digging, and so forth) pointed to a more temperate climate and landscape than Norway's. The use of many foreign words and such things as the constant references to "Welsh" cloth, gold, and steel indicated a proximity to Celtic culture. The evidence accumulated by Vigfússon led him to connect Eddic poetry with the southward emigration of the Scandinavians and their subsequent contact with southern culture.

Similar ideas were taken up by Sophus Bugge on a broader scale in his *Studier over de Nordiske Gude- og Heltesagns Oprindelse* (Vol. I, 1881–89; Vol. II, 1896). With uncommon erudition and ingenuity and by the use of bold etymological conjectures, Bugge traced the influence of medieval Christianity on Norse mythology, an influence he believed to have been transmitted by the Celtic and Anglo-Saxon inhabitants of the British Isles. He also looked for and found foreign influences in Norse poetry; the Helgi poems are traced to Britain on the strength of supposed loanwords and certain resemblances to Irish stories.

The first suggestion of similarities between the Irish and Icelandic *prose* traditions came from the Celticists Todd and Zimmer and from Eugen Mogk.[43] This hint too was followed up in detail by Bugge in his

---

42. *Corpus Poeticum Boreale*, ed. Guðbrandur Vigfússon and Frederick York Powell (Oxford, 1883), *I*, lvi–lxiv.

43. Sophus Bugge, *Norsk Sagaskrivning og Sagafortælling i Irland* (Kristiania, 1908), pp. 211–12, which quotes from William G. Todd, ed., *Cogadh Gaedhel re Gallaibh*

book *Norsk Sagaskrivning og Sagafortælling i Irland* (1908). The burden of the argument is devoted to a demonstration of a Norse *Brjáns saga* written in the Norse Dublin colony shortly after the Battle of Clontarf (1014). Proceeding from an allusion to foreign historians in the Irish account of the battle, *Cogadh Gaedhel re Gallaibh* (*The War of the Irish against the Foreigners*), Bugge tried to establish the source of the allusion. That it was Norse he concluded from the fact that it contained information available only to a Norse participant in the battle, from Norse expressions in the Irish text, from dramatic episodes foreign to Irish style and reminiscent of the Icelandic saga, and so forth. That it originated in a Norse settlement in Ireland was evinced by indications that the Icelander who used the same lost text in *Njáls saga* had misunderstood certain portions which would have been clear to a Norseman familiar with Irish language and Irish topography. (Bugge went so far as to restore the misunderstood passage of the original *Brjáns saga* in Old Norse.) He concluded his case for the existence of such a saga by theorizing that it had also been used by the author of a likewise lost and undated but largely reconstructible poem about the battle on Brávǫllr. The *Brjáns saga* thus brought to light documented, in Bugge's opinion, the existence of an Irish impulse in Norse narrative. He argued the general feasibility of such an impulse by pointing out resemblances of Irish stories to the Norse myths and legends, Loki and Geirrøðr, Þórr and Útgarðarloki, Ragnarr loðbrók, etc. The similarities satisfied him that there was "a historical connection between Icelandic saga writing and Irish saga writing. . . ."[44]

At the time of his death Bugge had not completed the plan of his book and left only scattered notes pertaining to the affinities between the Icelandic and Irish sagas proper. These notes were affixed to *Norsk Sagaskrivning* by his son. Of general similarities they mentioned attention to biographical and genealogical matters, an objective-dramatic style, a correspondence in subject matter—feuds, raids, vengeance, feasts, assemblies, etc.—the tragic ethos, attention to topographic details, and the use of dialogue. Of more specific likenesses they noted a possible indirect connection between *Gunnlaugs saga* and the Irish saga of the sons of Usnech, both stories built around a Helen motif. Further resemblances were observed in the use of stanzas, the citing

---

(London, 1867), p. XXVIII, H. Zimmer in *Keltische Beiträge, 3* (1890), 35, and E. Mogk, *Kelten und Nordgermanen im 9. und 10. Jahrhunderte* (Leipzig, 1896), p. 25.
44. Ibid., p. 210.

of authorities, the appearance of *fylgjur,* the detailed description of clothing, the *hvǫt,* burning in, the arts of certain magicians, and the custom of *mannjafnaðr.*

The systematization of the theory was left to Alexander Bugge. As early as 1903 the younger Bugge had investigated the basis for a cultural connection between north and west in a book dealing with historical, archeological, and linguistic influences and suggesting considerable interchange even before the Viking Age.[45] Seconded by Olrik and Deutschbein, Bugge then turned his attention to literary matters.[46] The result of researches conducted in British sources—chronicles, the *Historia Britonum,* Anglo-Norman poems, Irish texts—was the reconstruction of what was termed a viking saga, a genre which flourished in the western outposts of the Norse world in direct touch with Britain. This viking saga provided the impulse for saga telling in Iceland. Bugge's final summary described the development as follows: "Die mündliche sagaerzählung ist zwischen 950 bis 1000 in den wikingeransiedelungen auf den britischen inseln entstanden. während der folgenden 50 jahre hat man auf Island und in Norwegen diese saga kennen gelernt. dann haben es in der zweiten hälfte des 11 jh.s die Isländer angefangen, die mündliche tradition zu sammeln. während dieser zeit ist auf Island die mündliche saga entstanden, um achtzig bis hundert jahre später niedergeschrieben zu werden."[47]

Much of Heusler's important "Anfänge" is concerned with a critical review of Bugge's theory.[48] In his estimation the Irish hypothesis as conceived by Bugge failed to explain three points. 1. Only Iceland produced a saga literature. Bugge does not explain why the British viking saga did not galvanize a similar literature elsewhere in the north. (Heusler disputes at length Olrik's supposition that there were Norwegian *fornaldarsǫgur* underlying Saxo's stories.) 2. Icelandic literature shows complete thematic independence from its supposed model. None of the Irish tales and none of the Irish heroes reappear in Norse garb. 3. Against Bugge's theory that the viking saga (= *fornaldarsaga*) was

---

45. "Vesterlandenes Indflydelse paa Nordboernes og Særlig Nordmændenes Ydre Kultur, Levesæt og Samfundsforhold i Vikingetiden," *Vidensk. Selsk. Skr.,* II, *Hist.-Filos. Kl.* (1904), No. 1.

46. Max Deutschbein, *Studien zur Sagengeschichte Englands* (Cöthen, 1906); Axel Olrik, "Sigvard den Digre, en Vikingesaga fra de Danske i Nordengland," *ANF, 19* (1903). Alexander Bugge, "Havelock og Olav Trygvessøn," *Aarbøger for Nordisk Oldkyndighed* (1908).

47. Alexander Bugge, "Die Entstehung der Isländischen Saga," *ZfDA, 51* (1909), 37.

48. Andreas Heusler, "Die Anfänge der Isländischen Saga," *Abhandl. der K. Preus. Akad. d. Wiss. Phil.-Hist. Cl.* (1913), No. 9.

the point of inception, Heusler argues the primacy of the family saga. The famous record of saga telling at Reykjahólar in 1119 he regards as no "zeitloses Kulturzeugnis" but as the birth of the *fornaldarsaga.* The seeds of the family saga had in contrast been germinating since the Saga Age.

Heusler went on to argue that the traces of stories in the British Isles were insufficient to prove more than the existence of storytelling as practiced everywhere. They were only a *Vorstufe,* the raw material for a saga in the technical sense. Even the stylistically closest of the stories, the account of Siward digri in a Latin chronicle of the twelfth century, is too loose in its construction to be assigned to the same genre. The Icelandic saga developed not out of the Märchen, as Bugge claimed, but out of the genealogical traditions maintained in Icelandic families.

Against the proposed similarity of Irish and Icelandic sagas Heusler marshaled a fourteen-point program of differences. The Icelandic saga is sober and realistic, the Irish fantastic. Icelandic style is abstemious and shuns the lyric flights of its counterpart. The stanzas in the Icelandic sagas serve the purpose of corroboration; they are documentary, unlike the verse in the Irish sagas, which serves to sculpture a lyric or dramatic moment. The Icelandic accounts do not digress but stick to the plot. The standing epithet, epic repetitions, the accent on clinical details, the fondness for externalities, and the allusions to past events are all foreign to the Icelandic sagas. The Irish sagas project type characters and have no formal presentation of the dramatis personae. The Icelandic saga's descriptive technique is constant while the Irish descriptions pendulate between schematic brevity and luxuriant detail. In contrast to the commentarial propensities of the Irish saga the Icelandic technique evolves what Heusler calls a "berechnende Verschweigungskunst." Finally, the differences in dialogue are considerable. In the Icelandic saga the dialogue can be the dramatic skeleton of the action while it eschews the declamatory mood and the long monologues of the Irish saga, which in turn lacks the stichomythic technique of the Icelandic saga.

In view of these divergencies Heusler proposed to revise the theory of Irish origins. He reduced the influence to a mere external impulse. "Das irische Prosaerzählen wirkte auf sie als gesellschaftliche Sitte, auch ohne dass sein Inhalt ihrem Gedächtnis sich eingrub; und von der Weise des Erzählens beachteten sie nur das Äusserliche: dass man Verse in die Prosa einschob. . . . Was wir die entscheidende Wendung auf dem Wege der Isländergeschichten genannt haben: der Aufstieg der häuslichen Chronik vom Folklore zur Kunst: dies, denken wir uns, vollzog sich unter dem Eindruck des berufsmässigen Prosavortrags der Iren."[49]

The next page in the discussion was written by Emil Olson.[50] Olson reviewed much of Heusler's argument against direct borrowing and concurred. He emphasized that, in the absence of the viking sagas, which purported to be the missing link, the theory rested wholly on the similarities between the Icelandic and Irish genres. Like Heusler he found these similarities greatly outweighed by the dissimilarities. But Olson went further by denying any connection whatsoever. The idea of an abstract impulse was for him no tangible quantity and was superfluous. The genealogical traditions in Iceland were adequate to explain the rise of a saga literature.

A refutation on a much grander scale was Finnur Jónsson's book *Norsk-Islandske Kultur- og Sprogforhold* (1921). Jónsson's book was a broad revaluation and devaluation of British influence on the Norsemen and a frontal attack on the comparatists in the fields of linguistics, mythology, and literature. He proceeded, for example, by reducing to a mere handful the number of loanwords which entered Norse from Irish or English. He halved the number of Celtic settlers which A. Bugge found among the *landnámsmenn* and minimized the possibility that sea rovers would in the course of a brief contact absorb and rework the difficult linguistic and artistic formations of the Irish. He tried everywhere to focus the indigenous elements. Against Vigfússon he argued the Norwegian cliffs and fjords, bear and elk in the *Edda,* against Olrik and von Sydow the allusions to Norse myths in the earliest court poetry, against Bugge, Bragi's "fjǫlð sagna" already in the ninth century, and so forth. Jónsson granted considerable influence from the south via Denmark but found little room for an extensive cultural borrowing from the west.

The Irish hypothesis has not been revived. Among the more recent handbooks only Heusler was still inclined to believe that the existence of two prose epics so close together could not be explained as happenstance.[51] Otherwise the theory is only a shadow. Paasche found it

---

49. Ibid., p. 49.
50. Emil Olson, "Den Isländska Sagans Ursprung," *Nordisk Tidskrift* (1918), pp. 411–29.
51. Andreas Heusler, *Die Altgermanische Dichtung,* p. 207. Also positive were Axel Olrik, *Nordisches Geistesleben* (Heidelberg, 1908), p. 88, and Gustav Neckel, *Die Altnordische Literatur* (Berlin, 1923), pp. 113–14.

worth discussing, Helgason mentions it perfunctorily, de Vries and Nordal pass over it in silence, and Stefán Einarsson notes it only in passing.[52]

The Þáttr Theory

The *þáttr* theory can be dealt with more briefly. It grew out of the assumption that the sagas could not have existed from time immemorial in the complex form which we now know, but must have been assembled from smaller components. The theory occurs in various forms even in the older literature. It constitutes the thesis of Möbius' *Über der Ältere Isländische Saga* (1852), which dealt primarily with the composition of *Glúms saga.* "Die Glúmssaga stellt sich uns als eine Reihe von Erzählungen über Glum dar, welche der Sagaschreiber zu einer Biographie dieses seiner Zeit im Eyjafjord hochangesehenen Häuptlings vereinigt hat."[53] In Möbius' case the theory was directly modeled on the rhapsodic view of epic poetry. "Die Geschichte der epischen Poesie, sowohl der frühesten, als der wir später in der kunstmässigeren Form der Ballade, der Romanze, der kämpevisa begegnen, lässt uns als sehr wahrscheinlich annehmen, dass wie diese Gedichte, auch jene mündlich vorgetragenen Erzählungen auf Island nur von geringem Umfange gewesen, nur einer oder wenigen, mit jener engverbundnen, Begebenheiten gegolten haben."[54] Keyser's system rested ultimately on a kind of *þáttr* theory, inasmuch as he pictured the genesis of the saga as a forging together of oral "smaasagaer" in the eleventh century.[55] Sars adopted the same thinking: "One must surmise that even after saga writing began in earnest some time elapsed before people acquired the necessary skill in combining the bits of oral tradition or lesser stories (þættir) into larger units and in grouping them effectively."[56] The theory was given its classical form by the poet A. U. Bååth in his Lund dissertation, *Studier öfver Kompositionen i Några Isländska Ättsagor* (1885). Bååth analyzed four sagas, *Ljósvetninga saga, Vatnsdœla saga, Laxdœla saga,* and *Njáls saga,*

---

52. Fredrik Paasche, *Norges og Islands Litteratur indtil Utgangen av Middelalderen,* pp. 323–24; Jón Helgason, *Norrøn Litteraturhistorie,* p. 120; Stefán Einarsson, *A History of Icelandic Literature* (New York, 1957), p. 123.
53. Möbius, *Über die Ältere Isländische Saga,* p. 36.
54. Ibid., p. 12.
55. Keyser, *Efterladte Skrifter, 1,* 406.
56. Johan Ernst Sars, *Udsigt over den Norske Historie* (Christiania, 1877–93), 2, 287; cf. Heusler, "Anfänge," p. 74, note 1, and Baetke, "Über die Entstehung," pp. 70–81.

in an effort to show that the basic *þættir* were with progressively greater skill assimilated to the large saga form by the use of fate as a connecting thread.

As in the case of the Irish hypothesis, Heusler's critique in "Anfänge" intervened decisively in the *þáttr* discussion. Heusler granted the existence of *þættir* as documented by the *Ljósvetninga saga* complex, but he regarded them as a genre contemporaneous with and not prior or prerequisite to the saga. In the form proposed by Bååth and others he made the theory subject to six restrictions.

1. That the saga tellers were capable of longer tales is shown by Haraldr harðráði's *útferðarsaga* and by the saga which Sturla Þórðarson told on King Magnus' ship "mikenn hluta dags." [57]

2. The combination *þættir* was not the prerogative of the writer but could have begun at the oral stage.

3. It is impossible to subdivide many of the sagas into sections which could have led an independent existence (*Hrafnkels saga, Hœnsa-Þóris saga, Hávarðar saga, Bandamanna saga, Heiðarvíga saga*).

4. A saga such as *Grettis saga* could not have been built as a simple concatenation of *þættir* a + b + c, etc. The *þættir* must rather be thought of as accretions in the larger saga framework in the pattern G + a + G + b + G + c + G, etc.

5. The theory that sagas evolved from the combination of independent *þættir* is too exclusive. Sagas also grew by incorporating written sources such as *Landnáma,* by borrowing material from other sagas (the Gunnarr Þiðrandabani episode in *Laxdœla saga*), and by simple stylistic expansion. "Bei umfänglichen Werken wie der Vatns-dœla, Grettis, Njáls saga, am allermeisten aber bei Eigla und der Laxdœla, erscheint die üppige Ausformung des einzelnen vermöge der durchgebildeten, breitliegenden epischen Mittel als eine Hauptsache im Entstehungsgang." [58]

6. The insertion of *þættir* can also be the work of copyists.

In sum Heusler pronounces against the overemphasis on compilation in the genesis of the saga. "Ein kritischer Sammler und Ordner war Ari, war der Verfasser der Landnámabók. Bei den Aufzeichnern der Familiensagas sind andere Tätigkeiten ebenso wichtig gewesen: das Ausgestalten, das Erfinden und—in allererster Linie—das Nachschreiben." [59]

---

57. *Sturlunga Saga,* ed. Kristian Kålund (København, 1906–11), 2, 326.
58. Andreas Heusler, "Anfänge," p. 78.
59. Ibid., p. 79.

W. H. Vogt approached the *þættir* differently in his article "Frásagnir der Landnámabók." [60] He was chiefly concerned with the stylistic development of the saga and thought to find a key in the short narratives of *Landnáma*. By analyzing these passages he arrived at a distinction between "Erzählungen," characterized by their visual appeal, and "Berichte," more akin to annalistic exposition. Both styles he believed were fair representations of tenth-century storytelling, that is of a primitive form which later blossomed into the sagas. On the relationship of these *frásagnir* to the saga Vogt wrote:

> die erzählung denk ich mir durchaus gelegentlich: beim anblick des merkwürdigen orts, beim klang des namens von mann und gegend, auf der reise, beim handel, auf den dingen, auf der bierbank, da denk ich mir, kam eins zum andern; die eine geschichte von Aud rief die andre; die namen der vorfahren und geschwister tauchen auf und erhalten ihre farbe; da weiss der eine *den* merkwürdigen ortsnamen zu erklären und der andre den andern. die nachfahren melden sich und wissen von ihren gütern zu berichten. in einer halben stunde ist der ganze Aud-stoff zusammen und noch einiges andre—und das nächste mal kann einer das ganze auftischen.[61]

Vogt's departure from the traditional theory is in terms of flexibility.

One can in fact trace a pattern of progressive atomization in the *þáttr* concept since Heusler, from the solid narrative block to the undefined narrative scrap. But for both extremes the term *þáttr* has seemed inappropriate. In 1933, Kersbergen wrote: "Even less than Bååth's grouping can I accept his term *þáttr* for the subdivisions of the saga which once had an independent existence. For the dry memorials about genealogies, descendants, domiciles, etc., the term is completely inadequate, since such memorials lack any dramatic content. But also for the short episodes in the larger narrative complexes the term is not felicitous since it does not indicate an absolute independence. A *þáttr* is a subdivision of a larger whole; a strand in a rope." [62] The editors of *Fornrit* avoid the technical term altogether, emphasizing the heterogeneous nature of the oral material by a rich use of synonyms: "þættir" (*Fornrit, 4,* xxvii), "smáþættir" (*Fornrit, 8,* xv), "arfsagnir eða munnmælasögur" (*Fornrit, 6,* xxii), "óskýrðar sagnarleifar" (*Fornrit, 9,* lxxix), "einhverjar sagnir . . . sundurlausar og

---

60. *ZfDA, 58* (1920), 161–204.
61. Ibid., 199–200.
62. Anna Kersbergen, "Frásagnir in de Laxdœla Saga," *Neophilologus, 19* (1934), 54.

óljósar" (*Fornrit, 11,* lxxi), "hinar fjölmörgu sagnir" (*Fornrit, 7,* xliii). About the central part of *Bjarnar saga* Nordal says: "The basis is probably oral tradition, which existed in bits; the author is uncertain in what order to arrange these odds and ends and uncertain about how much time elapsed between the events" (*Fornrit, 3,* lxxix). In contemporary research one can therefore no longer speak of *þættir* as the saga base.[63] They have proved on the one hand to be too large and tough-cored to be absorbed by the saga and on the other hand too slight to furnish an adequate point of departure. Scholars are agreed on the inadequacy of the *þáttr* as an underlying principle without having concurred on a substitute. Some reckon with a greater source, the saga itself, others with lesser sources, a tradition of heterogeneous particles.

63. But for some reconsiderations see Wolfgang Lange, "Einige Bemerkungen zur Altnordischen Novelle," *ZfDA, 88* (1957), 150–59.

4

Freeprose versus Bookprose

The terms freeprose and bookprose were coined by Andreas Heusler and designate two contrasting opinions about the form and importance of the oral tradition on which the sagas are based.[1] The freeprose theory postulates a period of highly developed oral saga telling preceding the period of writing. During this period the saga style was developed and the narrative material was fully evolved in articulated stories. The relationship of the saga writer to his material was that of an editor rather than a creator. He enjoyed the same freedom as any previous teller in addition to specifically literary prerogatives denied the oral sagaman, but he was always bound by his oral source or sources. This is the theory propounded with individual variations by Meissner, Heusler, Neckel, Wieselgren, Liestøl, and others. A review of the evidence is made superfluous by Helgason's succinct summary in *Norrøn Litteraturhistorie*,[2] but for the sake of completeness I repeat the salient points.

The evidence is taken partly from the incidental information provided in the old literature and partly from considerations of style.

The sagas contain allusions to saga telling.[3] The reference cited most often is the recitation of Haraldr harðráði's *útferðarsaga* recorded in *Morkinskinna*. It is told how an Icelander entertains the court with

1. Heusler, "Anfänge," pp. 53–55.
2. *Norrøn Lit.*, pp. 109–20.
3. Rudolf Meissner, *Die Strengleikar* (Halle, 1902), pp. 7–9; Heusler, *Altgermanische Dichtung*, p. 204. Helgason, *Norrøn Lit.*, pp. 113–15.

stories for several months, then suddenly becomes morose and taciturn. The king divines the reason and the saga teller confesses that his repertory is exhausted with the exception of Haraldr's own saga. This the king bids him reserve for the Christmas festivities, during which he presents it bit by bit for thirteen evenings. At the conclusion the king thanks him for an accurate and well told account and asks who taught him the saga. The Icelander explains: "It was my custom out in Iceland to go to the Thing every summer, and every summer I learned something of the saga from Halldórr Snorrason." [4] The freeprose exponents lean heavily on this and other references. According to Heusler they prove the following points. 1. Saga telling was quasiprofessional; 2. The court was receptive to saga telling; 3. A saga can be told a few years after the events; 4. The saga is regarded not only as fact but also as entertainment; 5. The saga teller, like the scald, has a repertory; 6. The saga is learned piece by piece; 7. A saga could be of considerable length.[5]

It is emphasized that, compared to the one record of the recitation of Eddic poetry in the whole corpus of Old Norse literature, the several references to saga telling provide abundant evidence of the custom,[6] and whether or not the references are true in a documentary sense, they must contain an accurate cultural picture. Another reference to which much importance is attached is the recording of a sourceman at the end of *Droplaugarsona saga:* "Þorvaldr had a son, whose name was Ingjaldr. His son was named Þorvaldr and he told this saga." [7] To the freeprosaist the passage evinces the transmission of a complete saga from generation to generation. Furthermore there is the testimony of Saxo and Theodricus to the effect that the Icelanders were the saga people par excellence.[8] In line with these passages are the frequent references to oral tradition within the sagas, "menn segja," "sumir segja . . . aðrir segja," "þat er flestra manna sǫgn," etc.[9] While many of these phrases are formulaic or even refer to writ-

---

4. *Morkinskinna udgivet for Samfund til Udgivelse af Gammel Nordisk Litteratur,* ed. Finnur Jónsson (København, 1932), p. 200: "Þat var vandi minn ut a landino at ec for hvert sumar til þings oc namc hvert sumar af saugunni naucquaþ at Halldori S. s."
5. *Altgermanische Dichtung,* p. 204.
6. Heusler, "Anfänge," p. 60.
7. *Fornrit, 11,* 180: "Þorvaldr átti son, er Ingjaldr hét, Hans sonr hét Þorvaldr, er sagði sǫgu þessa." See Meissner, *Strengleikar,* p. 9, and Helgason, *Norrøn Lit.,* p. 110.
8. See Scovazzi, *La Saga di Hrafnkell* pp. 278–79.
9. Knut Liestøl, *Upphavet,* chap. 3, and "Reykdœla Saga, Tradisjon og Forfattar," *Festskrift til Finnur Jónsson* (København, 1928); Helgason, *Norrøn Lit.,* p. 112; Heinzel, "Beschreibung," pp. 133–35.

ten sources, it is argued that they are originally genuine allusions to storytelling.

The oral family saga is supported by the analogy of the oral *fornaldarsaga*. That this sister genre lived in tradition is shown not only by the wedding at Reykjahólar but by the recurrence of Icelandic stories in Saxo.[10] Common knowledge of saga tradition is presupposed in sections of *Landnáma* which do not borrow from written sagas, and by poetry, notably *Íslendingadrápa*.[11] The same knowledge is reflected by the existence of certain variants which do not seem to be literarily interdependent and must therefore be traceable to separate oral archetypes.[12] The genuineness of the stanzas as vessels of tradition is bespoken by the not infrequent conflicts between stanza and prose.[13] For example, the first stanza in *Bjarnar saga* is placed in the context of Bjǫrn's Russian adventures, although the *vísa* states that he was very near Oddný (therefore in Iceland) at the time. Under these circumstances the stanza cannot be regarded as the saga author's private fiction, since it would then have harmonized better with his prose. The dependence on tradition is further shown by the interest which the sagas take in antiquities and their preservation of old religious, legal, and historical matters.[14] Finally, an indirect indication of oral tradition is the consistent anonymity of the sagas. This has been interpreted to mean that the authors did not feel themselves as such but as transmitters of an impersonal tradition.[15]

The stylistic line of argument initiated by Meissner and Heusler was carried furthest by Liestøl. Meissner spoke of the curious combination of naïveté and art which he could only conceive of apart from the scribe. Heusler picks up the argument and, speaking of Maurer's "amusischer Blick," emphasizes the necessity of distinguishing sharply between the historical genre and the saga, which must not be regarded as "aktenmässige Geschichte." The *fróðir menn* conjured up by Finnur Jónsson and others Heusler regarded as totally inadequate to the artistic conception of the sagas. The clarity and pith of the style is only comprehensible in terms of oral refinement.[16] Liestøl went

10. Heusler, "Anfänge," p. 60, and Helgason, *Norrøn Lit.*, pp. 115–16.

11. Helgason, *Norrøn Lit.*, pp. 112–13.

12. Liestøl, *Upphavet*, chap. 2; Helgason, *Norrøn Lit.*, pp. 111–12.

13. Helgason, *Norrøn Lit.*, p. 112. For a radical rejection of this view see now Bjarni Einarsson, *Skáldasögur* (Reykjavík, 1961); on the first stanza of *Bjarnar saga* see p. 237.

14. Heusler, "Anfänge," p. 61; Liestøl, *Upphavet*, chap. 8; Helgason, *Norrøn Lit.*, pp. 125–30.

15. Heusler, "Anfänge," p. 61, and *Altgerm. Dichtung*, p. 214.

16. Meissner, *Strengleikar*, p. 7; Heusler, "Anfänge," pp. 53–54, 61.

further. The homogeneity of style which allows one to speak of a saga style as one speaks of a fairy tale style, the recurrence of stock phrases, the anacoluthon, the leveling of style and structure, the objectivity and the epic tendencies of expansion on the one hand and schematization on the other he interpreted as the product of oral processes comparable to the analogous processes studied firsthand in the Norwegian *sogor*.[17] At the same time the lack of artistic economy, weaknesses in composition and unevenness in the application of detail, the excess of genealogical matter, doubling of names, etc., show the author's dependence on his oral sources.[18]

In order to bring out the peculiar mettle of the sagas they have been compared to the relatively untempered narrative of other thirteenth-century writings, especially *Sturlunga saga*. Meissner spoke of a "reinere und höhere kunst der erzählung, eine strenge objektivität der darstellung, eine sicherheit und grösse der komposition, die ein feineres stilgefühl voraussetzt, als wir in den sagawerken finden, die wirklich in dieser zeit verfasst sind."[19] This idea was better crystallized by Liestøl in terms of epic laws, convention, anticipation, parallelism, contrast, and so forth.[20] The different use of dialogue has frequently been remarked on.[21] Heusler summarized: "Man fuhr fort, das menschlich Fesselnde zu verstärken; rein Stoffliches auszusieben, die Umrisse zu klären. Also ein Vereinfachen der Massen (auch der Namenhaufen) —zugleich ein Herauswölben und Bereichern des Wichtigen. Die Darstellung der Hauptsachen gerät umständlicher (Liestøl). Die Seelenzeichnung vertieft sich und wird mehr Selbstzweck. Das Werkzeug dazu ist der verfeinerte Dialog."[22]

The claim that the saga style is really a preliterary achievement is supported by the observation that it appears in perfected form at the very outset. The earliest sagas are not experimental and no development in the basic technique is perceptible. "It is fully developed at the first cast. That is to say: it was fully developed when one began to write sagas. But there must have been a period of growth."[23]

17. Liestøl, *Upphavet*, chaps. 2–3, and "Tradisjon og Forfattar i den Islendske Ættesaga," *Maal og Minne* (1936), p. 8; Helgason, *Norrøn Lit.*, pp. 116–19.

18. Liestøl, *Upphavet*, chaps. 2–3, and "Tradisjon og Forfattar," p. 11; Helgason, *Norrøn Lit.*, pp. 110–11.

19. Meissner, Strengleikar, p. 103.

20. Liestøl, *Upphavet*, chap. 3.

21. Werner Ludwig, *Untersuchungen über den Entwicklungsgang und die Funktion des Dialogs in der Isländischen Saga*, p. 50; Otto Springer, "The Style of the Old Icelandic Family Sagas," *JEGP*, *38* (1939), 120.

22. *Altgerm. Dichtung*, p. 212; cf. Helgason, *Norrøn Lit.*, p. 117.

23. Liestøl, "Tradisjon og Forfattar," p. 8.

In addition certain environmental factors have been adduced to explain the growth of the saga. Scholars have dwelt on the ability of an illiterate people, capable of memorizing laws and a large body of poetry, to remember stories in reasonably set form as well.[24] Some of the conditions which might have encouraged the saga are these:

1. The aristocratic and ancestral pride of the Icelanders, which gave them stock in the past; 2. Intimate familiarity with historic sites; 3. A peaceful period in the eleventh century, which contrasted to the feuds of the tenth century and cast these in a heroic light; 4. The centralization of tradition at the alþingi; 5. A small population in which the memory of an individual was not so quickly displaced; 6. The preservative influence of stanzas on the traditions surrounding them; 7. The tendency of tradition to begin anew after a migration; 8. The tendency of traditions to thrive where there are common interests, such as the colonization and the national issues of Iceland; 9. The ability of the chieftain to focus tradition as a king might; 10. The tolerance of the Icelandic clergy.[25]

In reviewing the so-called bookprose standpoint one runs a twofold risk of overgeneralization, on the one hand of absorbing all the sagas in one unnuanced statement of theory and, on the other, of throwing the various proponents of bookprose in a common lot without regard for individual differences. If there is one point on which the bookprose men are agreed, it is that no one theory of origins is adequate to all the sagas.[26] The demand set forth repeatedly is that each saga be studied with a view to its peculiarities; that the genre "saga" be de-emphasized in favor of the unique creation. This regard for the particular is perhaps the reason why no general statement of bookprose theory has been issued; the natural medium for a believer in bookprose is the monograph, as exemplified by the introductions to the *Fornrit* saga editions. In dealing with the theory one is therefore concerned with a broad area of agreement on procedure rather than a common explanation of how the sagas came into being. In the second

24. Liestøl, *Upphavet*, chap. 4.
25. Ibid., chap. 5; Helgason, *Norrøn Lit.*, pp. 118–20.
26. E. Ó. Sveinsson goes to the (specious) length of saying that the bookprose theory is no theory at all: "The chief difference between the two theories is that the bookprose theory is not, in the first place, a theory, not in the first place a doctrine, but rather an attempt to follow the tracks from the known to the unknown without prejudice, to pass with the help of experience and probability from one point to the other. On the other hand the free-prose theory, at least in its German form, is primarily a *Lehre*, a doctrine, which is set forth fully fashioned, and the origin of the Family Sagas is explained in accordance with it" (*Dating the Icelandic Sagas* [London, 1958], pp. 7–8).

place there are, fortunately, differences of opinion among the scholars who are assembled under the bookprose banner. There are conservatives and liberals, but the differences are slight enough so that they would perhaps not object to occupying the same benches.

The bookprose theory is associated with Iceland. Though its roots run to Maurer, it was for practical purposes the creation of B. M. Ólsen. His work was carried on by S. Nordal, E. Ó. Sveinsson, and their collaborators in the publication of the *Fornrit* series. An analysis of bookprose is based on the work of these men.

The lack of a concentrated statement of theory is paralleled by the absence of a methodical refutation of freeprose. The Icelandic objections must be gleaned from various works and are more often than not stated in passing. The Icelandic approach is predominantly positive. For a thorough critique it is necessary to look to Denmark and later to Germany.

In Denmark the literary historian Rubow cast himself in the role of a gadfly and attacked the problem of saga origins strictly from the point of view of literary method.[27] He placed the onus of misconception on the literarily unsuspecting generation of German-inspired philologists concerned only with the narrow matters of historicity and text criticism. The oral epic was the phantasm of a scholarly *horror vacui*. Against its existence he aligned the following arguments: 1. The highly valued references to saga telling are of late date or unhistorical. 2. The use of place names as corroborative evidence is not permissible since the place names are usually primary and in themselves the only historical part of the story surrounding them. 3. The reference to a saga teller in *Droplaugarsona saga* can be compared to H. C. Andersen's "det er fra ham vi har Historien" (it is from him we have the story). 4. It would be preternatural if oral sagas survived 200 to 300 years. Parallels taken from metrical traditions must be disallowed. 5. The *þáttr* theory is contradicted by the artistic harmony of the sagas. 6. The accuracy of topographic details proves nothing since these were available to the saga writers themselves. 7. That the Icelanders knew their genealogies does not support the historicity of the sagas. 8. The "menn segja" formulae mean no more than the "Det vil jeg for sanden sige" (That I say in sooth) of the Danish ballads.

Rubow's own theory was that Brother Robert's translation of *Tristram* in 1226 marked the point of inception for the saga genre.[28]

---

27. Paul V. Rubow, "De Islandske Sagaer," *Smaa Kritiske Breve* (København, 1936).
28. Possible influences of *Tristan* on the scald sagas have been traced at length and in detail in Bjarni Einarsson, *Skáldasögur.*

This erotic blueprint is particularly apparent in the scald sagas. He pointed out that the earliest saga manuscripts date from the middle of the thirteenth century and that the period 1226 to 1300 would represent the normal lifespan of a literary genre according to our modern experience. Adapting Bédier he suggested that the saga writers may have composed their works in honor of temporal or ecclesiastical patrons. But Rubow found no acceptance among the professionals, if for no other reason, then because *Fóstbrœðra saga* at least certainly antedates the efforts of Brother Robert.[29]

Certain aspects of the freeprose theory have been countered by Nordal. The belief in an oral prose epic he terms the explanation of one miracle by another miracle, pointing out that there are no good parallels. The demonstration of a possibility is not the demonstration of the existence of such an epic (*Fornrit, 2,* lx). Where the sagas can be compared with one another or with other sources, they show deviations, "inaccuracy, misstatements, and exaggeration" (*Fornrit, 2,* lxi). Against the idea of dictation put forward by Meissner and Heusler Nordal reminds us that the faithful reproduction of the storyteller's version is a technique originated by the modern folklorists. Furthermore the literary quality of the sagas forbids our regarding them as popular art.[30] The argument of stylistic homogeneity Nordal compares to a man's opinion that all babies are alike, or to an urbanite's view that all white sheep are alike. Close study of the sagas reveals that no two can be attributed to the same author. The argument of anonymity is accorded little patience: "All invented sagas are transmitted anonymously, like all Eddic poems. Do *Vǫluspá* and *Njála,* which are both anonymous, bear the stamp of their authors less than, for example, *Vellekla* and *Sverris saga?*"[31] In regard to Haraldr harðráði's *útferðarsaga* Nordal points out the great discrepancy between what must have been told at the king's court and the combination of truth and patent fiction in *Morkinskinna* (*Fornrit, 2,* lxi). The view that the sagas would lack their peculiar brand of realism and would be flat and stereotyped had they been the work of an author, involves, according to Nordal, an underestimation of the thirteenth-century Icelandic muse. (*Fornrit, 2,* lxi).[32] In his introduction to *Hœnsa-Þóris saga* he notes some errors in the saga's topography. While the bookprosaists do not admit that topographic accuracy constitutes evidence of oral stories, Nordal points out here that topographic inaccuracy

29. Sveinsson, *Dating the Icelandic Sagas,* p. 84.
30. Nordal, "Sagalitteraturen," *Nordisk Kultur, 8,* Part B (Stockholm, 1953), 233–34.
31. Ibid.
32. Nordal, *Hrafnkels Saga Freysgoða,* pp. 64–65.

proves the contrary, since it would have been rectified had the story circulated orally for a long time (*Fornrit, 3,* xxiv).

Like their predecessors the proponents of bookprose believe in oral tradition at the foundation of the sagas. B. M. Ólsen said: "It may be counted certain that oral sagas are to a large extent the basis of our *Íslendinga sögur.*"[33] The conviction is expressed more categorically by E. Ó. Sveinsson: "I regard it as a fact, as an indisputable fact, that nearly all sagas are based to a greater or lesser extent on unwritten tradition. . . ."[34] This unwritten tradition is however not conceived to have been crystallized and transmitted in sagas such as we know them. It existed rather in bits and pieces; the list of references on page 63f. gives an idea of the fragmentation.

The decisive moment in the birth of a saga was not the decision to transcribe tradition but the active intervention of an author. The author collected, scrutinized, interpreted, organized, formed, and altered available tradition (oral and written) and from it created a saga which bears the mark of his procedure and his personality. B. M. Ólsen's formulation is not outdated. He stated that:

> . . . they [the sagas] are works of art and it was an artist who held the pen which recorded them on parchment; behind them lies not a single integrated saga, but a variety of separate oral stories, which the author of the saga collected, excerpted, and tried to fashion into a whole. Sometimes there are also written sources behind the saga. In particular many saga writers had *Landnáma* before them; they took from it what they needed and sometimes used it unaltered or combined it with oral stories or sometimes even adapted it quite arbitrarily.[35]

The emphasis on written sources represents a departure from previous thinking. Heusler and Liestøl believed in the incidental use of written materials but did not assign them the same importance. Sveinsson wrote: ". . . in the family sagas, the Icelandic sagas proper, the oral tradition is the more prevalent feature. In spite of this being the case, there are probably few Icelandic sagas which are not, in one way or other, supported by written genealogical sources. Sometimes these sources have been, as it were, a kind of skeleton to which later

33. B. M. Ólsen, "Um Íslendingasögur," *Safn til Sögu Íslands, 6,* Parts 5–7 (1937–39), 10.
34. E. Ó. Sveinsson, "The Icelandic Family Sagas and the Period in Which Their Authors Lived," *Acta Philologica Scandinavica, 12* (1937–38), 72.
35. B. M. Ólsen, "Um Íslendingasögur," p. 11.

the flesh and blood of the oral tradition have been added, but sometimes they have been used for the correction and emendation of the
told story." [36] Full homage is paid to this belief in the *Fornrit* introductions, large sections of which are devoted not only to the tracing
of genealogical sources but also to the discovery of literary borrowing
from one saga to another.

Broad scope is allowed the discretion of the author. His freedom is
regarded as the artistic secret of the saga: "The saga art attains its
peak when the saga material is dealt with freely, without deviation
from the realism of the older sagas" (*Fornrit, 2, lxi*). The idea of invention or improvisation on the part of the author is indeed nothing
new. It was not only championed by mavericks like Jessen and Bley
but was recognized by Heusler and Liestøl. The departure is practical
rather than theoretical; the Icelandic school allows a greater latitude.
Not only are dialogue and characterization seen exclusively as the
work of an author,[37] but large sections of plot are detached from tradition. Nordal defended the view that the account of the burning in
Hœnsa-Þóris saga is a deliberate departure from the version which
Ari gives of that event (*Fornrit, 3, xx–xxi*). Björn Sigfússon regards
the role of Áskell goði in *Reykdœla saga* as the author's private fiction
(*Fornrit, 10, lxxv*).

Nor is the preoccupation with an author in itself an innovation.
Möbius had made some effort to isolate the author's activity in *Glúms
saga*. Vogt tried, with more finesse, to disentangle tradition and author
by applying folkloristic, stylistic, and psychological criteria. In *Vatnsdœla saga*, for example, he attributed Þorsteinn's egotism to the tradition and his milder traits to the author's intervention in his behalf.[38]
This system was, as we saw, applied on a complicated scale by Reinhard Prinz in his study of *Gísla saga*. But the Icelandic school goes
further. Björn K. Þórólfsson, who might be assigned to the conservative wing, believes that Prinz scotched the role of the author (*Fornrit,
6, xxvi–xxvii*). According to the thinking in Reykjavík the author's

36. E. Ó. Sveinsson, *Corpus Codicum Islandicorum Medii Ævi, 5* (Copenhagen,
1933), "Introduction," p. 11.
37. B. M. Ólsen, "Um Íslendingasögur," p. 98: "Jeg hef áður bent til, að samtölin í
sögunum hljóti ifir höfuð að vera tilbúin af höfundunum sjálfum og ekki tekin eftir
munnlegum sögum. Þetta er því áþreifanlegra sem samtölin eru samin af meiri
iþrótt." E. Ó. Sveinsson, "The Icelandic Family Sagas and the Period in Which Their
Authors Lived," p. 83: "People have been eager to suggest that the characters of Hallgerðr and of Skarpheðinn have been bungled in Njála. On the contrary, I believe that
the author has created these strange characters from something vague and insignificant."
38. *Altnordische Saga-Bibliothek,* vol. XVI: *Vatnsdœla Saga* (Halle, 1916), "Einleitung," LVII.

personality is more or less dominant throughout the saga, and though a tradition can be identified here and there, tradition as such never speaks.

The emphasis on the author is reflected in the disposition of the *Fornrit* introductions. One section is often entitled "Höfundur Sögunnar," a section in which, as some critics have felt, a game of identification is played.[39] The most famous instance is the attempted identification of Snorri as the author of *Egils saga*. First conjectured by N. F. S. Grundtvig, this idea was arrived at independently by B. M. Ólsen and Bley; combatted by Wieselgren, it has since been vigorously espoused by Nordal.[40] The most recent contribution in this field are Barði Guðmundsson's studies collected in *Höfundur Njálu* (1958). Where an actual identification of the author is not feasible, as almost always, an effort is made to define the milieu, if possible the family or monastery, in which a saga was written. This is done by circumscribing the district in which it originated on the basis of the author's topographical knowledge, and by dating the saga.

The emancipation of the author from a set oral tradition has further entailed the assumption that he was open to those cultural and biographical influences which play such a large part in the study of modern authors. Traces of contemporary life and events are sought out in the sagas. Long before the principle was actually stated Bley suggested that Snorri's relationship to King Hákon was the nerve of Egill's conflict with Erik.[41] B. M. Ólsen connected the slaying of Kálfr in *Glúms saga* with a similar event in Eyjarfjǫrðr, recorded in *Sturlunga saga,* and the same identification was later made independently by Björn Sigfússon.[42] Heusler was not backward and pointed out that the wiping of a bloody sword on Gudrun's clothing had a close parallel in an identical act of Ásbjǫrn Guðmundarson in 1244.[43] The

39. See Hallvard Lie, "Noen Metodologiske Overveielser i Anl. av et Bind av 'Íslenzk Fornrit,'" *Maal og Minne* (1939), pp. 105–14. This witty and penetrating article is still the only fundamental criticism of the "Icelandic school" to appear.

40. B. M. Ólsen, "Landnáma og Egils Saga," *Aarbøger for Nordisk Oldkyndighed* (1904); André Bley, *Eigla-Studien* (Gand, 1909); Per Wieselgren, *Författarskapet till Eigla* (Lund, 1927); Nordal, *Fornrit*, 2, "Formáli" and "Snorri Sturluson. Nokkrar Hugleiðingar á 700. Ártíð Hans," *Skírnir, 115* (1941). Most recently: M. C. van den Toorn, *Zur Verfasserfrage der Egilssaga Skallagrímssonar* (Graz, 1959), and Peter Hallberg, *Snorri Sturluson och Egils saga Skallagrímssonar* [*Studia Islandica,* 20] (Reykjavík, 1962).

41. Bley, *Eigla-Studien,* pp. 216–18.

42. B. M. Ólsen, "Um Íslendingasögur," pp. 359–62; Björn Sigfússon, "Ingólfsþáttur í Víga-Glúms Sögu," *ANF, 53* (1937), 62–69.

43. Heusler, *Kleine Schriften,* 2 (1943), 364. In general see E. Ó. Sveinsson, *Dating the Icelandic Sagas,* pp. 73–75.

contemporary background as represented by *Sturlunga saga* has been most ingeniously linked to the sagas in the articles of Barði Guðmunds-son.[44]

Similarly, scholars became aware of the literary context in which the saga writers worked and reacted against the idea that the saga was hermetically sealed off from other genres. The influence of the romantic literature which spread from the Continent to Scandinavia in the thirteenth century was studied in *Gunnlaugs saga* by B. M. Ólsen and in *Laxdœla saga* by E. Ó. Sveinsson.[45] The historical writings which predated the family sagas came to be viewed to some extent as stylistic models. "Is it not almost a miracle, if a Family Saga, written perhaps in the very same room as Heimskringla, is composed without any influence from the 'bookprose' of the Sagas of the Kings?"[46] The evolution of an Icelandic prose style is now seen as a gradual process, not unlike the development of Old High German from interlinear translations, to which Meissner had emphatically contrasted the apparently painless birth of Icelandic prose.[47] In opposition to Finnur Jónsson stylistic roughness became a characteristic of early writing, not of post-classical degeneration, whereas fluent style was no longer regarded as the true patent of oral tradition but as a sign of artistic ripeness gradually attained by several generations of saga writers. As a result of this viewpoint *Kormáks saga* and *Hrafnkels saga,* for example, exchanged places at the opposite extremes of the saga writing period.

A similar revolution took place in the outlook of the cultural historian. To the picture of decline and dissolution, both political and literary, painted in bleak colors by Heusler, E. Ó. Sveinsson in his book on the Sturlung Age opposed a thirteenth century filled with ambivalent currents. It was a period of violence, but also of great artistic achievement. "It was a period of contrast and of tension, a tragic period."[48] The sagas were a direct outgrowth of these tensions. Sveins-

44. See the vol. *Höfundur Njálu* (Reykjavík, 1958); Also Peter Hallberg, "Nyare Studier i den Isländska Sagan," *Edda, 53* (1953), 244–47, and "Njálas Författare och Hans Samtid," *Nordisk Tidskrift, 35* (1959), 524–35.

45. E. Ó. Sveinsson, *Fornrit, 5* (1934), "Formáli"; B. M. Ólsen, "Om Gunnlaugs Saga Ormstungu," *D. Kgl. Danske Vidensk. Selsk. Skr., 7* R. *Hist. og Phil. Afd.,* II:1 (København, 1911); See esp. Bjarni Einarsson, *Skáldasögur.*

46. E. Ó. Sveinsson, "The Icelandic Family Sagas and the Period in Which Their Authors Lived," p. 74.

47. Gabriel Turville-Petre, *Origins of Icelandic Literature* (Oxford, 1953), p. 142; Meissner, *Die Strengleikar,* p. 87.

48. E. Ó. Sveinsson, "The Icelandic Family Sagas and the Period in Which Their Authors Lived," p. 80.

son believes that *Fóstbrœðra saga* and *Glúms saga* reflect the gloomy age of lawlessness in the northern districts during this period, while *Egils saga* reflects the cultured surroundings of Snorri.[49] Baetke goes so far as to say that the feuds of the sagas in no way represent the peaceful tenth and eleventh centuries but must be seen in the light of the quarrels which rent the Age of the Sturlungs.[50]

The various aspects of the new approach were forged into a coherent theory of saga literature by Nordal. First outlined in his book on Snorri Sturluson in 1920, the theory was further developed in the introduction to *Egils saga* and is the skeleton of the essay "Saga-Litteraturen" in *Nordisk Kultur*. The basic assumption is that the saga is governed by the recognized rules of literary history and can be understood in the context of a literary development from 1100 to 1400. The movement began in the historical works of Sæmundr and Ari in the south of Iceland. The subjects of these works were history, genealogy, and chronology; the spirit was learned and the method critical. Somewhat later a counter-trend appeared in the literary center of the north. The monastery at Þingeyrar opened its doors to hagiographic and legendary tendencies, which compromised the critical spirit of the southern school. At the same time concessions were made to a taste for "light reading" by the inclusion of fuller details and anecdotal matter (*Sverris saga*). The two poles of literary activity—the learned and the entertaining (*vísindi og list*)—found a synthesis in the works of Snorri Sturluson in the west of Iceland. To the period of synthesis belong the family sagas with their combination of fact (real or supposed) and fiction, their genealogical and historical apparatus within a popular framework. Toward the end of the thirteenth century the synthesis began to break down and split into purely fictional sagas on the one hand and unadorned annals on the other. Thus there is a kind of rough symmetry between the twelfth and fourteenth centuries flanking a period of combination and concentration, the period of the classical saga.

Before progressing further it is well to define as precisely as possible the difference between the freeprose and bookprose theories. As we have seen, both believe to varying degrees in oral tradition, in the freedom of the author, in the use of written sources and in exposure to contemporary influences. At the same time, the monographic evidence compiled by the Icelanders has not been without its effect

49. Ibid., p. 79.
50. Baetke, "Über die Entstehung," p. 82.

on their opponents. Meissner wrote in a review: "Bin ich auch längst von der Schroffheit abgekommen, mit der ich 1902 (Die Strengleikar) mich ausgesprochen habe, so befestigt mich doch die Arbeit Gehls in der Ansicht, dass die Kunst der Sagaerzählung in der Zeit mündlicher Überlieferung ausgebildet, und geformter Stoff im allgemeinen treu in die Zeit des Pergaments gerichtet worden ist. . . . Dieser Glaube umfasst nicht die isländische Saga in Bausch und Bogen und entbindet uns nicht von der Pflicht, die Eigenart und Entstehungsgeschichte jeder einzelnen Saga ohne Voreingenommenheit zu untersuchen." [51]

Liestøl published a brief reformulation a few years after his book appeared. He by no means shifts his ground, but the approach is conciliatory.

> There is no reason to quarrel about words. One can perfectly well call the man who recorded the saga an author as long as one does not succumb to the easy temptation of putting so much in the word author that it begins to overshadow certain facts. If there are sagas, and some of them are among the best, which do not have any considerable basis in tradition, the oral saga is the stylistic prototype even for these sagas. For most of the others it is moreover the main foundation. This means that when one speaks of authors in connection with the Icelandic family sagas, the word can mean so many things. One time the saga writer can have been largely a transcriber, another time also a collector, a third time an editor, and a fourth time to a great extent a creative writer. But if one takes a broad view of the matter, one perceives that the oral saga was both the point of departure and the guide for the written saga. And the oral saga was not only the origin and the determining factor, but usually also the very nerve of the written saga. [52]

The Icelanders are very guarded in their statements about the form of oral tradition. Nordal's position is that oral tradition can only be a subject of fruitless speculation and that the student's first duty is to the written saga as we have it. This reticence he maintains with perfect and frustrating consistency throughout his work. His colleague E. Ó.

---

51. Meissner, *Anzeiger für Deutsches Altertum,* 57 (1938), 69. Per Wieselgren also showed himself to be tractable, *AfDA,* 52 (1933), 101: "Auch wenn man mit ihm [Nordal] nicht an auswendig gelernte Sagas oder Sagateile glaubt, gibt es keinen Grund, das Vorhandensein voll entwickelter Sagas—auch grösseren Umfangs—vor dem Hauptzeitalter der Niederschrift anzuzweifeln. Die Worte mag man selbst gewählt haben."

52. Liestøl, "Tradisjon og Forfattar," p. 14.

Sveinsson is a little less elusive on this point and a combing of his writings turns up a number of statements about the nature of Icelandic tradition. "In oral accounts a determined and fixed way of narrating developed gradually, with distinct features and methods which were preserved in the recital of skilful storytellers, however various the actual phraseology might be." And again: "Still more, however, of the nature of the Icelandic sagas is derived from the oral form of the narrative; hence the brief and vigorous, but simple and graceful, style which is not intended for silent reading, but is evidently designed for recital. Hence also the dramatic effect and the objective method: everything that takes place is described from the outside, as if the writer were a spectator; we are left to guess the mental state and emotions of the persons from their words and actions. And hence, also, various artistic methods which the saga writers have learned from the storytellers." (For the sake of the context it is fair to say that E. Ó. Sveinsson goes on to express his opinion that the saga *writers* did not follow these traditions closely.) "Le style des sagas est un style oral; et par là nous ne voulons pas dire que les sagas sont une transcription littérale de traditions orales. . . . Mais nous supposons que les auteurs ont mis à profit l'art des conteurs oraux." [53] These are statements which a believer in freeprose would applaud wholeheartedly, and it is reasonable to question whether the theories are really so incompatible and whether the distinction between bookprose and freeprose is not artificial.

Twenty years before the first volume of *Fornrit* appeared Heusler defined the difference as follows:

> In dem hier Ausgeführten liegt, dass im einzelnen Falle die Freiprosa- der Buchprosa-Lehre sehr nahe kommen kann. Aber der grundsätzliche Unterschied der Betrachtungsweise zeigt sich, wo man die Frage nach den Quellen der Saga stellt.
>
> Man kennt die oft gebrauchte Formulierung: Hauptquelle des Verfassers war die Tradition . . . eine weitere Quelle waren die Strophen oder die "poetische Tradition"; eine dritte waren geschriebene Werke. Hierin spricht sich die Buchprosa-Theorie aus. Vom andern Standpunkt stellt es sich so dar:
>
> Die prosaische und die poetische Tradition bildeten in der Regel eine Einheit (Die Strophen standen, Ausnahmen vorbehalten, seit

---

53. E. Ó. Sveinsson, *Corpus Codicum Islandicorum*, 5, "Introduction," p. 11; "Les Sagas Islandaises," *Archives des Lettres Modernes*, 36 (1961), 38; Also *Fornrit*, 4, xxv.

alters in dem erzählerischen Zusammenhang); diese Einheit war
die Saga—oder mehrere Sagas, gleichlaufend oder anders. Somit die
Quelle der Saga war—die Saga selbst. Umständlicher ausgedrückt:
die primäre Quelle der schriftlichen Isländersaga war in jedem
Falle die mündliche Saga, mit oder ohne Strophen. Dies kann
die einzige Quelle gewesen sein. Es können noch weitere, sekun-
däre Quellen bestanden haben, nämlich. . . .[54]

Heusler goes on to name unrelated stanzas, other related sagas or
þættir or learned sources (Ari, *Landnáma*), unrelated oral or written
works or migratory motifs, fragmentary local, family, or place name
tradition.

This distinction is difficult to improve on. Bookprosaists and freeprosaists can often be in substantial agreement on what the sources of
a saga were but rarely on the form of those sources or the way in
which the saga author used them. In most cases the adherent of freeprose believes in a central core of formed tradition which could (but
need not) be infinitely varied by the writer, but which imparted to
the saga its fundamental structure and narrative art. The believer in
bookprose for the most part rejects this central core and sees the lines
of a saga as the work of an author who imposed his artistic will on
heterogeneous materials. The gap between the theories is therefore real
and fundamental though it has often been much exaggerated in the
ardor of discussion.

An effort to supersede both schools was made by Baetke in his
book *Über die Entstehung der Isländersagas* (1956). Baetke's quarrel
is with the idea of oral tradition, which he believes to be a fiction agreed
on to support the historicity of the saga. He institutes a distinction between two kinds of oral tradition: an official tradition which preserved
legal, ritual, and to some extent historical matters, and a private tradition (*munnmæli*) which was volatile, unformed, and quickly displaced.
The family sagas had no share in the official tradition. Baetke therefore rejects Nordal's theory of a historico-fictional synthesis and classi-
fies them together with the *fornaldarsǫgur* on the basis that they are
exclusively entertaining in conception and execution. The study of
possible traditions behind them is irrelevant since the creative moment
must be looked for in the act of the author. "Ob ihre Verfasser die
Handlung erdichteten oder ob sie für sie Anekdoten, Sagen, Familien-
überlieferungen u.a. benutzten, ist von nebensächlicher Bedeutung." [55]

54. Heusler, "Anfänge," pp. 69–70.
55. Baetke, "Über die Entstehung," p. 54.

Against the freeprose theory Baetke produces these arguments:

1. The references to saga telling lose their value because they are themselves contained in fictional sagas. Furthermore the stories alluded to involve events contemporary to the speaker. The reference to a sourceman in *Droplaugarsona saga* is corrupt, chronologically improbable, and contained in a saga which Jón Jóhannesson and Nordal believe to be a bookprose product. Perhaps it is a device used to enlist the reader's confidence, a device similar to the claim of one manuscript of *Gunnlaugs saga* that it stems from Ari himself. The saga telling at Reykjahólar cannot be entered as evidence that *Íslendinga sǫgur* were told. 2. The anonymity of the sagas means nothing since it is shared with works which are manifestly bookprose. 3. Heusler's argument that many genuine details are preserved from the Saga Age is circular in so far as we have only the word of the sagas themselves and no corroborative sources. 4. The homogeneity of style is not as great as claimed and was modeled on the kings' sagas. Furthermore the oral quality is no more than we would expect, since it represents the writer's natural mode of expression. 5. Objectivity is also proper to other works of thirteenth-century Iceland. 6. It must be doubted that oral transmission was able to polish and perfect the style or composition of a story. 7. The differences between the family saga and *Sturlunga saga* are differences of genre and not of time or oral development. 8. It is improbable that the Icelandic colonists had time to devote to saga telling. They needed first to create the social and material basis from which a literature could spring. 9. Heusler's theory entails the metamorphosis of a *fróðr maðr* into an artistically talented *sagnamaðr*.

The failure of the bookprose theory Baetke blames on its willingness to make major or minor concessions to oral tradition in one form or another, *þættir, frásagnir,* or whatever. Any variation of this view suffers from the same internal difficulties which afflict the *þáttr* theory. The author is reduced to a collector, and a process of collection is not adequate to explain a work of art. Nor does the theory explain the genesis of formed *frásagnir*.

The element of oral tradition must therefore be disregarded in studying the sagas. They were the products of the Sturlung Age during which they were written. The feuds and vendettas are a reflection of the contemporary tumult, which contrasted so sharply to earlier conditions that the era after the settlement came to be viewed as a golden age and was cast in a heroic light. This nostalgic view of the past was nurtured by the imminent absorption under the Norwegian crown.

The threat from abroad brought a reaction against the preoccupation with Norwegian history and led to a literary concentration on Icelandic affairs (*Biskupa sǫgur, Kristni saga,* and large redactions of *Landnáma*). The literary counterpart to this historical activity was the creation of the family sagas. Viewed as a creation of the thirteenth century their development under the influence of the classical and medieval literature introduced by the church is set in better perspective. The saga cannot be regarded as the last offshoot of Germanic heroic poetry, rather it filled a gap left by the departed heroic age. Seen in this light it is apparent that the usual chronology of genres should be inverted to give the sequence: *fornaldarsaga, konungssaga, Íslendinga saga.* A form of *fornaldarsaga* existed already in the eleventh century. The *konungssaga* began around 1100. From these forerunners and from genealogical material the family sagas were derived. *Egils saga,* which still partakes of the historical type, shows how the transition was effected.

In his final chapter Baetke gives an account of the saga's origins in cultural terms. Though long winter nights, isolation, aristocratic pride, and so forth are not adequate to explain the rise of a literature, nevertheless the causes must be sought in the special social and political framework of Iceland. The democratic (or aristocratic-democratic) society of farmers was fundamentally different from the feudal organization of contemporary Europe and was in fact unique. The backbone of the system was the independent farmer; it was around him and in his image, rather than in the shadow of a court or an estate, that Icelandic literature developed. It is the central and dominant position of the farmer which explains the realism of the saga and its dependence on living models.

5

Critical Considerations

The bookprose theory has performed valuable services in promoting
a flexible view of the sagas. For one thing it has convincingly reas-
serted the point that the historicity of the sagas is a problematic affair.
The belief in historicity has always been a matter of persuasion rather
than demonstration and is therefore cyclical. In 1800 it was anathema,
only to become gospel again in 1900. The difficulty is that there is no
real evidence one way or the other. Liestøl gave a reasoned case for
historicity, but an analogical argument of this kind is little better than
a rational guess. Baetke's denial of historicity is no less likely to be
correct because it is less impressively reasoned. The only evidence
available is necessarily circular; a check against Ari and *Landnáma*
is fruitless since there is always the possibility of direct or indirect dependence. The discussion is therefore largely unenlightening, which
of course does not dispense us from weighing the evidence as objec-
tively as possible. This is the position to which the *Fornrit* editions
come nearest, avoiding intransigeance in either direction. It is a position which takes the problem as well as the inherent difficulties seriously without succumbing to a formula. Unlike more recent trends
it leaves the subject open and viable.

In another area bookprose has more than the merits of prudence.

It has jettisoned without regrets the environmental apparatus inherited from Müller and repeated down to Liestøl and Helgason. The notion that an oral narrative could be argued from long winter nights, democratic institutions, and insular curiosity persisted for a surprising length of time, but it can now be regarded as abandoned. Unlike historicity it is not an endemic issue and is not likely to be raised again after Nordal's censure.

But the chief contribution of the Icelandic school is its demand for hardheadedness, its ban on easy arguments and all too general considerations, its insistence on more minute study. The impact can be seen in the fact that we no longer dare take oral tradition for granted or imagine that an oral story was conjured onto parchment. We ask more questions and are less easily satisfied. Much else that is positive could be said about the bookprose or Icelandic method and the learned world has not been sparing of recognition. It is in fact a method which has held the field alone and almost unchallenged for the last thirty years, so that there would be danger of a consensus by default were it not for recent charges of conservatism. Yet there remains much that is uncertain, and the present state of the question is far from justifying any sort of consensus. I have therefore tried in this concluding chapter to present some of the conflicting evidence and point up a few of the difficulties which beset the bookprose theory.

Genealogical Sources

The de-emphasis of oral tradition in modern saga research has been accompanied by increased attention to the possibility that the thirteenth-century saga writers leaned heavily on written sources. Among the documents available to them *Landnámabók* occupies a prominent position.[1] In it could be found a wealth of genealogical information

1. *Landnámabók* is the record of Iceland's settlement. It is extant in five redactions: 1. *Sturlubók*, compiled by Sturla Þórðarson in the thirteenth century. 2. *Hauksbók*. According to his own testimony Haukr Erlendsson († 1334) established his text by harmonizing *Sturlubók* with a lost version of *Landnáma* by Styrmir Kárason († 1245). Where these texts were in conflict Haukr adopted the fuller version. 3. *Melabók* (two leaves of a parchment from about 1400). 4. *Skarðsárbók*, compiled by Björn Jónsson á Skarðsá († 1655), who combined the redactions of Sturla and Haukr. 5. *Þórðarbók*, a harmonization of *Skarðsárbók* and *Melabók* (then presumably complete) by Þórður Jónsson († 1670). Because of the fragmentary remains it is difficult to trace the textual history of *Landnáma*. Haukr informs us that the first men to write about the settlement were Ari fróði (1068–1148) and Kolskeggr hinn vitri (Ari's contemporary), and it is assumed that the tradition reaches back into the beginning of the twelfth century. The most authoritative effort at ordering the redactions is Jón Jóhannesson's *Gerðir Landnámabókar* (1941), in which he arrived at the following stemma:

and brief historical notes about the settlement period and the Saga Age. The systematic correlation of *Landnámabók* and the sagas was initiated by B. M. Ólsen in a series of articles from 1904–20.[2] The permanent value of these studies was to establish *Melabók* as the most primitive redaction of *Landnáma*, whereas *Sturlubók* was clearly shown to have expanded *Landnáma* with saga extracts. Ólsen further assumed that the sagas had in turn made use of an earlier redaction of *Landnáma*. Since the publication of his studies every saga editor has been obliged to account for possible connections with *Landnámabók*. This is a knotty problem and the task is made doubly difficult by the fact that we are dealing with lost redactions. A thorough summary of the problem to date would be of great interest. A few pages here cannot begin to unravel the complications but permit only a discussion of principles based on a few examples.

B. M. Ólsen believed that *Egils saga, Eyrbyggja saga, Hœnsa-Þóris saga, Laxdœla saga,* and *Gull-Þóris saga* all made use of an early *Landnáma* redaction. But because of the considerable discrepancies he was obliged to temper this conclusion with the corollary assumption that the sagas in question had alternate recourse to oral accounts and in some cases actually subordinated *Landnáma* to their oral sources. The evidence which Ólsen presents is slight and often treated by way of footnotes. Occasionally the involved argumentation becomes entangled in contradictions. For example Ólsen assumes that Blundketill Geirsson's genealogy in *Hœnsa-Þóris saga* was taken from *Landnáma:*[3]

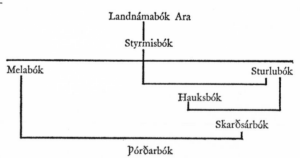

For a convenient summary see Jón Helgason, "Fortællinger fra Landnámabók," *Nordisk Filologi: Tekster og Lærebøger til Universitetsbrug* (København, n.d.), *3*, v–xii.

2. "Landnáma og Egils Saga," *Aarbøger for Nordisk Oldkyndighed* (1904), pp. 167–247; "Landnáma og Hœnsa-Þóris Saga," *Aarb.* (1905), pp. 63–80; "Landnáma og Eyrbyggja Saga," *Aarb.* (1905), pp. 81–117; "Landnáma og Laxdœla Saga," *Aarb.* (1908), pp. 151–232; "Landnáma og Gull-Þóris (Þorskfirðinga) Saga," *Aarb.* (1910), pp. 35–61; "Landnáma og Eiríks Saga Rauða," *Aarb.* (1920), pp. 301–07.

3. "Landnáma og Hœnsa-Þóris Saga," p. 76.

Ketill blundr

Geirr hinn auðgi

Blundketill

At the same time he assumes that the confusion between Þorkell Blundketilsson and Blundketill Geirsson arose in oral tradition. "It was no wonder that the tradition in Flokadalr and environs, where the memory of the district's old settlers, Ketill blundr and his grandson Blundketill, was still alive among the population, could confuse these two people with such similar names and transfer the legend of the burning from Þorkell Blundketilsson to the better known Blundketill Geirsson."[4] But if Blundketill and his forefathers were so well known to oral tradition, there was no reason to seek them out in *Landnáma*.

Again B. M. Ólsen regards the remark about "Arngrímr Helgason Hǫgnasonar, er út kom með Hrómundi" (chap. 1) as a loan from a *Landnáma* redaction related to *Sturlubók* 46 and *Hauksbók* 34. On the other hand *Hœnsa-Þóris saga* disagrees with this passage in *Sturlubók/Hauksbók* when it says that the farm Helgavatn was named after Arngrímr's son and not his father (chap. 2). Ólsen interprets this to mean that *Sturlubók/Hauksbók* followed an older *Landnáma* against *Hœnsa-Þóris saga,* but he overlooks the necessary conclusion that in this case *Hœnsa-Þóris saga* could not have used the same passage from the older *Landnáma*.[5] That is to say, when *Hœnsa-Þóris saga* agrees with *Sturlubók* 46/*Hauksbók* 34 in one instance and disagrees with the same passage in another, the relationship of the saga to the *Landnáma* tradition cannot be interpreted as one of dependence.

In *Egils saga* B. M. Ólsen specifies only two passages which are directly dependent on *Landnáma,* but in one case (chap. 23) the deviations are considerable and outweigh the factual correspondence.[6] In the other case, chapter 1 of *Egils saga* is derived from a *Landnáma* redaction behind *Sturlubók* 344/*Hauksbók* 303, but since this passage gives an account of Þórólfr's death manifestly borrowed from *Egils saga,* it is uncertain whether *Sturlubók* 344/*Hauksbók* 303 owes its

4. Ibid., p. 72.
5. Ibid., p. 76.
6. "Landnáma og Egils Saga," pp. 183 (note 2), 194–95.

genealogical information to an earlier redaction of *Landnáma* or directly to *Egils saga*.[7]

Ólsen's conclusions have not gone unchallenged in the painstaking investigations of the *Fornrit* editors. In his introduction to *Egils saga,* Nordal accedes to Ólsen's main thesis but rejects the idea that some redaction of *Landnáma* served as a source (*Fornrit, 2,* xxxiii–xxxiv). In his introduction to *Hœnsa-Þóris saga* he likewise finds no necessity to assume influence from a *Landnáma* text (*Fornrit, 3,* xvi, n. 2). But where some of the specific results are dismissed, the principle is retained. In the introductions to *Eyrbyggja saga* and *Laxdœla saga,* E. Ó. Sveinsson adheres to Ólsen's views while enunciating them with less assurance. Finnur Jónsson had regarded *Eyrbyggja saga* and *Landnáma* as reflections of different oral traditions. Sveinsson leans rather to Ólsen's opinion, according to which *Eyrbyggja saga* altered *Landnáma* on the basis of oral traditions "because it is more likely to follow a written source" (*Fornrit, 4,* xvii). About *Laxdœla saga,* which is notoriously difficult to square with *Landnáma,* Sveinsson does not commit himself further than to say that its author used a source close to an older *Landnáma* (*Fornrit, 5,* xxxix). But there are so many discrepancies that Ólsen was obliged to assume a certain amount of oral deformation[8]; the deviations are significant enough that they cannot have arisen in written tradition.

7. Ibid., pp. 184–85.
8. Ólsen was obliged to assume oral deformation in the account of Ketill flatnefr ("Landnáma og Laxdœla Saga," p. 202), the list of Óláfr pá's children (pp. 182–83), the chapter about Hrútr (pp. 183–84), and the report of Auðr's death (p. 190). The deviations are so great that they cannot have arisen in written tradition. The discrepancies can be explained in several ways: 1. The authors of *Landnáma* and *Laxdœla saga* used independent oral traditions. 2. The authors used independent written accounts of the colonization. 3. The author of *Laxdœla saga* revised *Landnáma* according to firsthand traditions. 4. *Laxdœla saga* used a written source dependent on *Landnáma* but altered to suit local traditions. 5. *Laxdœla saga*'s departures from *Landnáma* are to be interpreted as the inventions of the author. Possibilities 1 and 2 are excluded by the verbal correspondences between *Laxdœla saga* and *Landnáma,* while 3 and 4 amount to the same thing, inasmuch as they presuppose that at sometime between the composition of *Landnámabók* and *Laxdœla saga* oral tradition was alive enough to shake written tradition. The conjecture of invention on the part of *Laxdœla saga*'s author is subject to the following considerations. Finnur Jónsson and more recently Jón Jóhannesson argued that the common source for *Laxdœla saga* and *Landnáma* was Ari. Jóhannesson postulated that Ari's brief *Landnáma* was expanded by Styrmir in the sections dealing with the settlement of Snæfellsnes, whence the fuller and divergent account in *Sturlubók.* This hypothesis, likely in itself, only shifts the point at which oral tradition invaded written tradition. If not the author of *Laxdœla saga,* then Styrmir must have had access to supplementary traditions. And even assuming this to be the case, the explanation is still not adequate to define *Laxdœla saga*'s position in the tradition. Its version of Ketill flatnefr's death may, as Jón Jóhannesson suggested, be pure *skáldskapur* (*Gerðir Landnámabókar,* p. 213). Similarly, the very divergent account of Auðr's death may be a product of the saga writer's "viðleitni til að gera úr því sögu" (*Fornrit, 5,* xl). On

This combination of written and oral sources is slippery ground for bookprose. One wonders whether there is more than a difference of phrasing between the hypothesis that a saga and *Landnáma* drew on separate oral traditions and the hypothesis that a saga changed *Landnáma* on the basis of oral traditions. In either case the deviation is ultimately oral. The latter hypothesis supposes that the author of *Laxdœla saga,* for example, had oral traditions which were so secure that his confidence in them enabled him to disregard his written *Landnáma.* In the first place this speaks for a firm, not necessarily reliable, oral tradition. The written legacy stemming from the revered father of Icelandic historiography was with some probability a strictly controlled tradition, which was not tampered with lightly. In the second place it is questionable to what extent a saga writer was really dependent on *Landnáma* when he had alternate sources which he felt to be more trustworthy. In calculating the relationship between *Landnáma* and the sagas the divergencies should weigh at least as heavily as the congruencies, which may, after all, have a basis in fact. This principle can be clarified by further examples.

The first consistent application of the bookprose theory was Ólsen's study *Om Gunnlaugs Saga* (1911). The approach which Ólsen devised became the recognized model for the following generation of Icelandic scholars. It proceeds from an analysis of the saga according to the theory of heterogeneous origins. Wherever possible written sources are sought out from among earlier extant writings, especially *Landnámabók.* Where parallel documents are available, they are if possible considered as contributory rather than corroborative. Ólsen's study was sharply but not effectively criticized in Finnur Jónsson's *Samfund* edition of *Gunnlaugs saga,* but among contemporary scholars the essay

the other hand the discrepancies in the list of Óláfr pá's children are difficult to explain from a combination of a written prototype and invention. *Laxdœla saga* has two sons, Hǫskuldr and Helgi, in excess of *Landnámabók.* There is no reason for Styrmir or Sturla to have dropped these names. They must therefore be the responsibility of the author of *Laxdœla saga,* and why should he invent two names out of thin air? That they are not inventions is shown by the fact that they participate in the vengeance against Bolli, a chapter of the saga likely to have support in tradition. It is unreasonable to suppose that the saga writer invented two people in chapter 28 in order to have them available for nonessential roles in chapter 54. This genealogical discrepancy must therefore be anchored in separate traditions. It is even less conceivable that the extensive account of Hrútr's activity in *Laxdœla saga* is an embroidery on the very brief mention of his name, settlement, marriage, and children, which *Landnáma* may have inherited from Ari. Here too *Laxdœla saga* must have built on independent traditions. There seems to be no more satisfactory solution than the one proposed by Ólsen (Sveinsson, *Fornrit, 5,* xxxix–xl, is more evasive). At what point oral tradition encroached is impossible to tell, but the simplest assumption is to assign the author of *Laxdœla saga* himself the role of mediator.

87

appears to stand in full force (*Fornrit, 3*, xlii). It is divided roughly into three sections: a derivation of the genealogies from written sources, a study of the verbal resemblances with other sagas, and a consideration of compositional influences exercised by other sagas on *Gunnlaugs saga*. Only the first section concerns us here.

In order to make Ólsen's system clear I have reproduced the genealogies from the first chapter of *Gunnlaugs saga* and their supposed sources in Appendix I. These tables are intended to make graphic the curious eclecticism which Ólsen attributed to the saga writer. The picture for the rest of the saga is similar. It shows that the author neither used all (or most) of what he found in his genealogical sources nor did these sources suffice to provide all that he needed. The genealogies in *Landnáma* and *Egils saga* are not capable of explaining the entire cast of characters in *Gunnlaugs saga*. Ólsen is obliged to assume the use of oral traditions to account for Hrafn's two brothers and Helga's second husband Þorkell, none of whom are mentioned in *Landnáma*.[9] It is reasonable to question why, when the author had oral sources for three quite periferal figures, he was obliged to turn to *Landnáma* and *Egils saga* in order to establish the relationships of the saga's major characters. It is doubtful whether an oral tradition about Þorkell existed apart from an oral tradition about Helga and Helga's father Þorsteinn, or whether an oral tradition about Hrafn's brothers existed apart from a tradition about Hrafn and their father. Furthermore it is odd that the author who had gone to the trouble of looking up genealogies in *Egils saga* and *Landnáma* had sufficient self-discipline not to quote any of them *in toto*. There is not a hint of genealogical curiosity, no savoring of family trees. On the contrary, *Gunnlaugs saga*'s distinctly sub-average genealogical content can be conveniently summarized on one page. It is one of the fallacies of current saga research that it portrays the saga writer as a scholar, but the picture of our author accumulating information in his saga library, collating genealogies, and comparing sources is not persuasive. A saga does not look or read like a learned disquisition and shows remarkably few signs of the weighing and measuring in which bookprose would have us believe. There are, for example, no chronological speculations such as we find in Oddr Snorrason's *Óláfs saga Tryggvasonar*.

9. Björn M. Ólsen, "Om Gunnlaugs Saga Ormstungu," *D. Kgl. Danske Vidensk. Selsk. Skr.,* 7. R., *Hist. og Phil. Afd.,* 2, No. 1 (1911), 17–19.

Again it seems unnatural for a saga writer not to take his genealogical information from one source, which in the case of *Gunnlaugs saga* was entirely possible. The fact that Ólsen must resort to two written sources in addition to oral reports weakens his position. It is of course possible by combining the available genealogies from *Landnámabók* and other sources and by plugging the gaps with oral tradition to arrive at a solution, but to be convincing a source demonstration generally demands a greater degree of correspondence than this. Oral tradition which can be used like putty is too convenient.

Finally, let us not forget the saga audience in our concern with the author. Bookprose supposes that a thirteenth-century Icelander could write a saga about people of whom he knew so little that he was, in a manner of speaking, forced to look them up in a dictionary. Yet by common consent this research product was immediately accessible to the minds of the listeners, whether it was read or recited. The sagas cannot have been written as scholarly exercises for a limited group of literati, and they cannot have contained matter which was foreign to the audience. The numerous parchments of *Njáls saga* attest the reception accorded even this genealogical colossus. To account for such popularity we must assume that there was some kind of rapport between saga and listener (or reader). Even the genealogical paraphernalia, which try a modern reader's patience, must have had a familiar ring to the thirteenth-century Icelander.

Despite these reservations the comparison of *Landnáma* and the sagas has not been a blind alley. There are some very tangible connections, which are revealing both by their clarity and by their distribution. It is instructive to look at the list of *Landnáma* extracts in sagas given by Finnur Jónsson in the back of his *Landnáma* edition.[10] By far the greatest plagiarist is *Grettis saga*. The classical sagas are otherwise represented only by *Hænsa-Þóris saga* (chap. 1), *Eiríks saga rauða*, and *Grænlendinga þáttr*. The remaining sagas which demonstrably drew on *Landnáma* are post-classical: *Flóamanna saga, Sǫgubrot* I in *Fornmanna Sögur* XI, *Þorsteins þáttr uxafóts, Þórðar saga hreðu, Bárðar saga Snæfellsáss, Víglundar saga, Harðar saga Grímkelssonar, Gríms saga loðinkinna.*

The first three chapters of *Eiríks saga rauða* contain verbatim extracts from *Landnáma*, but Finnur Jónsson produced good evidence to the effect that they are interpolations and on this point found himself

10. *Landnámabók* (København, 1900), pp. 274–76.

in rare agreement with B. M. Ólsen.[11] In addition chapter 7 borrows from *Landnáma*. Here S. B. F. Jansson, who clarified Haukr Erlendsson's editorial policy, reinforced Finnur Jónsson's and B. M. Ólsen's supposition that chapter 7 is the work of Haukr himself.[12] *Grettis saga*'s debt to *Landnáma* was recognized by older scholars and Guðni Jónsson has shown convincingly that this is not a case of mechanical copying, but that the author of the saga skillfully constructed a narrative in chapters 1 to 8 from scattered notes in *Sturlubók* (*Fornrit, 7,* xvii–xxxi). But it is possible that in *Grettis saga* we are dealing with a special situation. If Nordal is correct in retracing the saga to the pen of Sturla Þórðarson, it is less surprising to find such a pervasive influence from *Landnáma*.[13] Sturla was himself a *Landnáma* editor and, like Haukr Erlendsson, had a unique familiarity with its content. In any case *Eiríks saga rauða* and *Grettis saga* combine to show that when *Landnáma* was used, it was plundered wholesale and not plucked for an occasional name.

Despite the fact that the comparison of *Landnáma* with the family sagas has produced meager results from the point of view of composition, the principle of borrowing has been extended by analogy. Where no connection to *Landnáma* is discernible, the *Fornrit* editors postulate loose genealogical tables from which the saga writers took their cast of characters. This approach was indicated by S. Nordal, who pointed out that there were in the twelfth and thirteenth centuries many genealogical records which were either absorbed in *Landnáma* or lost and which could have provided an important support for the traditions set down by the saga writers (*Fornrit, 2,* lxiv–lxv). That such genealogical tables existed, and perhaps in some quantity, is borne out by the mention of *ættartǫlur* in the *First Grammatical Treatise*. The crucial issue is not whether they existed but how they were used.

Nordal assumes their use everywhere, both in genealogically complicated sagas such as *Egils saga* and in genealogically simple sagas such as *Hœnsa-Þóris saga* and *Bjarnar saga Hítdœlakappa*. E. Ó. Sveinsson follows the same practice beginning in his book *Um Njálu*. The use of such genealogies may be granted on the common-sense basis that the author of *Njáls saga* could not have had six hundred names from the Saga Age in his head. But the *Fornrit* editors do not regard the genealogical matter as ornamental or external, they assign

11. F. Jónsson, *Historie*, 1st ed., 2, 648, and B. M. Ólsen, "Landnáma og Eiríks Saga Rauða," *Aarbøger* (1920), pp. 304–05.
12. S. B. F. Jansson, *Sagorna Om Vinland* (Lund, 1944), pp. 100–02.
13. S. Nordal, "Sturla Þórðarson og Grettis saga," *Studia Islandica, 4* (1938).

it a productive role in the conception of a saga. When Nordal suggests that the author of *Heiðarvíga saga* might have had written sources which provided the names of Barði's allies and the names of those who fell in the Battle of the Heath, the assumption must be that much of Barði's preparation and the account of the battle itself were drawn from these written sources, since the details of the action and names of the combatants are inseparable (*Fornrit, 3,* cxv). Similarly, Sveinsson assumes that the genealogical source at the disposal of *Njáls saga's* author contained brief notes about the events of the saga; these the author expanded imaginatively.[14] The analogy on which Sveinsson makes much capital is the two-page *Ævi Snorra Goða,* which he counts among the materials from which the author of *Eyrbyggja saga* worked. But a comparison of this fragment to the substance of *Eyrbyggja saga* is sufficient to show that it could not have breathed life into the saga. It contains only a fraction of the events described and none of the details. It may have served as a chronological and genealogical control, but it cannot have been the point of departure. The events mentioned in *Ævi Snorra Goða* are told with so much greater detail by the saga that the latter must have had access to extensive oral traditions. In other words *Ævi Snorra Goða* is superfluous.

Reykdœla saga was long regarded as one of those sagas closest to oral tradition. Liestøl viewed it as a prime example of how family traditions reached parchment in almost undiluted form, but the supposed homogeneous oral source was dismembered by Björn Sigfússon in his introduction to *Fornrit, 10.* Sigfússon sees the saga strictly in terms of an author who exploited a written *Þorlaugar þáttr* (used also in *Glúms saga*) as a basis for the section known as *Skútu saga* and then created the remainder of the story from a combination of extensive genealogical sources and oral traditions, embellished with his own innovations.

The genealogical source which Sigfússon postulates is an early redaction of *Landnáma.* He points out that the genealogies in chapters 1 and 17, and to a lesser extent in 5, 20, 23, and 30, nowhere conflict with and sometimes echo *Landnáma,* but the evidence is slight (*Fornrit, 10,* lxii–lxiii). Only in chapter 1 is the correspondence good, elsewhere only a fraction of the persons mentioned can be found in *Landnáma.* In chapter 5 *Landnáma* could have provided the name of Steingrímr Ǫrnólfsson but not the name of his wife Ástríðr or her father Þorbjǫrn or brothers Steinn and Helgi. In chapter 17 only five

14. *Um Njálu,* p. 93; *Fornrit, 12,* liii; "Njáls Saga," *Scripta Islandica, 1* (1950), 12.

out of nine names could have been found in *Landnáma*. Chapter 20 contains an allusion to the slaying of Hróarr Tungugoði, an event also recorded in *Landnáma*, but the saga clearly worked from a fuller account than the one provided by *Landnáma*. Chapter 23 gives two genealogies of three persons each, neither of which is to be found in *Landnáma*. The first one Sigfússon footnotes: "About this branch nothing is known except from *Reykdœla saga*." The second he footnotes: "In other sources there is no mention of these relatives of Víga-Glúmr" (*Fornrit, 10,* 221). In chapter 30 only one of the three names is known to *Landnáma*.

Sigfússon accounts for the poor agreement by assuming that *Reykdœla saga* used a *Landnáma* very different from the preserved redactions, one which was either more primitive and had not been shorn of material pertaining to the north, or one which had been expanded in the north to include more specifically northern genealogies (*Fornrit, 10,* lxiii). For the latter assumption there is at best no evidence and the former runs counter to *Landnáma* research, which assumes a gradual swelling rather than a tapering. The matter can be clarified statistically. Of the twenty-five persons in chapters 5, 17, 23, and 30 eligible to appear in *Landnáma,* only nine are to be found there. If this proportion is roughly average, it means that the *Landnáma* from which the author of *Reykdœla saga* worked was almost three times as large as the extant redactions. Such an elephantine document exceeds the license of hypothesis.

There is furthermore the problem of those saga characters who were not eligible to appear in *Landnáma*. No matter how we stretch the capacity of the redaction which nurtured *Reykdœla saga,* it cannot have included most of the minor figures in the saga. For example, chapters 2 to 17 contain the names of forty-two persons, of whom less than half were socially qualified to be listed in *Landnáma,* and who must therefore have dragged out their existence in oral tradition. This brings us to the inevitable question: if oral tradition could harbor the memory of so many *viri obscuri,* why could it not remember the elite? Wherever the theory of contaminated oral and written sources is pursued to its logical conclusion, it leads to this fundamental contradiction. We must either assume that oral tradition provided all or most of the names or take refuge in Baetke's logic and assume that all the names not explained by written sources were invented.

Two more brief examples will serve to point up the dangers of source multiplication. Jónas Kristjánsson perceived the illogicality of random combination in his introduction to *Glúms saga:* "If *Glúms saga* owes everything which it has above and beyond *Landnáma* to oral stories, then all of the genealogical material should be attributed to oral tradition" (*Fornrit,* 9, xxvi). But this realization does not bear fruit. "But it is much more probable that the author relied on one or more genealogical works which were unrelated to *Landnáma*" (ibid.). At the same time Kristjánsson believes that most of the action in *Glúms saga* is taken from oral tradition. This gives a curious picture of a saga's composition. On the one hand there are names without events, on the other events without names. From a combination of the two there somehow arises a saga.

The alternate supposition is that the lost genealogies were not restricted to names but gave a brief outline of action, on which the saga writer could build. This supposition is insidious since one tends unwittingly to exaggerate the resources of such a lost text. Jón Jóhannesson assumes an *Ævi* behind *Droplaugarsona saga,* but not content to attribute to it the general framework of the story, he also seeks to explain small details from it (*Fornrit, 11,* lxxxix). To vary an apt criticism by Anne Holtsmark, such an *Ævi* cannot serve both as a skeleton and as flesh and blood.[15] This would mean that the saga's source was another written saga, which still remains to be explained.

Much effort would have been spared us if a thirteenth-century Icelander had thought to record what he knew about saga composition. But even in the absence of such a document we can draw certain conclusions about the thirteenth-century view of a saga. If, for example, Sturla Þórðarson had considered the sagas to be constructions dependent on *Landnáma* or pure fictions, he would not have used them to revise a tradition which he knew to date from shortly after 1100. Sturla was born in 1214 and had firsthand knowledge of literary trends from 1230 or so to 1284, precisely the period during which saga writing is believed to have reached its height. If Sturla, from his contemporary perspective, knowing the modes of saga composition, as he must have, regarded the sagas as sources comparable and not subordinate to *Landnáma,* this testimony carries a certain weight. It suggests that the sagas were independent genealogical sources. We cannot of course place ourselves at the mercy of Sturla's judgment, but to question his selection of sources is a different thing from taxing him with palpable ignorance. He had at least some reason to believe that the sagas were valid sources with a claim to antiquity. Of Sturla's

15. "Om de Norske Kongers Sagaer," *Edda, 38* (1938), 162–63.

position in *Landnáma*'s history Jón Jóhannesson wrote: "At the beginning of the thirteenth century there still survived a great many traditional stories about men and events in the ninth and tenth centuries, but they had undergone various changes since the days of Ari. Many sagas were written which did not agree with *Styrmisbók* concerning these matters, though the disagreement was not due to pure invention. This provided the scholar with the task of harmonizing the diverse stories."[16] I believe this puts the problem in proper perspective and recognizes the probability that the saga genealogies were neither derived largely from *Landnáma* redactions nor invented from whole cloth.

The comparison of the sagas to *Landnámabók* has not outgrown its philological fostering. It has treated the sources strictly as manuscript variants, forgetting that the sagas are integral narratives. It is a simple matter to establish a correspondence between genealogies, but in order to establish a source relationship the saga passage must be evaluated in context. If the genealogy is organically connected with the rest of the saga and firmly anchored in traditional material, the chances are that its roots are oral. The first two chapters of *Eiríks saga rauða* and the first eight chapters of *Grettis saga* are inorganic and open to borrowing, but where scholars extend the principle to embrace the body of the saga, their results are more precarious. In the absence of the materials from which the saga writer worked, the way in which he worked remains a speculative matter, but the reaction against oral tradition, offered admittedly as a universal remedy in many cases, has brought about an equally unhealthy bias in the opposite direction. There is a conscious effort in the *Fornrit* introductions to explain as much as humanly possible on the basis of written sources, even when oral tradition is regarded as the major constituent. The unaccounted-for remainder is then thrown off as oral, but this remainder is often so inextricably bound up with the material supposedly taken from written sources that separate derivation is both unnecessary and improbable.

The evidence against the bookprose constructions is both explicit and implicit. As far as it can be ascertained from a comparison of *Landnáma* and the sagas, the former was not used productively in the body of the sagas, but rather as an inorganic supplement. Conversely, if the saga writers really did use *Landnáma* as a point of departure, it is curious that we have no sagas about those incidents connected with

16. *Gerðir Landnámabókar*, pp. 223-24.

the settlement in which *Landnáma* is so rich, no *Ingólfs saga Arnórs-sonar* for example. These considerations warn against overemphasizing the role which lost genealogies may have played in saga composition. As long as we define source as an *active* ingredient, it is difficult to admit genealogies as sources. A list of persons or even a skeletal record of events cannot have been the yeast in a saga recipe.

Literary Sources

Another facet of the emphasis on written sources is the theory of extensive inter-borrowing among the sagas. That a saga author knew other written sagas no one would deny, even if the knowledge were not vouchsafed by straightforward allusions. Nevertheless nineteenth-century scholarship did not find it advisable to assume that the sagas stood in literary debt to one another. It was even believed that the source allusions were to oral sagas, a belief which found some support in the fact that the content of the allusions is often inaccurate. As long as the theory of oral formation prevailed, it was possible to regard these inaccuracies as oral muddying and, conversely, the presence of striking parallels as the result of stereotype leveling in the tradition. When the theory of oral formation was jettisoned in favor of literary history according to the accepted rules, both parallels and divergencies appeared in a new light. The former were accounted for by the author's conscious participation in a literary school with written models, the latter by his poetic license. Like the modern author the Icelandic saga writer now emerged as an artistic innovator bound only by the rules of his guild and his literary tradition.

Björn M. Ólsen operated with the idea of full-fledged literary borrowing, for which Icelandic has the compound *rittengsl,* in *Om Gunnlaugs Saga,* and part of the impact made on his contemporaries was certainly due to the abruptness with which the new principle was thrust on them. Ólsen wasted no words on a theoretical justification of his departure from recognized procedure. A discussion of principle was left until twenty years later when E. Ó. Sveinsson prefaced his study of *Njála*'s sources with a brief section entitled "General Considerations about Literary Connections." [17] Sveinsson characterizes the old school as one which believed that the family sagas were composed without knowledge or at least without regard for what was written

17. *Um Njálu,* "Almenn Rök um Rittengsl," pp. 100–06. The substance of these remarks is repeated in *Dating the Icelandic Sagas,* pp. 77–80.

before them. He points out that this view is at odds with what several generations of research into the kings' sagas had established about their composition, and though the two genres cannot be thrown together indiscriminately, it is hard to believe that the *Íslendinga saga* could elude its written tradition entirely. He believes that the saga authors turned to other written sagas in search both of information and of narrative material. He recognizes the presence of chance correspondences between sagas and does not attach importance to similarities in proverbs, idioms, or standing phrases, but where there are verbal similarities not of this type, they carry more weight, and the greater their frequency the greater their significance. This revival of Maurer's doctrine that any extensive likeness in wording is proof positive of literary connection merits unreserved acceptance.

For thirty years now the Icelandic scholars have turned their intimate knowledge of the sagas to the task of unearthing such connections. The approach is legitimate and sufficient work has been done to allow a fair estimate of its success. The most thoroughly analyzed saga and the one best suited to exemplify the technique is *Njáls saga*.

According to Sveinsson and Kersbergen the saga which left the most obvious mark on *Njála* was *Laxdœla saga*.[18] Sveinsson goes so far as to say: "I believe that the author of *Njála* knew his *Laxdœla saga* almost by heart." [19] He finds a quantity of both motival and verbal borrowings. Among the former he lists seven which are, in his opinion, hardly disputable.

1. Gunnarr's inclination for Hákon jarl's *frændkona* Bergljót (*Njáls saga* 31) is akin to Kjartan's affair with Óláfr Tryggvason's sister Ingibjǫrg (*Laxdœla saga* 41–42). 2. Þjóstólfr's scuttling of Þorvaldr's boat (*Njáls saga* 12) might reflect Þuríðr's boring of Geirmundr's boat (*Laxdœla saga* 30), but contrary to Kersbergen (p. 177) Sveinsson does not believe that the connection is self-evident. 3. The strandings of Flosi and Njáll's sons (*Njáls saga* 153, 83) are similar to Óláfr pá's experience in Ireland (*Laxdœla saga* 21). 4. There are certain common features in the attack on Hlíðarendi (*Njáls saga* 77) and the attack on Helgi Harðbeinsson (*Laxdœla saga* 64), especially the slaying of Þorgrímr/Hrappr and the tearing off of the roof. 5. Njáll is able to identify Gunnarr's attackers from the description given by his shepherd (*Njáls saga* 69). The same motif is extensively developed in *Laxdœla saga* 63. 6. The first two marriages of Hallgerðr and Guðrún

18. Anna C. Kersbergen, *Litteraire Motieven in de Njála* (Rotterdam, 1927), p. 177: "Het belangrijkste is ongetwijfeld de invloed van de Laxd. geweest." Cf. Sveinsson, e.g. *Fornrit, 12,* xxxix.
19. "Njáls Saga," *Scripta Islandica, 1* (1950), 14.

are in some ways similar. 7. Hildiguðr's inciting of Flosi (*Njáls saga* 116) and Hróðný's admonishing of Ingjaldr (*Njáls saga* 124) are reminiscent of the scene in which Guðrún urges her sons to avenge Bolli (*Laxdœla saga* 60).

There are further similarities, but Sveinsson regards these seven as the most revealing. To do him justice it is necessary to emphasize that he is far from believing in a mechanical borrowing from *Laxdœla saga* or other written sources. He defines influence in the broadest possible sense:

> It can mean the direct borrowing of material from one work into another, but it can also mean something quite different. It can be interpreted to mean that material or aspects of material were used subordinately or as a model, and were transmuted. The mental process can have been conscious, but also unconscious. Or the influences may have functioned in still other ways. A word or a sentence, a bit of information, or a story could awaken an echo in the mind of the saga writer—and on his parchment appears a sentence or note which has been subjected to an "influence" from another work. Or the influences are a matter of tone, taste, tendency, or the interpretation of men and life. And it must not be forgotten that the value of "influences" is not determined least of all by how well fitted they are to release the latent powers in the writer's soul.[20]

It is of course as difficult to argue against as it is to argue for this kind of subconscious influence. The similarities are incontestable and no one is likely to venture the claim that the author of *Njáls saga* was not open to some direct or indirect influence from *Laxdœla saga*. On the other hand, influences of this sort can be so obscured by their transformation in a new context that they are imperceptible and therefore inconclusive. By defining influence so loosely Sveinsson tends to take with one hand what he gives with the other. Furthermore, there is a discrepancy between the definition and the examples. The definition is one we would expect from a student of modern literature, where influences are conceived not only in terms of matter but also in terms of attitude and technique. But these are not the influences which Sveinsson primarily pursues. His examples are drawn from motival and verbal similarities; the old philological approach is still intact. Regardless of the definition the examples must stand on their own merits.

20. *Um Njálu*, pp. 154–55.

As a matter of general principle, parallels are indicative of borrowing in proportion to their isolation as well as to their verbal proximity. That is to say that an item found in only two sagas is more likely to be a literary loan than an item which crops up in seven sagas. The latter is better classed as a formula. In Sveinsson's list of loans it is remarkable how many of them are motifs which are not restricted to *Njáls saga* and *Laxdæla saga* alone. Kersbergen counts six examples of shipboring, to which should be added a seventh from *Egils saga*.[21] The motif of stranding on foreign shores recurs in *Eyrbyggja saga* and *Fóstbrœðra saga*. The *hvǫt* is well known from *Vápnfirðinga saga, Hávarðar saga Ísfirðings, Harðar saga, Heiðarvíga saga,* and *Eyrbyggja saga*. It is not a striking coincidence that Gunnarr and Kjartan have attachments to highborn women in Norway. The adventurer and the princess is a common enough motif. One thinks of Haraldr harðráði's exploits in Constantinople. If Gunnarr's amorous adventure has a written model at all, it is more likely to be Hrútr's affair with Gunnhildr earlier in *Njáls saga*.[22] Lastly, the identification of men by their clothing is a widespread motif in the sagas; Kersbergen gives fourteen examples (pp. 69–70) and the one in *Njála* is no closer to *Laxdæla saga* than to other examples.

In all Sveinsson's comparisons the differences are quite as striking as the correspondences. In the onslaught on Gunnarr and Helgi Harðbeinsson, for example, an attacker is pierced with a spear through a window as he runs up on the roof, but the motif is fringed with very different dialogue. Both exchanges partake of the saga's grim wit, both are memorable, but they are plainly independent. The maneuver itself was not a literary feature but had a basis in experience, as is shown by an episode in *Sturlunga saga*.[23]

Worthy of consideration is the likening of Guðrún's and Hallgerðr's marriage sequences, but even here the analogy is not overwhelming. In crucial respects the first two marriages of both women are entirely different. Hallgerðr is responsible (willingly once, unwillingly the second time) for the death of two husbands. The function of these marriages is to foreshadow her role in Gunnarr's fate. In simplest terms it is a case of the epic three with final stress.[24] Guðrún's

21. *Litteraire Motieven*, pp. 83–84, and *Fornrit*, 2, 64.
22. Cf. Heinzel, "Beschreibung der Isländischen Saga," p. 156.
23. See Rolf Heller, "Laxdœla saga und Sturlunga saga," *ANF*, 76 (1961), 130. Cf. also *Fornrit*, 7, 260.
24. See Ari C. Bouman, *Patterns in Old English and Old Icelandic Literature* (Leiden, 1962), p. 12.

first two marriages do not play a part in her characterization or in the dramatic structure of the saga. Nor is she directly responsible for the death of any of her husbands.

In both of the latter examples we must reckon with what Heusler would have called "der unabhängige Grundstock." Sveinsson would probably grant this and would argue only that *Laxdœla saga* exerted a certain amount of attraction on *Njáls saga*. I am not persuaded that even an incidental influence need be assumed, but be that as it may, any influence which might have taken place is very slight. Motival borrowing which limits itself to a few details cannot be regarded as an important or productive element in the composition of a saga. The figure of Hallgerðr cannot be modeled after Guðrún, nor Gunnarr's defense after Helgi's. In order for the theory of written models to be important it should be able to show that *Laxdœla saga* in some way provided the germ for part of *Njáls saga*. As long as the loans are as problematic and as external as those suggested by Sveinsson, they do little to promote our understanding of the compositional process.

Whereas there is room for doubt as to whether *Njáls saga* may have borrowed a motif or two from *Laxdœla saga,* there is no ground at all for the assumption of verbal echoes. This is not a matter which can be argued abstractly, but anyone who looks through the proposed correspondences printed in *Um Njálu* will be struck by the modicum of resemblance to be found in them. A comparison with the parallel texts printed in works on the kings' sagas shows how much less exacting Sveinsson is in the degree of verbal congruence required to support *rittengsl*. In his review of the book Stefán Einarsson noted the criticism of this failing: "Probably it would not be difficult to find details in this work where one would say either: this is too much, or this is too little. Such objections have actually been forthcoming, f. inst. against his zeal in trying to establish verbal likenesses between Njála and other works." [25] The objections could be classed as follows: everyday phrases are regarded as constituting *rittengsl*,[26] *rittengsl* are estab-

---

25. *JEGP, 33* (1934), 569. See also Sveinsson's own cautious remarks, *Dating the Icelandic Sagas*, pp. 94–95.

26. *Njáls saga*   *Laxdœla saga*

Njót þú heill handa (39, 131)   Þorgerðr bað hann heilan njóta handa (55)

Sitr Gunnarr nú heima í sæmð sinni (56)   [Ólafur] sat í búi sínu í miklum sóma (31)

The dubiousness of the procedure is pointed up by the fact that the latter phrase from *Njáls saga* is repeated on page 141 of Sveinsson's book, this time as a loan from *Bandamanna saga*. To which of these sagas is the author of *Njála* indebted?

lished by similarity of word rather than of sequence,[27] idioms are taken to show *rittengsl*,[28] *rittengsl* are assumed where there is no coincidence of context, stock situations and motifs which necessarily have some degree of verbal resemblance are pressed into service as *rittengsl*.[29] As far as I can discover the hundred pages of Sveinsson's book devoted to these verbal correspondences produce nothing of significance.

In evaluating the similarities between *Laxdœla saga* and *Njáls saga,* Sveinsson does not forget to countercheck the deviations. There are some minor differences which, as he says, do not rule out the possibility that *Laxdœla saga* was known to the author of *Njála*. More important are the very divergent tales told about Hrútr Herjólfsson. For the sake of convenience I resort to a tabular summary.

27. *Njáls saga*

ok fóru menn ór hverri búð at undrask þá (33)	ok þótti mönnum þat mikit örendi ór öðrum sveitum, at undrask, hversu hann var ágætliga skapaðr (*Laxdœla saga* 16)
. . . bað hann færa Hallgerði ok kvað hana kenna mundu, hvárt þat höfuð hefði ort níð um þá (45)	Hér er nú þat höfuð, er eigi myndi undan teljask at mæla eptir þik. . . . (*Eyrbyggja saga* 27)

28. *Njáls saga*

Vel mun hann í höndum hafa (37)	Þú hefir vel í höndum við mik (*Heiðarvíga saga*, Kålund's ed., 103)
ok mun annars staðar meira slóða draga en hér (36)	Meira slóða mun draga. . . . (*Bandamanna saga* 21)
Heyr á endemi (48)	Heyr á endemi (*Bandamanna saga* 25, 31)

The significance of the last example is not enhanced by the fact that the phrase also occurs in *Hallfreðar saga* (*Fornrit, 8*, 143), *Vatnsdœla saga* (*Fornrit, 8*, 99), *Ljósvetninga saga* (*Fornrit, 10*, 82), *Reykdœla saga* (*Fornrit, 10*, 181), *Hænsa-Þóris saga* (*Fornrit, 3*, 46), *Hávarðar saga Ísfirðings* (*Fornrit, 6*, 312), and elsewhere.

29. The most vivid example is the portentous dream in *Heiðarvíga saga*, which is the star witness in Sveinsson's case for literary connection between *Njáls saga* and *Heiðarvíga saga*.

Njáls saga	*Heiðarvíga saga*
ek þóttumk ríða fram hjá Knafahólum. Þar þóttumk ek sjá varga mjök marga, ok sóttu þeir at mér, en ek snera undan fram at Rangá (62)	hann segir draum sinn, at honum þótti, sem þeir væri þar staddir á Gullteig ok kæmi at þeim vargar margir ok ættisk þar við, ok var mikit um, ok ek þóttumk vakna við þat, er ek hljóp undan heim til bæjarins. (Kålund's ed., 84)

Ominous dreams containing wolf *fylgjur* are rampant in the sagas (*Droplaugarsona saga*, *Gísla saga*, *Heiðarvíga saga*, *Harðar saga*, *Hávarðar saga Ísfirðings*, *Þórðar saga hreðu*) and are ill-suited to prove *rittengsl*; cf. *Fornrit, 11*, lxxiv. In general Sveinsson's method is reminiscent of one described by E. K. Rand: "Sometimes, after reading dissertations, let us say, on the plagiarisms of Virgil, one pictures the poet at a large desk on which ten or a dozen volumes of his more worthy predecessors are displayed, from which he filches a line here, a half-line there, a quarter-line there, an epithet there, constructing in this way a painful mosaic or picture-puzzle" (*Founders of the Middle Ages* [Cambridge, 1928], p. 163).

Laxdœla saga	*Njáls saga*
Hrútr's birth and characterization.	Hrútr affronts Hǫskuldr with his remark about Hallgerðr's thief's eyes.
He leaves the service of Haraldr gráfeldr and Gunnhildr in order to claim his inheritance from Hǫskuldr in Iceland. The claim is rejected and the brothers feud, but they are ultimately reconciled.	Hrútr courts Unnr on Hǫskuldr's advice.
	Hrútr's uncle comes from Norway and urges him to collect his inheritance there. The marriage is postponed three years.
A marriage with Unnr ends in divorce. From two later marriages (Þorbjǫrg and an unnamed woman) issue sixteen sons and ten daughters.	Hrútr becomes Gunnhildr's paramour and Haraldr gráfeldr's liegeman.
Hrútr quarrels with Þorleikr Hǫskuldsson and participates in the elimination of a brood of sorcerers.	Hrútr's viking expedition; Gunnhildr recovers his inheritance from Sóti.
	Hrútr takes leave of the Norwegian court; Gunnhildr's curse.
	Marriage to Unnr and divorce.
	Mǫrðr's effort to recover the dowry fails when he is intimidated by Hrútr.
	Hrútr advises his brother in the matter of Hallgerðr's marriage and the ensuing difficulties.
	Gunnarr exacts payment of the dowry from Hrútr.
	Hrútr warns Gunnarr about Hallgerðr's temperament and advises him in his suit against Otkell.

The differences are plainly considerable and it is doubtful that any poetic initiative can explain them.[30] The author of *Njáls saga* did not

30. Sveinsson weighs the possibility that *Njáls saga* disregarded *Laxdœla saga* in favor of another tradition, but he prefers to think that *Njála*'s account is best under-

utilize the material available in *Laxdœla saga,* and where there is common material the sagas give conflicting versions. Furthermore, *Njála*'s account of the quarrel precipitated by Unnr's divorce is shown to be traditional by the fact that the earlier saga alludes to "the quarrel of the Laxdœlir and the Fljótshlíðingar" (p. 48). If so much was traditional, it is reasonable to suppose that the whole story had an oral foundation.

Sveinsson is unable to make a convincing case for literary connection with *Laxdœla saga.* He asks us to believe that *Njála*'s author knew *Laxdœla saga* so well that he remembered little phrases but so badly that he forgot whole chapters. Had he really approached his task like the author of a king's saga, he would have taken at least some passage from *Laxdœla saga* almost as it stood. But whereas Sveinsson's arguments for literary connection with *Laxdœla saga* are weak, his discussion of literary connections with other sagas is much weaker. One is therefore inclined to submit to Sveinsson's irony and join those who hold "that the saga writers sat each in his own corner

stood as a historical emendation of its source. For, according to *Laxdœla saga*'s chronology, Hrútr must have been in Iceland before taking service with Haraldr gráfeldr. "Gunnhildarsynir koma svo seint til ríkis í Noregi, að vér verðum að ætla, að Hrútur fari löngu fyrir þann tíma til Íslands—tveim tugum ára eða meira, og þá er eðlilegast að hugsa sér, að þau Gunnhildur hafi alls ekki kynnzt, fyr en þá í utanförinni. Hér er því engu líkara en höfundur *Njálu* sjái tímavilluna og lagfæri frásögnina eftir því" (*Um Njálu,* pp. 113–14). I am unable to discover what in *Laxdœla saga*'s chronology obliged Sveinsson to date Hrútr's arrival in Iceland twenty years before Haraldr gráfeldr's succession to the throne. Hrútr is first introduced into the story after the chapter about Þorsteinn surtr's drowning, which Sveinsson dates between 955 and 959 (*Fornrit, 5,* lix). Haraldr gráfeldr's accession is usually dated to 961. In the chapter following the fraternal feud Hǫskuldr is described as "hniginn á inn efra aldr." Since he was probably born about 900, these words cannot well apply before 970. The chronology at this point is flawless. (It is another matter when *Laxdœla saga* over-prolongs Hrútr's youth. To judge by his mother's age he cannot have been born much after 915 and it seems excessive, even making allowance for his viking constitution, that he should have sired twenty-six children after the age of fifty.) Perhaps Sveinsson was led to assume an error because of *Njáls saga*'s chronology, according to which Hrútr must have been in Iceland not much later than 950 in order to comment on the child Hallgerðr. But the author of *Njáls saga* cannot have been motivated by a gross error in *Laxdœla saga.* Where there are divergencies in two accounts the Icelandic scholars have taken pains to explain the differences in terms of a consistent principle applied by one author or the other. A case in point is *Ljósvetninga saga,* another is the discrepancy between *Hœnsa-Þóris saga* and Ari's *Libellus,* which will be discussed later. The method has not always produced satisfactory results. A return to oral variants in the present era may seem unenlightened, but there is evidence for the old position. It is striking that two identical motifs recur in both sagas, thinly disguised by contrasting details: fraternal hostility and the claiming of an inheritance. In *Laxdœla saga* the temporary hostility is motivated by Hǫskuldr's withholding of his brother's share in the maternal legacy. In *Njáls saga* the same kind of rift is caused by Hrútr's comment on Hallgerðr. In *Laxdœla saga* Hrútr travels to Iceland expressly to claim his inheritance. In *Njáls saga* the route is reversed and goes from Iceland to Norway. We may be dealing here with one hostility and with one inheritance blurred and confused by tradition.

and wrote their sagas according to living tradition without caring about one another, and even if they did know about one another, they assiduously avoided making use of the fact." [31] The author of *Njáls saga* may well have known *Laxdœla saga,* but in this case he went to some lengths not to take advantage of his knowledge.

This criticism is not intended as a blanket rejection of written sources. Good evidence was produced long ago by Lehmann and Schnorr von Carolsfeld to support the view that *Njála*'s author used written laws. That he used written genealogies, a written *Kristni þáttr,* and perhaps a written *Brjáns saga* is not improbable. But there is only the thinnest evidence that he used written *Íslendinga sögur.* In his *Fornrit* introduction Sveinsson was in fact more cautious and mentioned only *Laxdœla saga, Eyrbyggja saga,* and *Ljósvetninga saga,* plus some unspecified *Austfirðinga sögur* and *konunga sögur.* On the other hand he supposed *Njáls saga* to have used no fewer than four lost sagas: *Gauks saga Trandilssonar, Saga Hróars Tungugoða, Fljótshlíðinga saga,* and *Þáttr af Þorgeiri Skorargeiri (Fornrit, 12,* xli–xliii). It is a dubious procedure to suppose that *Njáls saga* used lost sagas before demonstrating unequivocally that it used extant sagas.

That *Njáls saga*'s author learned his art by reading as well as by listening is a supposition that one can readily accept, but that the influence from written family sagas involved content has not been shown.

The *Fornrit* introductions have gradually built up a theory of written sources which now overwhelms the student of saga literature. To test each case on its own merits, as it deserves, would fill many pages. I have purposely chosen *Njáls saga* because it is the largest, one of the latest and most literary sagas, and the one which perhaps lends itself best to bookprose analysis. The fact that it does not pass the test enjoins caution in the similar analysis of other sagas. This does not mean that source hunting among the written sagas is fruitless or futile. We should continue to accumulate and evaluate as many similarities as possible, but we should show more prudence in distinguishing fortuitous or formulaic correspondences from literary borrowings and more restraint in burdening small similarities with mighty consequences. Above all we should be wary of hypothetical written sources, which are no more susceptible of proof and no less an article of dogma than oral tradition, the indemonstrability of which has been so firmly impressed upon us by the adherents of bookprose.

31. *Um Njálu,* p. 101.

The preceding paragraphs dealt with the written sources which the saga writers are believed to have used and considered what part it is reasonable to suppose these sources played in the creation of a saga and to what extent they can displace the notion of oral stories. But no matter what role we assign the written sources, we are obliged to add a second quantity in order to satisfy the modern theory of saga authorship. We must substitute for the well articulated oral tradition an author who possessed all the virtues of the dethroned tradition. We must envisage a poet who could form the available material and stamp it with his artistic will. The most striking and concrete declaration of this artistic will to come out of Iceland was made by S. Nordal in his introduction to the *Fornrit* edition of *Hœnsa-Þóris saga*.

The relation of tradition to poetic fiction in the sagas is, as previously stated, an area of study which suffers from a lack of evidence. In general only a few details can be compared with older sources, the rest is left to the uncertain discretion of the student. Only in one instance are we fortunate enough to be able to verify the main outline of a saga against a reasonably reliable historical source. The plot of *Hœnsa-Þóris saga* is recorded briefly by Ari in chapter 5 of *Íslendingabók*. The accounts are close but have enough irreconcilable differences to suggest their independence. For a few decades scholars felt secure in the belief that they possessed one sure example of a saga's degree of faithfulness and the extent of oral metamorphosis. But Nordal's introduction swept this certainty aside.

Nordal argued the improbability of an author's failing to know that his material was incorporated in the works of Ari. He hypothesized that despite the deviations in the saga's version the author was fully aware of his precursor and consciously departed from him partly in the interest of private chronological speculations and partly in the interest of enlivening the story. His premise is that the author was the arbitrary master of his material (*Fornrit, 3,* xv).

Nordal gives a complete list of the differences between the two accounts under eight points and tries then to explain the departures in *Hœnsa-Þóris saga* in line with the theory of poetic license. Of these eight points three (2, 5, 6) do not necessarily show a direct conflict and can be dropped from the discussion. Nordal's explanation of two other differences (3, 8) seems to me improbable but not impossible, and objections might appear carping. It should be remembered however that these five differences remain differences and give no positive evidence of a poet's intervention. The other three points (1, 4, 7) are crucial and with them Nordal's thesis stands or falls.

The saga and Ari do not agree on the fundamental point of who the protagonists of the story were. Ari states that it was Þorkell Blundketilsson who was burned in. The saga says that it was Blundketill himself. According to Ari, Hersteinn is Þorkell's son. The saga has no knowledge of Þorkell and makes Hersteinn Blundketill's son. Nordal's explanation of this genealogical confusion picks up an idea of Maurer's.[32] He supposes that the author of *Hœnsa-Þóris saga* falsely connected the name Þorkell Blundketilsson, which he found in *Íslendingabók,* with the name Blundketill Geirsson, which he found in a loose genealogical table. (In reality the Blundketill referred to by Ari was the son of Ǫrnólfr, as *Melabók* shows us.) The author knew that Geirr was Skalla-Grímr's son-in-law. This presented him with a chronological dilemma since Geirr could not have married before about 920 and his great grandson could not have been full-grown in 962 at the time of the burning. He solved the problem by dropping the most expendable link in the genealogy, namely Þorkell.

There is an uneasy neatness about the construction. A judgment of the hypothesis depends partly on whether one believes that, in view of the chronological nonchalance in other sagas, a saga writer was given to this type of conjecture. But even granting the premise certain reservations are in order.

Nordal recognizes that the author could not have used a *Landnáma* redaction, as B. M. Ólsen supposed, because this source clearly distinguishes between Blundketill Geirsson and Blundketill Ǫrnólfsson and would have obviated the confusion in *Hœnsa-Þóris saga.* By analogy any genealogical record of the district would have been apt to make the distinction clear. But even if we suppose that the genealogical table at the disposal of our author said nothing about Blundketill Ǫrnólfsson, it must have contained more than the mere name of Blundketill Geirsson, since, in order for the author to have a basis for his chronological calculations, he must have known a good deal about Geirr hinn auðgi's family. It would, for example, have included Blundketill's children and would have shown that he had no son named Þorkell or Hersteinn. The information given in a genealogical work would thus rather have tended to prevent than promote a confusion. It seems likely that the confusion proceeded from a dearth

32. "Über die Hœnsa-Þóris Saga," p. 56.

and not from a surplus of information. One can better imagine that the author saw or heard the name Blundketill Geirsson outside of a genealogical context. But if this is the case, there is of course no sufficient basis for the chronological construction.

Nordal does not in fact make clear from where the necessary dates were taken. Unless we are to postulate a lost chronology as well as a genealogy, the only available chronological source was *Egils saga*.[33] The supposition might then be that the author of *Hœnsa-Þóris saga* knew the chronology of *Egils saga* so well that a discrepancy of ten to twenty years worried him into departing from Ari's authority. For it must have been an extremely close knowledge of *Egils saga* which led him to date Geirr's marriage to 920 rather than to 900. However a good case can be made for the belief that the author of *Hœnsa-Þóris saga* did not use *Egils saga* at all, and least of all its chronology. The only person about whom he could have learned from *Egils saga* was Tungu-Oddr. It is therefore significant that *Hœnsa-Þóris saga* dates Tungu-Oddr's death to around 970, before the marriage of Jófríðr and Þorsteinn Egilsson, while according to *Egils saga* Tungu-Oddr was still alive after the marriage and after Þorsteinn's quarrel with Steinarr, that is to say around 980. It seems unlikely that the author of *Hœnsa-Þóris saga* would be so painstaking in one case and so careless in another, that he would feel alternately bound and emancipated from his source. Further evidence that he did not use *Egils saga* is that he makes no use of the information about Geirr inn auðgi which was available there. He seems not to have known of Blundketill's brothers since, as Maurer pointed out,[34] Hersteinn was obliged to seek aid outside the family. Finally there is a basic incongruity in the assumption that the saga writer would go to such scholarly lengths to reconstruct a chronology while regularly according such cavalier treatment to the authority of Ari. His concern for accuracy is hardly consistent. That the confusion of Blundketill Ǫrnólfsson and Blundketill Geirsson resulted from a learned conjecture and that Þorkell was dropped for chronological reasons does not therefore strike me as a plausible hypothesis.

Another crucial area of disagreement is the first encounter between Þórðr gellir and Tungu-Oddr. In Ari's account the battle is fought on the Thinggrounds while the saga never allows Þórðr to arrive at the Thing. Nordal explains the difference by supposing that *Hœnsa-*

33. Nordal suggests the use of *Egils saga* (*Fornrit, 3*, xvi).
34. "Über die Hœnsa-Þóris Saga," p. 27.

Þóris saga modeled its account after the episode in which Snorri goði was turned back at the Hvítá in *Heiðarvíga saga*. This seems to me to be an exceptionally speculative thought. If the author was simply improvising, what did he have against a good Thingfight such as the one later described in *Njála*—or the impending battle between Christians and heathens described by Ari himself? Nordal's explanation entails an arbitrary sacrifice in accuracy by our chronologically fastidious author with no corresponding gain in literary effectiveness.

The last point involves the slaying of Hœnsa-Þórir after the verdict in *Íslendingabók* but before the verdict in *Hœnsa-Þóris saga*. Nordal brands the saga's version as pure invention because it is illogical that Hersteinn should ride to Ǫrnólfsdalr instead of accompanying his allies to the Thing. This is symptomatic of the equation between historical improbability and firsthand invention with which recent saga research works. What might formerly have been regarded as oral distortion is now rather taken to be the author's fancy. But the argument cuts both ways. This episode is so improbable that it is unlikely to be the author's invention. Furthermore Nordal does not explain what needed explaining, namely why the episode was inserted before the verdict in defiance of Ari, when it could just as well have been reserved until after sentence was passed.

Nordal argued well for the use of *Íslendingabók*, but the case is inherently too weak. The issue is not whether the author of *Hœnsa-Þóris saga* knew Ari or not. He may have known Ari and in this case it is even more striking that he took no account of Ari's version. His disregard would evince a variant with enough vitality to maintain itself against any source. That the writer did in fact draw from such a variant is adequately shown by the *þáttr* of Gunnarr Hlífarson and Þóroddr at the end of the saga. The story has no foundation in Ari and cannot be invention since it has no compositional function.[35] Yet it presupposes the rest of the saga, which must therefore also have a foothold in tradition. And let us again not forget the weight of Sturla's opinion. Nordal asks how the author of *Hœnsa-Þóris saga* could fail to know Ari. In turn it is fair to ask how Sturla could fail to know that *Hœnsa-Þóris saga* was an imaginative deviation from Ari's authority, if this were really the case. It is possible, as Nordal says (*Fornrit, 3*, xii), that Sturla was a poor judge, but that his obliviousness could go to the extreme of confusing contemporary fiction with bona fide history is hardly a tenable position. If he used a saga

35. Cf. Sigurður Nordal, *Hrafnkels Saga Freysgoða*, p. 34.

to correct *Landnáma,* that saga, right or wrong, must have had some generally accepted basis in tradition. It is therefore unwise to part with *Hœnsa-Þóris saga* as an essentially oral story or to reject the discrepancy between it and Ari as a measure of oral distortion.

Oral Sources

The emphasis on the saga author is an understandable reaction against earlier views. Keyser's belief in a hard and fast tradition was gradually compromised by the demonstration of an author behind each saga, an author with poetic prerogatives. Among these prerogatives was the use of free invention. No one since Keyser has felt that a saga writer was incapable of resorting to fiction where he felt the need, though most, and among them the Icelanders, have believed that the sources from which he drew exercised a considerable degree of restraint. The most recent trend in saga study has veered toward the view that even this idea of restraint constitutes too great a concession to oral tradition and too slight a recognition of the author. According to Baetke and his students, traditions, if there were any, could be followed or rejected, retained as they were, or altered at the author's option. Even if they were still in circulation, they were so fragmentary as to afford no basis for a detailed narrative. A few scraps of disconnected information from the Saga Age were perhaps available and became entangled in the author's web of fiction, but they provided at most the seed for speculation.

This view, though it may seem like an extension of the bookprose theory, is in fact a drastic departure. It severs the family sagas resolutely from any preliterary or traditional phenomena and pictures them as a creative outburst peculiar to the thirteenth century. If the arguments for such a view are cogent, we must abjure the belief, held by several centuries of scholars, that the sagas were in some way the outgrowth of an oral literature. But for all the consistency of its viewpoint and boldness of its presentation Baetke's theory is not securely anchored. His basic criticism of freeprose theory rests on a misconception, and this misconception biases not only his own premises but in a visible way the work of his disciples. It is the notion that freeprose depends primarily on the assumption that the sagas are historical.

Baetke taxes his precursors with a fateful confusion of historicity, genesis, and oral tradition, but this criticism is at most applicable to Keyser and his kith; Heusler and Liestøl never argued oral tradition predominantly from historicity. Heusler's unequivocal disavowal has already been quoted (p. 50). Liestøl significantly reserved the study of historicity for the last three chapters of his book, which he prefaced with the statement that he was unwilling to shirk the matter of historicity and had therefore tried to define the historical element as closely as possible in an admittedly speculative area.[36] Thus the discussion of historicity is a kind of appendix and is not a link in the argument for oral tradition. When much of Baetke's book is devoted to assurances that the saga can contain very little history, these protestations miss the mark. Even if it were possible to prove that the sagas contain not one iota of history, Liestøl's main thesis would not be impaired. Baetke's criticism skirts the mechanics of oral transmission, a description of which was the central issue in Liestøl's book. No folklorist would reduce the matter to an either/or in which reliable history and pure fancy are the only alternatives. Liestøl assumed a multitude of intermediate stages and degrees of historicity. But Baetke's system has no place for oral deformation. The syllogism is essentially this: the sagas are unhistorical, therefore there is no historical tradition; since there is no historical tradition, the sagas are invented. The idea that a historical tradition could be transformed into an unhistorical tradition is circumvented.[37]

This short-cut became the basis of the method employed by Baetke's

36. *The Origin of the Icelandic Family Sagas,* pp. 181–82: "But the problem of reliability or unreliability, of truth or fiction, cannot be burked; it is the most interesting and probably the most controversial issue in the critical study of the sagas. Some writers endeavor to evade it, or to treat it as a secondary matter. They argue that the real value of the sagas lies in their artistic merit, and that the percentage of historical truth is of less moment. In any case the question is so difficult that one is tempted to cry 'sour grapes.' "

37. Symptomatic of Baetke's misunderstanding is his citing of Caskel's authority for the slight historical value of the Arabic aijām stories ("Die Entstehung," pp. 47–48). These stories apparently do not contain much fact, but it is not their historical accuracy which stands in question. Caskel should have been quoted at more length, for he assumes that the stories were written down from family traditions, originally with little contribution on the part of the transcriber. In other words he imagines the procedure to have been rather similar to what the freeprosaists postulate for the Icelandic family sagas. See Werner Caskel, "Aijām-al-'Arab, Studien zur Altarabischen Epik," *Islamica,* 3, 82–99, esp. 86. Liestøl made his position clear in "Tradisjonen i Hrafnkels saga Freysgoða," *Arv,* 2 (1946), 110: "Men spørsmålet: historisk eller tildikta er ikkje det same som spørsmålet om kva forfattaren av Hrafnkels saga fann føre seg og kva han dikta til. Når det levde tradisjonar om Hrafnkell, som vi i minsto av Landnáma ser at det må ha gjort, laut desse tradisjonane fylgja dei vanlege lovene for det som lever i minnet. Levde tradisjonen rik, ville han lett auka opp ved tildikting og meir og meir få ein kunstnarleg sving. Mellom dei sogemennene som fortalde om Hrafnkell, kan det ha funnist ein eller fleire kunstnarar som med ein gong kunne gjeva det heile ein sterk framskuv i kunstnarleg leid." Cf. Jan de Vries, "Die Isländische Saga und die Mündliche Überlieferung," *Märchen, Mythos, Dichtung* [*Festschrift Friedrich von der Leyen*] (München, 1963), p. 175. Hans Kuhn, *AFDA,* 75 (1964), 1–5.

disciples in the series *Saga*. An episode is established usually with good probability as unhistorical and is then unceremoniously labeled as the saga writer's invention.[38] A similar simplification is the automatic equation of art and author. Anything which is dramatically effective in the sagas is adjudged the work of the writer.[39] That dramatic technique could have been a legacy from the storyteller is not considered as a possible alternative, so that a large part of the central proof is left unessayed. It is not adequate to exhibit the lack of historicity or the presence of dramatic economy in order to prove oral tradition a chimera. It is necessary to prove that these unhistorical and dramatic qualities were not products of an oral process. This is the fundamental blind spot in Baetke's theory, but there are a number of other points which prompt reservations.

The distinction between carefully maintained official historical traditions on the one hand and quickly displaced private rumors on the other is not acceptable.[40] There is no evidence that a historical tradition in the custodianship of quasi-professionals existed. Ari and Snorri are in no way official guardians of a centralized historical tradition; they gathered their information where they could find it and compiled their books as private scholars. Equally unacceptable is the idea that there was a clear distinction between national history and family history. *Sturlunga saga,* which Baetke cites as an example of the first, shows precisely how the two were blended. National history could be seen only in terms of the feuds and machinations within and among the prominent families. That the great national events, which at the same time were the great family events (e.g. Njáll's burning and Snorri's murder), could be remembered clearly as national history and only vaguely as family reminiscences is an impracticable division.

The allusions to saga telling in the sagas have always been regarded as genuine in so far as they indicated some kind of oral tradition. That is to say the allusions have been regarded at least as culturally true. Now Baetke characterizes this argument as circular since the allusions appear in fictional sagas and must therefore themselves be fictional.[41] This makes doubtful sense. If the institution of saga telling never existed, would a saga writer be likely to invent it? Baetke sees

38. E.g. Ernst Walter, "Studien zur Vápnfirðinga Saga," *Saga, 1* (1956), 23, 35, 41; Rolf Heller, "Die Literarische Darstellung der Frau in den Isländersagas," pp. 23, 49, 75, 98.

39. Walter, pp. 27–28, 56; Heller, p. 80.

40. "Über die Entstehung," pp. 15–20, 38–46.

41. Ibid., p. 29.

the allusions as so many efforts to substantiate the truth of an account, but the idea of inventing an institution, which everyone knew to be nonexistent, in order to allay doubts is hardly logical. Let us imagine how much belief a saga of George Washington, ostensibly fashioned from what "some men say," would enlist. In order to have any power to convince, such allusions must have a basis in reality. The analogy of H. C. Andersen's fairy tale device is out of order since the purpose here cannot be to verify a report but simply to tease the reader's imagination with an illusion of oral storytelling. The reader is a party to the fiction.

The allusion to Þorvaldr in *Droplaugarsona saga,* which is so important to the freeprose theory, is dismissed summarily. After pointing out the defectiveness of the text, the chronological improbability, and the bookprose features of the saga, Baetke concludes: "Vielleicht ist sie nur als einer der mannigfachen Kunstgriffe aufzufassen, die die Sagaverfasser anwenden, um den Glauben der Leser an die Wahrheit ihrer Geschichte zu bestärken." [42] He compares the fiction to the attribution of *Gunnlaugs saga* to Ari in the Stockholm manuscript, attaches importance to the fact that there is either a copyist's error or an omission in Þorvaldr's genealogy, and characterizes the whole genealogy as "sonst unbekannt," which implies that the people in it did not exist. This "sonst unbekannt" is used frequently in the Baetke school to impeach the credibility of the genealogical matter in the sagas, but by good fortune we are able to verify the traditional status of some saga personages in other sources. Should we automatically dismiss all those persons who cannot be so verified as the author's fiction? This is part of the hyper-criticism transplanted by Baetke from the historical to the literary discipline: everything which cannot be demonstrated as true or traditional with documentary evidence (of which we have little) must be regarded as the author's invention. Would it not be curious if only those saga personages who happen by chance to be verifiable really existed in tradition?

It is a question whether the defectiveness of the text in which Þorvaldr appears has any bearing on the problem. The fact that the genealogy and perhaps the chronology are not in good order does not reflect on the possibility that a Þorvaldr or some other descendant of Grímr could have told the saga. To reject the gist of the author's statement on the basis of a textual corruption is a confusion of spheres.

It is quite unlikely that the allusion to Þorvaldr is a device used to

42. Ibid., p. 59.

substantiate the story. Would the author invent a genealogy, which Easterners at least must have known to be unreal, in order to gain credence for his story? Would he then further have claimed that a Þorvaldr told the saga if everyone knew that neither Þorvaldr nor anyone else would or could have told such a saga—again for the purpose of making his story credible?

The ascription to Ari in *Gunnlaugs saga* is not comparable. In the first place Baetke adheres to B. M. Ólsen's view that the plusses in Stockholm 18 are original without considering Nordal's more recent and more probable view that they are late additions. In the second place it is one thing to attribute a saga to Ari, the father of Icelandic historiography and a familiar name to all, and another to attribute a saga to a Þorvaldr, whom no one could have known, since, as Baetke thinks, he was a fiction.

It is of course rather a matter of faith whether one believes that family sagas were told or not. It is true, as Baetke points out, that the oral sagas referred to in our extant works dealt with contemporary events.[43] The one allusion to an oral family saga which would have saved much speculation is missing. Nevertheless most people have seen no reason to deny that family sagas were told. Sveinsson writes: "It is reported of a certain marriage feast, held at Reykhólar in the West of Iceland in the year 1119, that in order to entertain the guests tales were told, which in this instance were indeed exaggerated accounts of ancient heroes and vikings, but doubtless tales of real events from the saga period have also been told by way of amusement."[44] Baetke believes in the oral *fornaldarsaga* but balks at the oral family saga.[45] At the same time he assigns both types to the same category of entirely entertaining literature. This suggests the improbable sequence that within the area of fiction the Icelanders first proceeded with the painstaking combination of vague indications, invention, genealogical and chronological speculation to produce *ex vacuo* a family saga, before bothering to record the *fornaldarsǫgur,* which had circulated at least since the beginning of the twelfth century and required much less expenditure of effort or ingenuity on the part of the author.

There are other things which mystify in this creation from chaos. One wonders what confluence of spirit circumscribed the genre to such an extent. Why did the inventors of the sagas restrict themselves

43. Ibid., p. 58.
44. E. Ó. Sveinsson, *Corpus Codicum Islandicorum Medii Ævi,* 5, "Introduction," 10.
45. "Über die Entstehung," p. 59.

to the period known as the Saga Age without being tempted into the preceding or following periods? One wonders why the artistic achievement could not be matched in the *fornaldarsaga,* since the artistic aspects were the work of the author and could presumably be applied to any material. An explanation should be offered for why the dramatic scheme of a *Njáls saga* was not transferred by a capable artist to events around 900, or, let us say, to events in Norway contemporary to the Icelandic Saga Age. Somehow we must imagine a tacit agreement among saga writers that their literary technique was applicable only to the period 950–1050 in Iceland.

One concession Baetke has made to tradition is the existence of genuine stanzas.[46] But he regards them not as nuclei of tradition but as fragments without context or connection. It is indicative of this mode of thinking that Heller regards the plot of *Bjarnar saga* as pure invention because, though the stanzas indicate a quarrel, they are not explicit about the reason for the quarrel.[47] Heller assumes that the author had no more knowledge of Bjǫrn and Þórðr than we would if we looked at their stanzas as they are printed in *Skjaldedigtning.* This is possible, but contrary to the almost universal assumption that the stanzas could not have survived in an isolated state.[48] We would have to imagine that they had a tough constitution indeed if they could weather two centuries stripped of all tradition. Baetke and Heller would have us think that people were able to recite thirty-eight stanzas attributed to Bjǫrn and Þórðr, but until the composition of the saga they would have been unable to answer the question of an inquisitive listener about the identity and dealings of the two men. It is not credible that this question went unanswered in the eleventh or twelfth century any more than after the saga was written. We need not assume that the answers were always the same, but we cannot obviate the certainty that there were answers and that some of them must have been known to the author of the saga. We have proof that scaldic stanzas depended on traditions in *Íslendingadrápa,* which could have meant very little to the listener unless he knew as much or in fact a little more about the saga heroes than we do.

The new school, consistent with its tenets, places much emphasis on the Christian ground from which the sagas sprang. The Þorleifr

46. Ibid., p. 36. Cf. the important article by Siegfried Beyschlag, "Möglichkeiten Mündlicher Überlieferung in der Königssaga," *ANF,* 68 (1953), pp. 109–39.
47. Heller, "Die Literarische Darstellung der Frau," pp. 9–12.
48. See *Fornrit,* 2, v; 3, xxiii; 7, xlvi. For the opposite view, Bjarni Einarsson, *Skáldasögur.*

kristni episode in *Vápnfirðinga saga* reflects for E. Walter a conscious Christian bias, even a touch of propaganda. The Christian element has always been regarded as surprisingly small in the sagas, but there is no reason to believe that it is not present, perhaps in a discreet form not yet sufficiently appreciated. Christian intrusion in greater or lesser degree does no injury to a freeprose view. On the other hand those who believe that the sagas were a product of the thirteenth century, and the thirteenth century alone, must establish a Christian predominance to the exclusion of the heathen viewpoint. This is difficult in view of the sagas' inconsistency. How well does the miracle of Njáll's saintly glow and unsinged state jibe with the rest of the saga? Phrased another way, is *Njáls saga* the work of an Icelander steeped in hagiography? The question is of course rhetorical. Christian sentiment cannot be the core but only a small excrescence, external to the substance of the saga. It will hardly be possible to demonstrate an underlying Christian slant comparable to that in an *Óláfs saga* in any of the family sagas. Where the Christian bias becomes apparent, we are dealing with a superimposition, or at least with two layers. In other words the author betrays a personality independent from the saga matter, or stated in reverse, the matter proves its autonomy and priority in relation to the author. We have now been provided with a perfect example of the disparity between author and matter in the proof that M represents the more original version of *Fóstbrœðra saga*. It is not conceivable that the author of what Finnur Jónsson called "romantisk-teologisk-anatomisk tøjeri" was also the firsthand creator of such plastic and dramatic scenes as Butraldi's death. Such contradiction of purpose and taste could not have been the lot of one man. The idea long held that the medieval learning is interpolative has a kernel of truth in so far as this learning is incongruous and foreign to the style and spirit of the narrative. The author is a prey to old and new traditions and neither can be disregarded if we are to form a fair picture of his sources.[49]

Perhaps the least satisfactory link in Baetke's theory is the explanation of the style.[50] According to Baetke the famous saga style was all but inevitable. It was the only way the Icelanders could have written because it represents the way they spoke. Aside from the fact that this explanation ignores the very stylized and literary idiom of the sagas,

49. J. M. C. Kroesen explains the difficulty by supposing that two authors had their hands in the composition of the saga: *Over de Compositie der Fóstbrœðra Saga* (Leiden, 1962).
50. "Über die Entstehung," p. 61.

the "ausseralltägliche Natürlichkeit" (Heusler), that is, a style which transcends an everyday tone especially in the dialogue, the process would be unique. We are asked to believe that, once equipped with an alphabet, a man had only to write as he had always spoken. This makes the difficult transition from speaking to writing too easy. No other people was, such a short time after receipt of the alphabet, able to compose idiomatic prose works because they had always spoken that way. The ability to write a vernacular is not natural and presupposes discipline, more so than a learned style perhaps. The freeprose hypothesis of oral antecedents and the bookprose assumption of a gradual stylistic evolution both satisfy the basic requirement of an organic explanation; what Baetke offers is not a substitute.

The natural upshot of Baetke's view of the saga style is Heller's view of saga realism. Of the saga authors he says: "Wollten sie ihre Werke lebensnah gestalten, mussten sie zu kleinen Zügen greifen, die das Leben ihrer Zeit in gleichem Masse bot wie sicherlich auch das vergangener Jahrhunderte. Auf diese Weise müssen wir auch bei der Mehrzahl der 'echt' scheinenden Berichte mit dem Wirken dichtenden Geistes rechnen. Das heisst, dass sich Vorgänge wohl so abgespielt haben könnten, in ihrer uns vorliegenden Form aber von den Saga-verfassern gestaltet sind."[51] The idea that the sagas were based on everyday experiences rather overestimates the color of daily routine in Iceland. There is plainly more than a little legendary matter in the sagas, which is, for example, not found in *Sturlunga saga*. The clearest case is the grandiose heroics and feats of arms which are a trademark of the sagas. It is not probable that these were inspired by the sober events of the day; they are more likely to be a draft on the gilded traditions of early Iceland.

Baetke's viewpoint is an interesting tangent to saga research, like Schlözer's revolt two centuries ago and like Rubow's more recent adventure, but it is unlikely to strike roots. There remains too much evidence in favor of oral tradition for us to ignore it entirely. It is sufficient to recall the references to saga telling, which cannot be wished out of existence, the great probability that there were traditions to explain scaldic stanzas, the fairly numerous allusions to specific traditions which are not explained and which cannot have been inserted for artistic reasons,[52] the recurrence of famous Saga Age per-

---

51. Heller, "Die Literarische Darstellung der Frau," p. 85.
52. *Reykdœla saga* refers to the slaying of Hróarr Tungugoði (*Fornrit, 10,* 214–15), *Laxdœla saga* to the quarrel between Laxdœlir and Fljótshlíðingar (*Fornrit, 5,* 48), *Egils saga* to the feud between Gunnlaugr and Hrafn (*Fornrit, 2,* 300), *Hreiðars þáttr* to

sonalities such as Snorri goði and Guðmundr ríki in contexts which are in no way dependent on one another, the analogy of the oral *fornaldarsaga,* and the availability of tradition when Sturla revised *Landnámabók.* These are the traditional arguments of the freeprose theory and they have not yet been effectively discredited.

Conclusion

Icelandic scholars, as well as Baetke, have placed an almost exclusive emphasis on the uniqueness of each saga and have criticized earlier scholars for failing to penetrate the individual work of art as well as the general characteristics shared by all sagas. This new emphasis is entirely justified and has been fruitful. The more one reads the sagas, the keener is one's awareness of those peculiarities which set a given saga apart from the group—the sobriety of *Egils saga,* the pathos of *Gísla saga,* the burlesque of *Hœnsa-Þóris saga,* the curious intrusion of the author in *Fóstbrœðra saga.* The analysis of these differences has led to a concern with the genesis of each individual saga and a corresponding unwillingness to speak of the genesis of the saga genre. Implicit in the new orientation is the question: to what extent do the sagas really constitute a homogeneous genre? Yet no one denies that they are bound closely together by common features; the proponents of bookprose are as conscious of this as the defenders of freeprose. B. M. Ólsen put it this way: "If we compare our sagas, it is clear that the art which is revealed in their composition is uneven. Some are composed with greater skill than others. Nonetheless they all adhere to set rules in their art, rules which are common and peculiar to them. But it is doubtful whether the saga writers were conscious of these rules." [53] E. Ó. Sveinsson also recognizes the presence of norms: "These strict rules were second nature to a whole group of saga writers in a certain period: it seems to have been quite natural for them to abide

---

an unknown slaying by Glúmr (*Fornrit, 10,* 247), *Svarfdœla saga* (*Fornrit, 9,* 165), and *Vatnsdœla saga* (*Fornrit, 8,* 52) to the quarrel between Kolbeinn and Uni (see *Fornrit, 9,* 150, note 1). *Þorleifs þáttr jarlsskálds* alludes to stories about Þorleifr's brothers (*Fornrit, 9,* 216), *Valla-Ljóts saga* alludes to hostilities between Halli and Einarr Þveræingr (*Fornrit, 9,* 239), Broddi's diatribe in *Qlkofra þáttr* (*Fornrit, 11,* 91–92) alludes to unknown events, *Hávarðar saga Ísfirðings* notes traditions about those of Hávarðr's allies who were exiled (*Fornrit, 6,* 356), *Eiríks saga rauða* refers in passing to the career of the otherwise unknown Þorgils Leifsson (*Fornrit, 4,* 210). These allusions presuppose knowledge on the part of the reader. Whether or not the events referred to were historical, they must have been real to the Icelandic audience and a part of Icelandic tradition.

53. Björn M. Ólsen, "Um Íslendinga Sögur," p. 44.

by these rules, just as a great composer creates his works of art in conformity with strict rules of which he may or may not be aware." [54] What is surprising in these formulations is the notion of unconscious canons. The strict rules, of which Ólsen and Sveinsson speak, are more likely to be imposed by tradition than by second nature; there is after all nothing natural or archetypal about them. The saga writers must have consciously acquired and practiced their technique before arriving at such a uniform and specialized form of narrative, and since there is no evidence of a written apprenticeship, this practice must have taken place at the oral stage. [55]

The saga is characterized by a number of laws. Ólsen stressed the dramatic presentation and strict objectivity of the narrative, Bååth studied fate as a compositional feature, Koht dwelt on the effective use of suspense, Baetke attached special importance to the saga's psychological preoccupation, and so forth. These principles apply to all of the family sagas and taken together they circumscribe a genre. But a genre has antecedents. The saga manner did not spring Venus-like almost simultaneously from many minds. In Liestøl's words, "the sagas must have had a period of growth." [56] This is the recognition which underlies the freeprose theory. Heusler and others were not misled by a deficiency of literary insight; on the contrary, they were too keenly aware of the high degree of technical mastery in the sagas to suppose that they blossomed without roots. *Nam nihil simul inceptum et perfectum esse constat.*

This does not mean that the Icelandic scholars are unaware of saga art as a hereditary given. If one looks carefully, one can find statements such as these: "About the writing of the ancient sagas everything is uncertain; of course the authors learned the saga art from older sagas. Perhaps they learned it so well that they had what they wanted to say at their fingertips when they stood face to face with the parchment." [57] One can even find laconic admissions of oral forerunners to the extant sagas: "It should be mentioned that there is every reason to believe that the core of *Laxdœla saga* was an integral story, which

---

54. E. Ó. Sveinsson, "The Value of the Icelandic Sagas," *Saga-Book, 15* (1957–59), 6–7.

55. The persistence of stereotype situations points in the same direction. This has been most recently commented on by Jacoba Kroesen, *Over de Compositie der Fóstbrœðra Saga,* p. IX. It is instructive to read the description of the formulaic performer's learning process in Albert Lord's *The Singer of Tales* (Cambridge, Mass., 1960), pp. 21–26.

56. See above, p. 68.

57. E. Ó. Sveinsson, "Njála og Skógverjar," *Skírnir, 111* (1937), 18.

dealt with Guðrún, Kjartan, and Bolli." (*Fornrit,* 5, xlv). Most important but striking in its isolation is this statement: "The saga writer is, to a certain extent, bound to unwritten tradition, sometimes to its contents, at any rate to its narrative style. In spite of the enormous rift which, certainly, has often separated a written from its corresponding oral saga, the written saga as a whole must be regarded as an ennobled continuation of the oral one, and not a complete departure from it, not an absolutely new Formwille." [58] In general, however, there has been no effort to define the oral element in the sagas. Instead the *Fornrit* introductions have adhered to the typological system set up by Nordal, according to which saga writing experienced a gradual evolution from primitive to refined art during the thirteenth century. As Anne Holtsmark pointed out, the initial difficulty is that two of the best sagas, *Egils saga* and *Njáls saga,* stand at opposite ends of the evolution.[59] At the beginning of the development Nordal places *Heiðarvíga saga,* which is unanimously regarded as a very early work. In his introduction he emphasizes the primitive aspects of the style, the unclear mixture of exposition and dialogue, Þórarinn's clumsy description of topography and personalia well known to Barði, the constant recurrence of certain words such as *nú.*[60] But these quirks are not enough to separate the style of *Heiðarvíga saga* appreciably from saga style in general. It is precisely Þórarinn's drawn-out recital of a plan of attack which constitutes a sure mark of saga technique, the construction of a dramatic high-point by anticipation and retardation. Stylistic typology is at best a matter of degree, not of kind, and it should not obscure the solidarity of the saga genre.

Nordal's reticence about the oral stage leads one to suppose that the first, or one of the first, men who tried his hand at saga writing was, on the basis of heterogeneous scraps of tradition, able to evolve a very intricate and, despite some stylistic roughness, highly effective

58. E. Ó. Sveinsson, "The Icelandic Family Sagas and the Period in Which Their Authors Lived," p. 77.

59. Anne Holtsmark, "Det Nye Syn på Sagaene," *Nordisk Tidskrift,* 35 (1959), 521.

60. Cf. the remarks of Ulrike Sprenger, *Praesens Historicum und Praeteritum in der Altisländischen Saga* (Basel, 1951), pp. 14–16 and 121–22; and Walther Gehl, *AfDA,* 58 (1939), 112: "Der Verfasser der Heið. wäre damit der Schöpfer der Íslendinga saga als Gattung. Er wäre der erste, der aus zerstreuter Tradition eine Familiensaga gestaltete. Die 'Fehler und Mängel' der Saga, ihr ungelenker Stil sollen darauf hindeuten. Nordal hebt mit Recht hervor, dass eine gründliche Untersuchung des eigenartigen Stils dieser Saga von besonderem Wert wäre. Was er selber an Einzelbeobachtungen zusammenträgt, scheint mir willkürlich herausgegriffen und ebenso willkürlich gedeutet zu sein. Man hat den Eindruck, als läge das Ergebnis für N. von vornherein fest. Die wichtige Frage, wie denn nun dieser 'Bahnbrecher' aus zerstreuten Traditionen, deren Charakter überaus dunkel bleibt, die erste Familiensaga gestaltet hat, wird gar nicht ernsthaft aufgenommen."

mode of storytelling. This is characteristic of a tendency to regard the sagas as a spontaneous effervescence of Icelandic spirit in the thirteenth century, but this expression of spirit is not as fresh as it seems. Some seventy years ago Ker made the irreverent but sage observation that the sagas with all their stylized heroics were on the brink of decay.[61] This applies to early sagas as well as late. Even B. M. Ólsen spoke of hyper-art (*oflist*) in connection with *Heiðarvíga saga* and hyper-art is seldom a beginner's frailty.[62]

If we are prepared to concede that the art of the family saga was available to the earliest saga writers, we must go a step further. Liestøl insisted that traditional material could not exist apart from some kind of form. Conversely form could not exist without content. A structure such as the one in *Heiðarvíga saga* could not have been a disembodied phenomenon. To concede a pre-saga narrative style is as good as conceding an oral saga. This does not of course mean that our written sagas are transcriptions of oral sagas. No one will claim today that the author of *Heiðarvíga saga* simply wrote down a saga by heart. There is no evidence for the memorization of whole sagas and the freeprose doctrine is no longer the doctrine of verbatim retention.[63] In fact much of what the Icelanders have claimed as the saga writer's due is compatible with the supposition of oral stories. The writer undoubtedly could and did use written sources, supplementary oral sources, his own imagination, and above all his own words, but his art and presumably the framework of his story were given him by tradition. The inspiration of the sagas is ultimately oral.

61. William Paton Ker, *Epic and Romance* (London, 1896), chap. 3, part 3, "The Heroic Ideal."
62. "Um Íslendinga Sögur," p. 208.
63. There has been a natural tendency for the spokesmen of bookprose to achieve polemical effects by concentrating on the most doctrinaire and dated aspects of freeprose, especially the assertion of a rigid tradition, while disregarding the freeprose concessions discussed above (p. 77). Heusler's view that the two versions of *Bandamanna saga* were oral variants shows to what extent he overplayed the idea of oral rigidity, and Liestøl's discussion of the variant problem indicates a similar exaggeration. However, the fundamental article of the freeprose theory, as I understand it, is not some unascertainable degree of fixedness in the oral transmission, whether it be 25 per cent, 50 per cent, or 75 per cent, but the assumption that the written sagas were preceded and preconditioned by oral sagas. These oral forerunners cannot be disposed of by drumming on the dead issues of strict historicity and inflexible wording.

Appendices

Appendix I: The Genealogies in "Gunnlaugs Saga"

In order to make Ólsen's compositional system clear I reproduce the genealogies from the first chapter and their supposed sources, bracketing those sections which the author of *Gunnlaugs saga* referred to.

The first genealogy in *Gunnlaugs saga* chapter 1 is this:

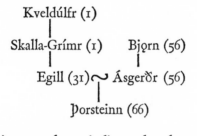

The numbers in parentheses indicate the chapters in *Egils saga* which provided the names. The genealogies in these chapters are as follows:

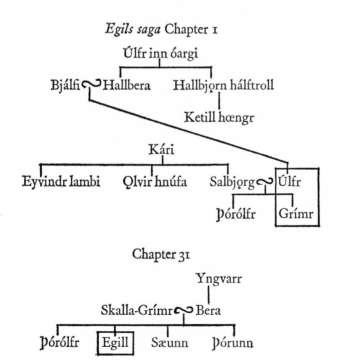

Chapter 56

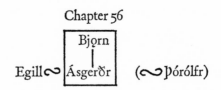

Chapter 66

Chapter 79

Þorsteinn ∽ Jófríðr

Helga   Grímr   Skúli   Þorgeirr   Kollsveinn   Hjǫrleifr   Halli   Egill   Þórðr   Þ

The remainder of the genealogy in the first chapter is this:

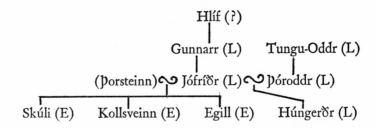

These names are taken from *Landnáma* (*Stb.* 37 or 329) and *Egils saga* 79.

Stb. 37

(most of genealogy)

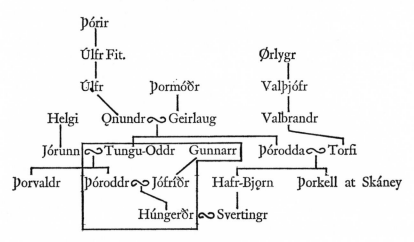

Stb. 329

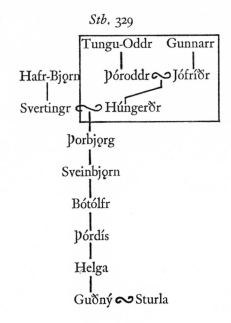

Gunnarr's matronymic is assumed to come from *Egils saga* 79.

The evidence which Ólsen presents for his view has a number of weaknesses which Ólsen points out himself. These in themselves compromise his results rather seriously.

1. It is unlikely that *Gunnlaugs saga* used *Stb.* 37 because chapter 11 of the saga gives a genealogy which deviates from *Landnáma.*

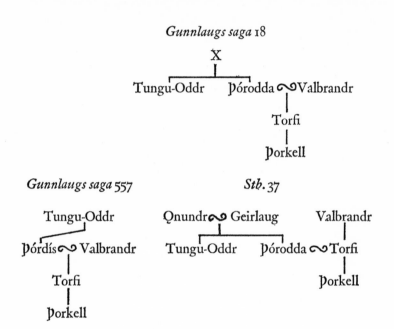

Ólsen suspects an orthographical error in the saga: *Torfa* (*Fornrit, 3,* 88, 5) should probably be emended to *hans* or *Þorkels*.

Of the three versions 557 is least probable for chronological reasons. Tungu-Oddr († around 965 according to the chronology of *Hœnsa-Þóris saga*) could not have died younger than about fifty since his son Þorvaldr was full-grown during his lifetime. His daughter Þórdís (not in *Landnáma*) could therefore not have been older than about twenty-five and her son Torfi in his infancy in 965. Torfi could then have been full-grown and married in 990, but his son Þorkell would have been only sixteen in 1006, at the time of Húngerðr's wedding, and too young to be an independent proprietor.

There is however no reason to change the reading *Torfa* which is supported by both manuscripts. The defective reading includes only the words *Þórodda systir/Þórdís dóttir* and the simplest explanation is to assume the faulty expansion of an abbreviation by the scribe of 557.

2. The reading *Þorgerðr* in chapter 2 is likewise supported by both 18 and 557 and shows independence from *Landnáma*'s *Þorbjǫrg*.

3. The saga lists three sons of Þorfinnr at Rauðamel, Þorgils, Þórir and Eyjólfr (Eyvindr, 557). B. M. Ólsen assumes that these names derive from *Stb.* 68 and that Eyjólfr/Eyvindr is a corruption of one of the names there. The seven sons in *Landnáma* are Þorkell, Þorgils, Steinn, Galti, Ormr, Þórormr and Þórir. None of these names has the vaguest resemblance to Eyjólfr/Eyvindr, while these are very easily explained as orthographic variations. This is another sign of independence from *Landnáma*.

Further objections to Ólsen's analysis are these:

1. An important point overlooked by Ólsen is contained in chapter 5 of the saga, where Þóroddr is called *inn spaki*. In *Landnáma* and *Egils saga* Þóroddr is always referred to as *goði,* and nowhere does the epithet *inn spaki* occur. The author of *Gunnlaugs saga* must therefore have had an independent source about Þóroddr since it is unlikely that he would invent the honorific title for a minor character.

2. If the author really took the names of Þorsteinn's sons from *Egils saga* 79 and the names of Þorfinnr's sons from *Stb.* 68, we must suppose that he made a completely random selection on a basis which is not clear from the sources or from the saga. It is more satisfactory

to assume that the selection was dictated by knowledge which the author happened to have at his disposal.

3. It is unlikely that the author combined *Stb.* 365 and 75 to arrive at Hrafn's father. This kind of combination presupposes either an enormous familiarity with *Landnáma* or the use of an index.

4. There is an absence of any telltale verbatim correspondences with *Landnáma*.

Appendix II: Variants

The discussion of Icelandic oral tradition lies very much in the region of speculation and logic. The records at our disposal tell nothing about how a saga was told or how it was conferred to parchment. The establishing of what oral form was and what its relation to the written saga was depends on the utilization of inadvertent clues secreted in the texts themselves. As long as these exist in one form, they afford no foothold for back-projections, but there are a few texts in the old literature which are extant in different versions. They permit a study of the nature and extent of narrative variation in the sagas and provide a tangible basis for discussing whether the variation was oral or scribal. As in most chapters of saga research agreement in this area is at a premium.

As far as I can determine, the variant problem was first brought into the lists by Rudolf Keyser. Keyser speaks of the "talrige Bearbeidelser af eet og samme Emne" and explains them as independent reflections of an oral tradition. "Begge Bearbeidelser toge Sagnet om den enkelte Begivenhed af Folkemunde, saadant som det i mundtligt Foredrag havde formet sig. . . ."[1] It does not lie in the nature of Keyser's book to give examples and he does not specify which variants he has in mind. But it is apparent that he is alluding to the variant versions of a given episode which appears in more than one saga rather than to divergent redactions of one and the same saga.

Keyser pictured the genesis of a saga as the forging together of oral "smaasagaer" in the eleventh century. Whereas the sagaman did not venture to alter the phraseology of his miniature sagas, he did feel competent to arrange them in the order he saw fit. When the larger saga had once been fashioned, it lived on intact until it was copied down in the twelfth century. This method of composition resulted in occasional overlapping; the same episode could be incorporated into different sagas by different sagamen, but it continued to exist in its primitive form in both contexts. Where the same episode appears in forms so different as to forbid derivation from an identical source,

1. Rudolf Keyser, *Nordmændenes Videnskabelighed og Literatur i Middelalderen*, p. 418.

Keyser assumed that we are dealing with originally distinct traditions.

In his extensive discussion of Keyser's book Maurer took a different view of the variants. He pointed out that they could better be explained as interdependent. "Aber dergleichen deutet meines erachtens eben doch nur darauf hin, dass von diesen mehrfachen bearbeitungen entweder eine die andere benützt, oder dass beide mittelbar oder unmittelbar gleichmässig aus einer dritten quelle geschöpft haben; ob aber letztenfalls diese ältere quelle eine mündliche oder schriftliche gewesen sei, ist damit noch keineswegs gesagt. Für nicht wenige fälle lässt sich nachweisen, dass es eine schriftliche und nicht eine mündliche quelle war, welche benützt wurde." [2] He went on to show scribal relationship for a number of examples taken from the historical sagas. To these he added a counter-example provided by *Fagrskinna* and *Jómsvíkinga saga,* in which the same report is ascribed to the same sourcemen and yet has a very different complexion in the two texts. "Uebereinstimmungen in der wortfassung deuten demnach, wo sie nicht rein zufällig sind, auf die benützung schriftlicher quellen; die benützung gemeinsamer mündlicher traditionen dagegen führt nicht zu solchen, sondern sie gestattet sogar immer noch ein weites auseinandergehen sogar in bezug auf den inhalt der erzählung." [3]

These positions as they were drawn up about a hundred years ago have been argued with alternate warmth since. The initial victory belonged to Keyser, while Maurer's dissenting opinion seems often to have gone unheeded until the advent of the modern Icelandic school. The general acceptance of oral variants is reflected in Heinzel's study of the *Hervarar saga* tradition: "Die Erscheinung, dass zwei Erzählungen desselben Inhalts in der Form abweichen, kommt in der altnordischen Literatur häufig vor; auch in der vorzugsweise sogenannten isländischen Saga . . . und beruht gewiss auf der gut bezeugten mündlichen aber kunstmässigen Tradition der Sagas. . . ." [4] The concept was one which Finnur Jónsson adopted and with which he operated throughout his career. He took his cue from the chapter common to *Glúms saga* and *Reykdœla saga,* believing that these variants should be attributed to two saga tellers from different parts of

2. Konrad Maurer, *ZfDPh, 1* (1869), 74.
3. Ibid., p. 76.
4. Richard Heinzel, "Über die Hervararsaga," *Sitzungsberichte der Wiener Akad. d. Wiss., 114* (1887), 435.

Iceland. Their close agreement constituted for him proof that two sagamen could relate the same story in very much the same way.[5]

The possibility of oral variation entered the study of a number of manuscript traditions. But the first treatment which made an effort at viewing and weighing manuscript variation in perspective was Liestøl's chapter "Stil og Variantar" in his *Upphavet til den Islendske Ættesaga*. Liestøl recognized the existence of both oral and scribal variants in the sagas and tried to establish principles for distinguishing between them.

Though the scribe could take considerable liberties with his model, his presence is always betrayed by the *kind* of liberty he arrogated to himself. His work is characterized by misreading (the confusion of words which look alike, but do not necessarily sound alike), by deviations in detail, but faithfulness to the plot and the order of events. An episode is not skipped deliberately in order to be inserted in a later spot. The scribe could resort to interpolations, but the presence of such can be determined by the comparison of manuscripts and by telltale stylistic differences. If the scribe chose to shorten or expand his model, the changes are constant throughout the work. Finally, the scribe may have had a tendentious motive in altering his model. In such cases the tenor of the changes is usually readily apparent.

Oral variation has different characteristics. Words or names which sound alike are confused. Whole episodes can be forgotten or inserted from other sources because the stories became confused in the saga teller's memory. The order of events is subject to transposition. There is a tendency for those things to be remembered which are especially important or pithily phrased or which for some reason arouse particular interest.

Liestøl concludes that it is not the degree of correspondence but rather the type which determines whether we are dealing with oral or written variation. He gives a list of fourteen variants, of which he feels some are oral, some written, and some doubtful. Of the fourteen he is able to claim oral variation for five with some confidence. He admits that the possibility of secondary oral tradition—the influencing of one written saga by another via the oral route—must be reckoned with, but maintains that this does not obviate the consideration that stories could be remembered approximately as they were told (or

5. Finnur Jónsson, *Den Oldnorske og Oldislandske Litteraturs Historie* (Kjøbenhavn, 1898), 2, 219.

read). Furthermore there are no signs of secondary tradition in many cases. Some of the episodes must have belonged in both sagas from the very beginning. For example they show details original to both versions, or, despite identical circumstances, they present a man's character and role in an entirely different light.

Having established the principles of variation Liestøl tries to determine the nature of Icelandic tradition by extracting the common traits from variants which are demonstrably oral. On the basis of principles listed above he regards as such the scene in which Þórdís vainly attempts to avenge her brother (*Eyrbyggja saga* and *Gísla saga*) and the *sæter* episode between Hallfreðr and Kolfinna (*Hallfreðar saga* and *Vatnsdæla saga*). In the former the variants are similar both in insignificant details and in psychology. In the latter example the characterization is different but some of the dialogue is identical. "Dette viser at dialogen er gamal i fråsegni og ligg attum den kløyving som den ulike samanhengen hev ført med seg." [6] The balance shows that dialogue, psychology, and descriptive detail could belong to the oral stage of a saga; in other words the oral saga must have had narrative breadth and articulation. Liestøl draws from his material essentially two conclusions: the cleavage into variants is old, and the oral saga was a detailed and artistic narrative.

The same conclusions hold true for the second group of variants, the double redactions of a single saga. Liestøl gives a list of five such variants: *Bandamanna saga, Ljósvetninga saga, Gísla saga, Harðar saga, Hallfreðar saga*. In the case of *Hallfreðar saga* we are probably dealing with a purely literary reworking. The variants of *Gísla saga* and *Harðar saga* represent such radically different stages in the literary development of Iceland that a comparison yields no useful results. *Bandamanna saga* is a very doubtful illustration of oral variation. The only good example is the section of *Ljósvetninga saga* preserved in different versions, but this case Liestøl finds particularly instructive. The presence of oral variation is best evinced by four characteristics.

1. Some of the divergencies must be attributed to a failing of memory; each version contains certain things omitted in the other. 2. Episodes are transposed. 3. Unimportant details are subject to the greatest variance. The names of the chief characters are alike, but there are discrepancies in the names of the minor characters. 4. The verbal correspondence is greatest in what must be the oldest and most

6. Liestøl, *Upphavet*, p. 48.

stylized part of the variants—the only migratory motif to be found in the family sagas.

Again Liestøl reckons with the possibility of secondary oral tradition, but he believes that the type of variation involved points clearly to a gradual evolution of the narrative material during a succession of years. The presence of two variants is ascribed to a lacuna in the manuscript before the scribe of one redaction. To fill in the gap he resorted to oral tradition. The close correspondence to what was lost shows that ". . . den munnlege forteljingi hev vore fyldig og fast. Ulikskapane ligg i mindre ting; hovudhendingane er dei same, og stundom er det mest ordrett samsvar. Forteljaren hev kunna ikkje berre handlingsgangen, men i stor mun det språklege uttrykket med." [7]

Of Liestøl's categories I will consider the latter first. Since he attaches importance only to one example, it might seem sufficient to restrict the discussion to *Ljósvetninga saga*. But in order to form an idea of the overall nature of manuscript variation and to establish a basis for comparison, it is advisable to include the other examples as well.

Hallfreðar saga

Hallfreðar saga is extant in two forms, as an independent saga in *Mǫðruvallabók* (M), and as an insert in *Óláfs saga Tryggvasonar hin meira* (Ó) and in *Flateyjarbók* (F). There has never been any doubt that both versions represent only one saga. The discussion has centered on the relationship of both versions to the original. G. Vigfússon and, following him, Finnur Jónsson assumed that M was clearly the more faithful copy whereas Ó (together with F) represented an expanded reworking. W. H. Vogt propounded the same view. [8] A careful comparison of the manuscripts brought v. Eeden to the opposite conclusion, namely that M more often than not represents a shortening of the original text. His results have been accepted by Einar Ólafur Sveinsson, Jan de Vries, S. Nordal and Bjarni Aðalbjarnarson. [9] The

7. Ibid., p. 54.
8. *Fornsögur*, ed. Guðbrandur Vigfússon and Theodor Möbius (Leipzig, 1860), p. X; Finnur Jónsson, *Historie*, (1898), 2, 475; W. H. Vogt, "Die Überlieferung der Hallfreðar Saga," *ANF*, 41 (1925), 57–81.
9. W. van Eeden, "De Overlevering van de Hallfreðar Saga," *Verhandl. d. K. Akad. v. Wetenschappen te Amsterdam, Afd. Lett.*, N. R., Deel 19 (1919), No. 5; *Fornrit, 8*, lxxiv–lxxviii; Jan de Vries, *Altnordische Literaturgeschichte* (Berlin, 1941–42), 2, 295; Sigurður Nordal, "Sagalitteraturen," p. 239; Bjarni Aðalbjarnarson, "Om de Norske Kongers Sagaer," *Skrifter Utg. av d. Norske Vid.-Akad., Hist.-Filos. Kl.*, 4 (1936), 91. Cf. also Bjarni Einarsson, *Skáldasögur*, pp. 167–68, etc.

results are in almost every way convincing. The scholar is favorably situated. He knows the methods used by the compiler of *Óláfs saga Tryggvasonar hin meira*. In addition the text in *Flateyjarbók* occupies in some cases a middle ground between M and Ó and can be used to confirm readings which would otherwise be doubtful. Finnur Jónsson notes that the compiler of the large *Óláfs saga* copied mechanically.[10] This can be established satisfactorily by comparing his excerpts from *Laxdœla saga,* where he follows the original closely without copying word for word. It is therefore unlikely that he expanded the text of *Hallfreðar saga* which he had before him.

In addition M gives manifestly too little information in some instances. To the conclusive evidence given by v. Eeden[11] I can add the following examples. When Ávaldi and Óttarr are introduced, Ó says: "Voro þeir Óttarr ok Ávaldi miǫk jafngamlir ok gerðuz þeir brátt fóstbræðr." M omits the sentence, but some pages later refers to them in passing as "fóstbræðr." When Galti proposes to the foster brothers that they sail to England, the motivation is dropped in M. Ó informs us that the sons of Gunnhildr had come to power and that Sokki was in their favor. Since Sokki would anticipate revenge, it was unsafe for the foster brothers to remain in Norway. Without knowing of the favor enjoyed by Sokki, Galti's statement in M, ". . . en nu er sú ǫld í Nóregi at ek treystumz eigi at halda ykkr hér með mér," hangs in the air.[12] Likewise the decision to sail to Iceland is unmotivated in M, whereas Ó ascribes it to the conditions in Norway[13] (perhaps "sú ǫld" in M is an anticipation of this). The tendency toward synopsis in M cannot be confused with classical terseness.

There is one transposition of importance. In M the Ingólfr-Valgerðr episode precedes the visits which Hallfreðr pays Kolfinna. In Ó the order is reversed.[14] W. v. Eeden (pp. 84–86) argued that Ó preserved the proper order while E. Ó. Sveinsson defended M.[15] It is difficult to decide which scribe had the better motive for transposing the stories. There are no obvious reasons for the change. Sveinsson finds the sundering of Hallfreðr's trip to Norway in Ó unnatural. Hallfreðr sails from Iceland, but only after the Ingólfr episode has been interposed is his arrival in Níðarós described. I tend to find M less natural. The

10. *Historie*, 2d ed., 2, 767.
11. "De Overlevering," esp. pp. 78–88.
12. *Hallfreðar Saga*, ed. Bjarni Einarsson, *Samfund til Udgivelse af Gammel Nordisk Litteratur* (København, 1953), pp. 4–11.
13. Ibid., p. 12.
14. Ibid., p. 23.
15. *Fornrit, 8,* lxxviii. Cf. Bjarni Einarsson, *Skáldasögur,* pp. 175–76.

Ingólfr episode is told complete: "Ok eptir þat réz Óttarr suðr í Norðrárdal ok bjó fyrst á Óttarsstǫðum."[16] Then Hallfreðr's infatuation is recounted, but in order to make this sequence possible, the scribe must retrace his steps and insert the explanation: "Þetta var áðr en Óttarr fór norðan." Then again at the end of the story he must repeat what has already been said: "Þá fór Óttarr einum vetri síðarr suðr til Norðrárdals." It is also more logical to suppose that Hallfreðr was not in Vatnsdalr while his sister was being seduced, since both his character and the literary stereotype would have demanded more of him than the passivity implied in M. Perhaps the scribe of M felt as did the editor of *Fornrit* and transposed the scenes in order to integrate Hallfreðr's *útanfǫr,* but he failed to cover his tracks adequately. Be this as it may, we are faced with a deliberate and not easily explainable scribal transposition.

Bandamanna saga

Bandamanna saga is preserved complete in two parchments: AM 132 fol. (M) and a fifteenth-century vellum 2845, 4° (K) in the Royal Library in Copenhagen. G. Vigfússon was the first to call attention to and champion K. His lead was followed by Cederschiöld and Maurer.[17]

The manuscripts are almost identical in plot and in detail, but M is one fifth longer and the verbal deviation throughout goes beyond the usual limits of scribal licence. The relative merits of the versions and their relation to one another have proved to be one of the more ticklish manuscript puzzles in Old Norse literature.

A thorough analysis is contained in the second edition of Heusler's *Zwei Isländergeschichten*.[18] Heusler summarized the divergencies under the headings a–l.

a. Exact verbal correspondence never extends over more than two lines.

b. Judging by the sense of direction in the saga the narrator of M lived in the east or northeast of Iceland. The narrator of K seems to have seen the events from the west or south.

16. *Hallfreðar Saga*, ed. Bjarni Einarsson, pp. 29–40.
17. *Ný Félagsrit, 18* (1858), 156–57; "Bandamanna Saga efter Skinnboken No; 2845, 4° å Kongl. Biblioteket i Köpenhamn," ed. Gustaf Cederschiöld, *Acta Universitatis Lundensis, 10* (1873), i–xiv, 1–26; Cederschiöld, "Bidrag till Kritiken af Bandamannasagas Text," *ANF, 5* (1889), 150–54; for a review of Cederschiöld's edition see *Germania, 19* (1874), 443–48.
18. *Zwei Isländergeschichten* (Berlin, 1913), pp. XXXV–XLIV.

c. The texts have contradictory proper names.

d. The figures do not agree.

e. Each version has passages not found in the other.

f. Sentences are transposed.

g. Certain details are differently phrased.

h. There is a difference in syntax which favors M. "Die sätze in A [M] sind fast durchweg klar und wohlgebaut, ihre verbindung gewandt und nicht einförmig."

i. The transitions are smoother in M.

k. In eleven instances K has direct discourse where there is indirect discourse in M.

l. There is a difference in point of view. K emphasizes ethical considerations whereas M has an eye for irony.

Heusler rejects the idea that M represents an expansion of K. The younger manuscript contains too much additional material to permit the hypothesis of consistent amplification. Furthermore M maintains a classical tone; viewed alone it does not make the impression of a younger puffed-up reworking. The extra material is not verbiage but genuine narrative. Heusler would prefer to regard K as a shortening, especially in view of its stylistic abruptness and the schematic ending. However the ambivalent indices lead him to favor a solution which avoids the issue of scribal emancipation: "Alles erwogen, und hauptsächlich im blick auf die vielen umstellungen (oben punkt f), halte ich dies für die zutreffende erklärung: die beiden versionen sind aus dem mündlichen vortrag geflossen, schon in ihrer urhandschrift waren sie erheblich verschieden."[19] To the considerations under a–l he adds the fact that the manuscripts do not provide more than one example of those common errors which betray scribal derivation from a common source. This error is the lack of alliteration in the *fjórðungr*:

> Brák ór slíðrum
> skǫlm nýbrýndri.

It could presumably have been present already in the oral stage.

Heusler's theory has not found much support among scholars since 1913. According to G. Jónsson (*Fornrit*, 7, xcv) only G. Indrebö and B. Sveinsson in the introductions to their editions and S. Undset in the introduction to her translation have been willing to believe in oral variation.

In the second edition of *Historie* Finnur Jónsson returned to the

19. Ibid., p. XLIII.

view propounded by G. Vigfússon, and in his edition of the saga he gave a detailed refutation of Heusler's argument: [20]

An explanation of the deviations in proper names need not be sought outside of scribal tradition. Almost all stem from simple mistakes in copying. The direct contradictions cited by Heusler are these: [21]

M	K
Ásmundar hǽrolangs	Ásmundar ǽþekolz
Þórarenn Langdǿlagoþe	Þorarín laxdǽla goda
Geller Þorkels son	Geller Þórðar son (but correct 9,15 and 11,32)
Hallr Styrmes son [22]	son Hallsteins frá Ásgeirsǫ
Rangárleiþ	Árnesleiþ
Þorgauzstaþe	Hǫgguandastaþe
Síþomúla	Reykiaholt
Bialfe	Øluer
Hildes	Hildar

Nos. 1–4 and 9 bear the marks of miswriting. Rangárleiþ must be an error because Þórarinn did not live in Rangárvallasýsla but in Árnessýsla. The next two place names represent a route which differs but is equally feasible in both versions. F. Jónsson supposes that there were two traditions current about the route, but it is not in itself unlikely that one scribe or the other simply altered the route from some personal motive. The name Bialfe, F. Jónsson regards as a change made by M in order to characterize the person ("åndelig stakkel"). I defer a general discussion of name deviation until dealing with *Ljósvetninga saga*.

The numerical discrepancies (Heusler d) are likewise scribal. F. Jónsson is able to show that the number "30" in K is a misreading for "13" in M because "13" is the figure later referred to in both texts.[23]

A year after this rebuttal Jón Helgason cut the Gordian Knot by questioning the existence of any tradition whatsoever behind the

20. *Historie*, 2d ed., p. 464; *Bandamanna Saga*, ed. Finnur Jónsson, *Samfund til Udgivelse af Gammel Nordisk Litteratur* (København, 1933), pp. v–xi.
21. *Zwei Isländergeschichten*, p. XXXVII. The names are quoted according to Heusler's orthography or, where names from K are not given, according to Cederschiöld's edition.
22. Cf. Cederschiöld's edition, p. 22, note to p. 12, where the mechanics of the error are explained.
23. *Bandamanna Saga*, ed. Finnur Jónsson, pp. vii–viii.

saga, "som langt snarere gør indtryk af at være en enkelt mands digterværk."[24] This is the opinion expressed in very certain terms by Jan de Vries and Guðni Jónsson: "Bandamanna saga *byggist als ekki á munnlegum frásögnum* nema að litlu leyti. . . ."[25] In S. Nordal's recent handbook the novelistic composition of *Bandamanna saga* is a tacit assumption.[26]

The problem is not one of those which has become a bone of contention between bookprosaists and freeprosaists. Neutrals such as de Vries and Helgason agree in rejecting the theory of oral variation. Even assuming a live tradition behind the written saga Heusler's argumentation lacks a firm footing. Some of his criteria do not weigh heavily; others rather speak in favor of literary relationship.

Among those points to which Heusler seems to have attached special importance are c, d, and f:

Aside from the misreadings made probable by Finnur Jónsson the deviation of proper names can only be used very cautiously as an index of oral variation. In such a plain case of editorializing as *Fóstbrœðra saga* names have not escaped the scribe's arbitration. Kratz notes these examples:[27]

H	M
Glivfra	Norðr aa
Ravnhofn	Slettu

As far as the numbers go Heusler himself mentioned in a footnote the tendency, seen by B. M. Ólsen, of a younger saga to swell numbers.[28] It is precisely the younger manuscript of *Bandamanna saga* (K) which in seven out of eight cases shows a higher figure.[29]

There remains the matter of transpositions, which Heusler regarded as the strongest buttress of his argument. The initial qualification must be made that transpositions apply only to phrases and sentences and do not extend to whole episodes. Nevertheless a scribe's motive in

24. *Norrøn Litteraturhistorie*, p. 172.
25. *Altnordische Literaturgeschichte*, 2, 401; *Fornrit*, 7, xcvi.
26. "Sagalitteraturen," p. 257.
27. Henry Kratz, "The Fóstbrœðrasaga and the Oral Tradition," *Scandinavian Studies,* 27 (1955), 129–30. Kratz's argument for oral variants is not impressive.
28. *Zwei Isländergeschichten*, p. XLII. Cf. Hallvard Magerøy, "Sertekstproblemet i Ljósvetninga Saga," *Afhandl. Utg. av d. Norske Vid.-Akad., Hist.-Filos. Kl.*, 2 (1956), passim.
29. *Zwei Isländergeschichten*, p. XXXVII.

making such slight changes is not immediately discernible. The cases must be investigated systematically with a view to discovering a common denominator. As an experimental sampling I take the first transposition listed by Heusler. It involves the words: "Þat er mér ofráð, þó at nú flytisk fram, er þú ert við" (*Fornrit, 7,* 302), which are attributed to Váli in K and to Óspakr in M. A good case can be made for M's priority. Oddr is about to sail from Iceland and wishes to entrust his property to his friend Váli. But Váli prefers to accompany Oddr abroad and replies in M: "Svá er háttat, frændi, at ek em ekki því vanr, ok vil ek heldr annask um fé okkart ok kaupeyri." Oddr then turns to Óspakr with the same request and Óspakr replies: "Þat er mér ofráð, þó at nú flytisk fram, er þú ert við." To this the author adds a psychologizing note: "Oddr leitar eptir, en Óspakr ferr undan ok er þó óðfúsi til"; the passage is thoroughly meaningful. Óspakr has been at great pains to ingratiate himself. Now he sees an opportunity to further his cause and goes about it methodically. His answer involves a calculated flattery: "The job is really too much for me though everything goes well enough as long as *you* are in charge." The flattery is eminently successful; Oddr turns over not only his property but also his *goðorð* to Óspakr, an act of trust which causes a few raised eyebrows around the district. In K, Óspakr's reply is put in the mouth of Váli where it has no meaning. Váli is Oddr's foster brother and equal and "var með honum, hvárt sem hann var hér á landi eða útan lands." He has no motive for false modesty or flattery. In fact the words as spoken by him contain a slight logical kink. Assuming that the "þat er mér ofráð" at the beginning of the sentence motivates the "ok vil ek fara" at the end, the implication is that Váli is choosing the easier lot by accompanying Oddr. M's implication, namely that a post as caretaker is beneath Váli's dignity ("ekki em ek því vanr"), makes far better sense. The transposition could be due to a visual slip on the part of the scribe. There is a double sequence of question and answer and his eye may have skipped over the first sequence and fallen on the second. So much is indicated by Óspakr's answer in K. "Ekki hefi ek vit til þess at vera fyrir slíkum stóreignum" is simply a paraphrasing of "þat er mér ofráð," which the scribe had used once and could not repeat.[30]

Heusler's final argument is the lack of errors traceable to a common

30. Cf. Hallvard Magerøy, "Studiar i Bandamanna Saga," *Bibliotheca Arnamagnæana, 18* (Hafniæ, 1957), 29.

written source. Guðni Jónsson pursued this line further and listed the following lapses: *hagvirkr* in K (301_{4-5}) misread as *harðvirkr* in M (301_{12}), *upp bú* in M (306_{17}) misread as *umboð* in K (306_6), *hætt* in M (311_{19}) misread as *helzt* in K (311_5), *Þorkelsson* in K (326_{13}) misread as *Þórðarson* in M (326_{24}) (*Fornrit, 7,* xcvi). These errors prove that both M and K are copies and at least not direct reflections of oral tradition.

Of those points which make scribal activity probable I would emphasize h (clearer style in M), i (smoother transitions in M), and k (the favoring of direct discourse in K). The third criterion is admittedly equivocal, but it has been shown that younger texts sometimes have a predilection for substituting direct for indirect discourse.[31]

Hallvard Magerøy has subjected *Bandamanna saga* to an exhaustive literary analysis. If further proof that we are dealing with literary variants were needed, it has now been provided. Magerøy's methodical comparison of the texts shows very persuasively that M is primary, and this section of his book is likely to stand. K is demonstrated to be less logical and the departures from the original are well explained from the principles of "anticipation" and "repairing," as illustrated in the example above.[32]

Gísla saga

Gísla saga is extant in two versions (M and S), which were printed one after the other by Konrad Gíslason.[33] The main body of the saga is alike in both versions. The deviations do not extend beyond the normal limits of scribal prerogative. Only the introductory sections dealing with Gísli's antecedents in Norway are radically different. In this part S is much longer (400 lines plus a lacuna of unknown length as contrasted to 150 lines in M) and contains some historical matter not in M.

In his *Prolegomena* Vigfússon spoke of S as "late, wordy, and amplified, especially the beginning, which is quite rewritten and stuffed up by a person ignorant of the topography of Norway." [34]

---

31. Heusler, *Zwei Isländergeschichten,* p. XLII, note 1.
32. Magerøy, "Studiar i Bandamanna Saga." But cf. the dissenting opinion of Walter Baetke in his introduction to *Bandamanna Saga und Ǫlkofra Þáttr* (Halle, 1960).
33. "Tvær Sögur af Gísla Súrssyni," ed. Konrad Gíslason, *Nordiske Oldskrifter Udgivne af det Nord. Lit.-Samfund, 8* (Kjöbenhavn, 1849).
34. *Sturlunga Saga,* ed. Guðbrandur Vigfússon (Oxford, 1878), *1,* lii.

In the first edition of *Historie* Finnur Jónsson postulated that the scribe of S had lost the beginning of his manuscript and filled it out on the basis of traditions and reminiscences, which were however paled and distorted by this time (ca. 1300).[35] The stanza which S has over and above M is an item wrung from living tradition, which the scribe of M had somehow missed. In his edition of the saga he adhered to the same theory, adding that the scribe of S did not need to betray his topographical ignorance if he had had the essentially accurate M before him.[36]

The editors of *Origines Islandicae* give a more detailed analysis of the manuscripts. They see in the scribe of S a deliberate remodeler. "He accordingly manufactures names, events, and scenes; he also brings in pieces from the Kings' Lives which have really nothing to do with Gisle's Saga." After the opening chapters he tired of his project and adhered more faithfully to his model. The same applies in somewhat lesser degree to the scribe of M. "The early part of the Saga, where the characters are in Norway, is poor in both texts, and is, saving a few lines, the compiler's composition, working on a hint or two in the original text or drawing from books rather than from genuine tradition." [37] The supposition seems to be that each scribe developed a very brief archetype according to his own lights. Jón Helgason simplified this explanation by assuming that S simply expanded the material in M while retaining the same order of events.[38]

Sophie Krijn and Reinhard Prinz returned to F. Jónsson's view but extended it to cover the whole saga; the cleavage is to be retraced to the oral stage. Krijn lists five considerations which lead her to this conclusion: [39]

1. She assumes that Liestøl is correct in deriving the frustrated attempt by Þórdís to avenge Gísli, which *Eyrbyggja saga* and *Gísla saga* have in common, from oral tradition. But S and M have independent correspondences with *Eyrbyggja saga*. Therefore the tradition cannot have been fixed. The best explanation is that S and M themselves derive from oral tradition.

---

35. *Historie*, 1st ed., 2, 460.
36. "Gísla Saga Súrssonar," ed. Finnur Jónsson, *Altnordische Sagabibliothek* (Halle, 1903), *10*, xxiii.
37. *Origines Islandicae*, ed. and trans. Guðbrand Vigfusson and F. York Powell (Oxford, 1905), 2, 190.
38. *Norrøn Lit.*, p. 175.
39. "Om Gíslasaga Súrssonar," *ANF, 51* (1935), 70–75.

2. The confusion between the names Þorkell and Þórdís is of an oral nature.

3. "En Afskriver sætter sig ikke ned for planmæssigt at ændre Sætning efter Sætning. Og det sker i Gísl.s. to Bearbejdelser."

4. The confusion between the names Þorgerðr and Þórunn is oral. "Man kan bedre forestille sig den Fremgangsmaade end at en Afskriver to Gange paa forskellige Steder har læst fejl."

5. The use of direct discourse in S for indirect discourse in M could well be ascribed to the individual technique of a storyteller.

Krijn distinguishes among three scribes in the history of S: a scribe who copied down the oral tradition; a scribe who copied the first manuscript while filling in the initial missing section according to memory; and a scribe who interpolated passages from Ari and the kings' sagas.

Whereas Krijn adapts Liestøl's principles, Prinz's analysis is visibly influenced by Heusler's introduction to *Zwei Isländergeschichten*. The differences between the manuscripts are summed up under the headings: "Wörtliche Übereinstimmung, Wortschatz, Satzbau, Direkte Rede, Erzählart, Auffassung des Stoffes." His conclusion matches Krijn's. "Hält man sich die durchgehende und bei der Übereinstimmung des Inhalts geradezu eigenwillig erscheinende Verschiedenheit der Ausdrucksformen vor Augen, so möchte man meinen, dass es sich hierbei weniger um Umgestaltungen durch Abschreiber handelt, als um eine verschiedenartige Aufnahme und Erinnerung der Urform durch zwei verschiedene Hörer. (Eine typische Verhörung scheint mir z.B. zu sein: S[eite] 71,6 M grjótinu: S græntóinni.)"[40]

B. M. Ólsen theorized that the scribe had read the complete saga, lost the first section, and repaired the gap with what he remembered plus a certain amount of extraneous material in *fornaldarsaga* style.[41]

Jan de Vries accepted F. Jónsson's theory *in toto*: "Der Schreiber der Redaktion S hat als Vorlage eine Handschrift gehabt, der der Anfang fehlte; diesen hat er durch eine viel breiter angelegte Einleitung ersetzt, die er teilweise aus eigener Phantasie geschöpft hat."[42] The remainder of S is no more than a stylistic revision of M.

The *Fornrit* editor, Björn K. Þórólfsson, reintroduced the concept of the conscious remodeler propounded by Vigfússon and Helgason

---

40. Reinhard Prinz, *Die Schöpfung der Gísla Saga Súrssonar*, (Breslau, 1935), p. 8.
41. "Um Íslendingasögur," pp. 118–24.
42. *Altnordische Literaturgeschichte*, 2, 307.

(*Fornrit*, 6, xlv). In the most recent discussion of the saga Anne Holtsmark seems inclined to fall in with this opinion though not excluding the possibility of reconstruction by memory.[43]

There are then three lines of thought:

1. Redactions M and S are oral variants (Krijn and Prinz), but in a late stage of the MS history of S the initial section was lost and reconstructed from memory (Krijn).

2. S is simply a stylistic reworking of M or another manuscript in the M branch. The early chapters were missing in the model and were rewritten in *fornaldarsaga* style on the basis of young and distorted traditions (F. Jónsson and Jan de Vries) or on the basis of what the scribe remembered from a previous reading (B. M. Ólsen).

3. S is a young adaptation of M. The remodeling was most drastic in the Norwegian prelude, after which the scribe tired and stuck more closely to the text of his model (Jón Helgason, B. K. Þórólfsson, Anne Holtsmark).

The arguments for the first theory, brought forward especially by Krijn, are: the oral confusion of names, the persistence of small changes, the use of direct discourse in S for indirect discourse in M. In answer to point one it can be granted that sound sequences are subject to confusion in oral tradition, but sexes are probably not. The substitution of Þórdís for Þorkell suggests the inadvertence of a scribe who is for the moment not following the story rather than the confusion of a man who knows the story intimately. If the confusion arose in taking dictation, it seems unlikely that the scribe would hear wrong twice. On the other hand he might have misread once and regarded the second Þorkell as a mistake on the part of his model. The confusion between Þorgerðr and Þórunn has a slightly better chance of being oral, but it is well to remember that proper names were abbreviated in the manuscripts and names beginning in Þor- were particularly subject to incorrect resolution. That a scribe can indeed go about changing sentence after sentence is shown by numerous examples: *Hallfreðar saga*, *Bandamanna saga*, *Fóstbrœðra saga*, *Eiríks saga rauða*, the *Mǫðruvallabók* texts of *Egils saga* and *Glúms saga*. The substitution of direct for indirect discourse has already been mentioned as a scribal peculiarity.

F. Jónsson supports his stand especially with the consideration that

43. "Studies in the Gísla Saga," *Studia Norvegica Ethnologica et Folkloristica* (Oslo, 1951), 2, 6, 3.

the scribe of S would not have made such topographical blunders had
he had M before him. In addition the striking divergence in personal
names speaks against literary derivation. There are seven differences:

M	S
Þorkell skerauki	Þorkell gullhjálmr
Ingigerðr	
Þóra Rauðsdóttir úr Friðarey	Ísgerðr úr Fresseyjum (i.e. Freys-eyjum)
Bárðr á Granaskeiði	Bárðr á Hellu
Kolbjǫrn á Hellu	Kolbeinn á Granaskeiði
Styrkárr	
Árni (Skeggjason)	Sigurðr

There are also some differences in the narrative. In M Bárðr seduces
Þórdís, in S it is Kolbeinn. In M the Súrnadœlir escape from their
burning house by breaking open a wall. In S they escape through a
hidden door which Gísli had constructed in advance. S has a *drótt-
kvætt* stanza missing in M.

Helgason pointed to the exact agreement in the sequence of events as
indicative of conscious editing. The chapters in question can be sub-
divided into the following eight phases:

1. Þorkell skerauki (gullhjálmr) in Norway
2. the Bjǫrn blakki episode
3. the quarrel over Grásíða
4. Þorbjǫrn Þorkelsson's household
5. the seduction of Þórdís
6. the departure of Þorkell (M and S) and the duel with Skeggi
(M)
7. the burning in of Þorbjǫrn's family
8. the revenge and emigration of the Súrnadœlir

The comparative sequence with the number of lines in parentheses is
as follows (I: interpolation; L: lacuna):

M	S	
	I (1–21)	+21
1. (3–11)	1. (22–34)	+ 4
2. (11–38)	2. (35–121)	+59
3. (38–45)	3. (122–51)	+22
4. (46–60)	4. (152–69)	+ 3

144

M	S	
5. (60–79)	5^1. (170–77)	
	I (178–229)	+66
	5^2. (230–308)	
6. (80–120)	6. I . . . L(I . . .)I +?	
	(309–33)	
7. (121–37)	7. (334–66)	+16
8. (138–52)	8. (367–406)	+25

This comparison shows a number of things. S is not missing any of the story in M. Every episode is included in its proper order. In addition each section is, as it would seem, systematically expanded. This means that the distortion of which F. Jónsson speaks can only apply to details, proportion, and style, while the narrative itself is preserved strangely intact. Yet the order of events is, by testimony of the folklorists, that aspect of a story most vulnerable to oral distortion. The possibility that a scribe would hit on the same sequence if he were reproducing a story on the basis of imperfect information is almost nil. The tradition must have been very strictly preserved in order to account for the identity of plot, but the romantic and historical accretions indicate that the scribe was not the servant of an ironclad tradition. That the accretions did not belong to an oral stage is clearly shown by the clumsy insertion of Hákon Aðalsteinfóstri's investiture between 5^1 and 5^2. Þórdís' seducer Kolbeinn is introduced together with Bárðr. Then they are dropped while the scribe inserts a fifty-line digression as a sort of afterthought. Finally the strand of the seduction story is picked up again. Such a sundering of a logical unit shows a careless and indiscriminate expansion of the model. Krijn's solution is to assume that a third scribe inserted the passage from a written source, but the multiplication of scribal links to explain a text is a last resort.

The same objections apply to B. M. Ólsen's hypothesis. A man who had read the saga could not remember so well and so badly at the same time. And if his aim were to reproduce what he remembered, he would not have reason to insert so much foreign matter. It is impossible to escape from an element of conscious alteration on the part of S, though not all the changes have yet been adequately explained.

Harðar saga

The case of *Harðar saga* is analogous to that of *Gísla saga*.

The complete saga is preserved only in one parchment, AM 556, 4°, from around 1400. This redaction is the fountainhead of all extant paper manuscripts. Among the fragments of *Vatnshyrna* (AM 564a, 4°, from around 1370–80 according to Nordal) [44] there is one leaf which contains the same account given in the first eight chapters of AM 556, but in a much briefer version. In this fragment (and *Landnáma*) the saga is entitled *Harðar saga*, in 556 *Hólmverja saga*.

In his *Prolegomena*, G. Vigfússon wrote: "We have but one vellum, AM 556, of the whole Saga, which yields a very 'stuffed-out' text, but a leaf of Vatzhyrna shows the primitive form of the story." [45] The same opinion was voiced in both editions of *Historie*. Finnur Jónsson saw particularly in the terseness of the *Vatnshyrna* fragment a guarantee of its primacy and had harsh words for the prolix expansion in 556.[46] This was the authoritative view until 1932 when Vera Lachmann devoted a book to the rehabilitation of 556.[47] Lachmann's thesis was that in the redaction represented by 556 "die Harðarsaga einer mittleren Schicht klassischer Sagas angehört, vielleicht mit Gíslasaga und Eigla zusammen, später als die Hrafnkelssaga, früher als die Njála. . . . Mindestens aber zur Abfassungszeit der Landnámabók und vor dem Tode Styrmirs (1248) [sic] muss sie ihre jetzigen Züge getragen haben." (pp. 241–42). Roughly stated her method is first to refute F. Jónsson's assertions and then to demonstrate those aspects which *Harðar saga* has in common with classical saga writing. She lists F. Jónsson's contentions under seven headings (pp. 1–2):

1. Die Saga is stilistisch "die Weitläufigkeit selbst,"
2. sie enthält eine Menge Fornaldar-Motive (Hügelraub, usw.),
3. "ungereimte" Geschichte von der Heerfessel,
4. unsinnige Ortsnamen-Erklärungen,
5. der Anfang ist "ganz unsagamässig,"
6. die späten Vísur,
7. die vorliegende Saga ist in den vergleichbaren Partien nichts

44. "Sagalitteraturen," p. 268.
45. *Prolegomena*, p. L.
46. *Historie*, 2d ed., 2, 422.
47. *Das Alter der Harðarsaga* (Leipzig, 1932).

als eine Ausweitung eines erhaltenen Bruchstücks, das in der sogenannten Vatnshyrna steht und ein Teil der echten, verlorenen und bereits in der Landnáma zitierten Saga ist.

Lachmann argues the contrary point by point:

1. She cites four examples of terse style and concludes: "Der Stil scheint also mindestens nicht überall redselig zu sein."

2. Very few sagas are completely free of *fornaldarsaga* motifs. A saga cannot be dismissed as post-classical simply because it contains such motifs.

3. The *Heerfessel* is magic personified in the shape of valkyrie-like spirits akin to those in the first "Merseburger Zauberspruch." "Aus einer Steigerung muss die unnaturalistische Erscheinung der anklammernden 'Heerfessel' begriffen werden."

4. Lachmann finds only one place-name explanation which is untenable and places special emphasis on the fact that *Harðar saga* does not borrow etiological stories from *Landnáma*.

5. She cites similar saga beginnings from *Hrafnkels saga*, *Gísla saga* (II), *Kormáks saga*, *Svarfdœla saga*, *Eyrbyggja saga*, *Laxdœla saga*, and *Gullþóris saga*.

6. Many of the manifestly post-classical stanzas belong to a younger stratum than the prose.

7. The assumption that 556 is simply an expansion of *Vatnshyrna* would be justifiable if the nonexpandable facts were identical in both redactions, but 556 gives information which in some ways exceeds, in some ways falls short of, and in some ways contradicts what is contained in *Vatnshyrna*.

Lachmann points out a number of passages in which she believes 556 gives a better text. It seems to her more likely that *Vatnshyrna* represents an abbreviated version, but it cannot be a shortening of a manuscript in the 556 group because of the contradictions. These divergencies must be ascribed to a cleavage in oral tradition.

The remainder of the study tests the historicity, composition, and style of the saga. Particularly exhaustive is the third section of 150 pages in which Lachmann draws parallels from the corpus of classical sagas in an effort to vindicate *Harðar saga*.

In his dissertation Werner Ludwig accepted Lachmann's view of the manuscript relationship.[48] He reasoned that there can be no literary dependence because of the differences in proper names. At the same

---

48. *Untersuchungen*, p. 25.

time the versions cannot belong to separate oral traditions because of the congruence of the plots and occasional verbal echoes. They must then be two independent recordings of the *same* tradition.

In *Arkiv, 51*, Finnur Jónsson took up the gauntlet.[49] The thesis of his article is that expansion is the normal tendency of young Icelandic manuscripts. He gives thirteen examples of expansion against one of condensation. The rest of the article is devoted to a detailed criticism of Lachmann's book. His main points are:

1. The stanzas are undeniably young and are so closely intertwined with the prose that they cannot be regarded as a separate stratum.

2. The vocabulary is young.

3. A high percentage of the parallels cited by Lachmann connect *Harðar saga* with young sagas such as *Flóamanna saga, Bandamanna saga, Grettis saga, Svarfdœla saga, Bárðar saga, Finnboga saga, Kjalnesinga saga, Þórðar saga hreðu,* etc.

4. The presence of a few terse passages does not change the fact that the predominant impression is one of verbosity.

5. The amount of *fornaldarsaga* material goes beyond what is customary in a classical saga.

6. Lachmann's explanation of the "Heerfessel" is "den rene gisning, rent grebet ud af luften."

7. F. Jónsson lists a number of dubious place-name explanations.

8. The parallel saga beginnings cited by Lachmann are from post-classical sagas.

9. The use of direct discourse for indirect discourse is typical of fourteenth-century manuscripts.

Finnur Jónsson concludes by maintaining the position held in *Historie*. His only concession is to admit a certain number of manuscript intermediaries between *Vatnshyrna* and 556 in order to explain the factual divergencies.

The defense is very solid. Lachmann's whole approach is questionable in that she compares parts of *Harðar saga* to parts of other sagas rather than basing her comparison on the saga as a whole. But as Finnur Jónsson pointed out, even this method leads to an alignment with notably post-classical counterparts.

Though Finnur Jónsson's principle of text expansion as the normal tendency has been somewhat restricted by recent scholarship, his judgment of *Harðar saga* has not been challenged. Sigurður Nordal

49. "Harðar Saga Grímkelssonar," *ANF, 51* (1935). The article is dated Feb. 1933. Cf. Jan de Vries, *Altnordische Literaturgeschichte, 2,* 317.

arrays it together with *Hávarðar saga, Svarfdœla saga,* and *Þorskfirðinga saga* and writes: "Vi har her altsaa for disse sagaers vedkommende med en *senere omarbejdelse af ældre sagaer* at gøre, en slags bastarder af ældre og yngre sagaer." [50] (Nordal's italics.)

There are only the briefest verbal correspondences between the two texts, but the order of events is identical.

Vatnshyrna	556
1. genealogies	Bjǫrn gullberi's flight from Norway and genealogies
2. Grímkell's marriage	same
3. Grímr inn litli episode	same
4. Signý's dreams	same
5. Signý visits her parents, dies in childbed after giving birth to Þorbjǫrg, etc.	same

The contradictions in names are these:

Vatnshyrna	556
Grímkelsstaðr	at Fjǫllum
Þórunn	Þuríðr
Fjǫllungr	Svartfaxi

Þuríðr/Þórunn is almost certainly an orthographic confusion. Finnur Jónsson suggested that at Fjǫllum was not a place name but a topographic indication, but the context makes this unlikely. There remain two changes which cannot be dismissed as visual lapses.

In addition 556 mentions nine people absent in *Vatnshyrna.* Six of them occur in the short compass of *Sturlubók* 137–39, but Þorgeirr Finnsson Halldórssonar Hǫgnasonar is probably not taken from this source since Hǫgni is not mentioned and Þorgeirr is not the husband of Signý. The two other new characters, Þorbjǫrn and Rannveigr, are nowhere to be found in *Landnáma.* However the amplification of genealogies can be regarded as one of the scribal prerogatives. Though *Hauksbók*'s version of *Eiríks saga rauða* is in places abbreviated, it gives added personalia at two junctures.[51]

---

50. "Sagalitteraturen," p. 262. Cf. also *Harðar Saga,* ed. Sture Hast (København, 1960), pp. 96–102.

51. Sven B. F. Jansson, *Sagorna om Vinland* (Lund, 1944), pp. 57, 81.

The variants of *Harðar saga*, like those of *Gísla saga*, are a curious blend of agreement and disagreement. Literary dependence is dictated by congruence of sequence, but 556 seems to have tapped additional sources.

Ljósvetninga saga

The most crucial case of variation is the one in *Ljósvetninga saga*. Liestøl writes: "Det einaste trygge dømet [of oral variation] er Ljósvetninga saga, men det er til vederlag sers forvitnelegt og lærerikt." [52] Because of its pivotal position in Liestøl's system the saga has attracted a good deal of commentary.

There are two redactions of *Ljósvetninga saga*. One is contained in AM 561, 4°, a fragmentary vellum from around 1400 (A). The other is preserved fully only in paper manuscripts from the seventeenth and eighteenth centuries. They all derive from a lost fifteenth-century manuscript, of which only a few leaves are extant in AM 162c, fol. (C). The first four chapters correspond in both versions. At this point A has a lacuna which corresponds to chapters 4_{21}–13_{130} in C. These chapters include three *þættir* which are loosely connected with the matter of the saga. Scholars seem agreed that considerations of space make it improbable that the lost leaves of A contained the same *þættir*. From 13_{130} to the end of the eighteenth chapter, A and C present texts which are very different in order, plot, and language. Again from chapter 19 to the point in chapter 21 where A breaks off, the manuscripts follow each other closely. Whether or not A ever contained the remaining ten chapters of C in the same form can only be a subject of speculation.

The variation is passed over by G. Vigfússon in his *Prolegomena*. In *Origines* he gives a detailed analysis of the manuscripts, but is uncertain about how to interpret the divergent aspects of chapters 13–18. "It almost seems as if the story of Acre-Thore had been retold imperfectly from memory." [53] In the first edition of *Historie* Finnur Jónsson simply notes that 561 has an order different from that in the other manuscripts. [54] In the second edition he accepts the explanation offered by A. Erichsen in her Berlin dissertation. [55]

52. *Upphavet*, p. 50.
53. *Origines Islandicae*, 2, 348.
54. *Historie*, 2, 500.
55. *Historie*, 2, 494; Adolfine Erichsen, *Untersuchungen zur Liósvetninga Saga* (Berlin, 1919).

In her study Erichsen prints the texts side by side and compares
them carefully. She finds them about equal but concedes a slight artistic edge on the side of C. In explaining the variation she rules out
the possibility of scribal interdependence chiefly because of two considerations: the order of events is different, and there is no perceptible
principle underlying the changes. She proposes either that the manuscript available to the copyist contained a lacuna, which was then
filled in according to the oral story, or that the scribe for some reason
rejected the version he had and substituted one that he preferred. She
takes A to represent the insert since a number of tests show it to be
stylistically isolated. Erichsen's results are endorsed by Liestøl and
by Helgason.[56]

As the bookprose doctrine was evolved in Iceland, such apparently
tangible evidence of set oral tradition caused discomfort. In 1937
Björn Sigfússon set himself the task of removing the irritation in his
study *Um Ljósvetninga Sögu*.[57] Sigfússon's thesis is that A contains
the primary version, which is deliberately but clumsily reshaped in C.
The motive behind the recasting is a desire on the part of the scribe
to place Guðmundr ríki in a more favorable light. According to Sigfússon A is a cohesive, logical story while C suffers from omissions
which betray its dependence on A.

The main discrepancies which the author has to reproach C with
are these:

1. According to A, Einarr Konálsson advises Guðmundr to in-
stigate as much litigation as possible against Þórir Helgason's *þingmenn* in order to collect enough fines to defray the cost of Þorkell
hákr's indemnity. Einarr is to keep the money until it is needed. C
fails to mention the purpose of the money and Einarr's caretakership
so that the subsequent statement in C, "Fé þetta var stórliga mikit, ok
tók Einarr Konálsson við," [58] is unmotivated and hangs in the air.
Thus C breaks the logical build-up of A, in which the suits against
the *þingmenn*, Þorgils Akrakarl, and Þórir Helgason are links in a
chain of events which leads to Þorkell's murder.

2. C omits mention of Guðmundr's prosecution of Þórir's *þingmenn*
so that the words of the herdsman in C, "Fédrjúgir verða þeir nú,
þingmenn Þóris," (p. 31) make no sense.

3. It is less logical that Þórir Helgason should be exiled because of

56. Helgason, *Norrøn Lit.*, p. 112.
57. Björn Sigfússon, "Um Ljósvetninga Sögu," *Studia Islandica, 3* (1937).
58. Erichsen, *Untersuchungen*, p. 33. The following page references are to Erichsen's
text.

his guilt as in C, than because of Guðmundr's false accusation as in A.

4. C accounts for Þórir Helgason's three years of exile before it concludes the episode at the Allthing. This is a chronological break caused by the writer's wish to rid himself of Þórir Helgason before initiating the story of Þorkell hákr's death. The order is so unnatural that it suggests arbitrary change.

This type of argumentation can be very striking, as in the case of v. Eeden's study of the *Hallfreðar saga* tradition. But I do not think that Sigfússon has been able to apply it successfully to the problem at hand. His conclusions are based on the over-exploitation of minor differences.

1. The failure on the part of C to make Einarr's plan explicit can be explained as unwillingness to trample the motivation. The pattern remains perfectly clear. In the first interview with Guðmundr, Einarr suggests that he avail himself of every opportunity to prosecute Þórir's *þingmenn* and adds: "ok mun þat fé brátt safnaz" (p. 20). In good saga style the reason is temporarily veiled for the reader as well as for the persons in the saga. (Þórarinn's elaborate plan in *Heiðarvíga saga* is comparable; the reasons for his plan are divulged much later.) After the outlawing of Þórir Akraskeggr the men assembled at the Thing suspect "at annat mundi meir búa undir fiándskapinum, en þá var bert gǫrt" (p. 30). The plot thickens, so to speak. When Þórir's property is confiscated, we learn that "fé þetta var stórliga mikit er Guðmundr fekk; ok tók Einarr Konálsson við" (p. 33). There is more mystery, but it is resolved immediately after Þorkell's slaying (where A and C coincide again) when Einarr reveals the plan by saying to Guðmundr: "ætla ek nú at þú munir taka við fé þínu, ok bjóða bœtr Ljósvetningum" (*Fornrit, 10, 53*). Everything is clear. What we are dealing with is simply a case of retardation as treated by Heinzel in *Beschreibung:* "Eine Tatsache wird unvollständig mitge-theilt, nur angedeutet. Dann Erklärung durch eine Person der Saga." [59] To rearrange the section as drastically as he did, Sigfússon's scribe must have had the details firmly in mind, including the sentence "ætla ek," etc. Therefore it is not credible that he forgot the connection between the assessment of fines and the payment of Þorkell's indem-nity. He simply gives a more discreet presentation of the material.

2. I do not understand Sigfússon's claim that C omits mention of the prosecution of Þórir's *þingmenn*. It says very plainly: "Líða nú

59. Richard Heinzel, "Beschreibung der Isländischen Saga," *Sitzungsberichte d. K. Akad. d. Wiss. Wien, Phil-Hist. Cl.*, 97 (1880), 94.

eigi langar stundir, áðr Guðmundr hendir sakar á þingmǫnnum Þóris" (p. 21). Since only one sentence separates this from Einarr's prediction "ok mun þat fé brátt safnaz," it is understood that Guð- mundr now begins to pocket fines. The words in A, "ok tók fé af hverium þeira" (p. 21), are not necessary to prepare the goatherd's statement: "Fédrjúgir verða þeir nú, þingmenn Þóris" (p. 31).

3. Sigfússon's assumption of Þórir Helgason's innocence in A de- pends on the interpretation of the text. When Guðmundr confronts him with the secreted goats, he says (A): "eigi vissa ek þetta; en nú er ok bæði, at þú ferr geystr, enda má vera, at eigi hafi vel verit til gǫrt" (p. 32). Erichsen assumes a translation something like: ". . . and yet it is possible that I am somewhat at fault." She writes: "Bei der Frohnung in A9 kann Thorir sich nicht damit entschuldigen, dass ihm die Hämmel geschenkt seien. Seine Lage ist ungünstiger. Kleinmütig gibt er zu: 'enda má vera etc.'" (p. 47). B. Sigfússon be- lieves that the admission refers not to the theft but to the libel against Guðmundr (*Fornrit, 10,* 26 n.1). Magerøy sees no admission at all in the words but interprets them as an inkling of foul play.[60] Again the "eigi vissa ek þetta" may be an elliptical reference to ignorance of the appropriate legal clause. Assuming that C is a reworking of A, the scribe seems to have interpreted the exchange in this way, since he lets Guðmundr say: ". . . myndi sú gjǫf nøkkut lǫglig, meðan sakar váru hafðar á hendr honum? en þú vissir, at féit var allt dœmt" (p. 32). If on the other hand A is dependent, the words "eigi vissa ek þetta" look like a reflex of Guðmundr's accusation in C. The problem is ticklish. It is quite possible that Björn Sigfússon or less likely Magerøy is right, but clearer evidence is needed. If Þórir's innocence is provisorily accepted for A, that version is in fact more satisfactory from an artistic standpoint. But Sigfússon is surely not a party to the Jónssonian doctrine that the younger version always represents a corruption of the "classical" text.

4. I am prepared to concede that C's insertion of Þórir's exile in the middle of the Allthing is less good technique than that which is exhibited in A, but again the superior text need not be the prior text.

I have allowed myself some detail in this matter in order to em-

---

60. Magerøy, "Sertekstproblemet," p. 42. Erichsen's translation still seems the most natural to me. Against Magerøy's interpretation I submit the following passages, in which the concessive force of the expression is apparent: "Ok var bæði, at ek hafða illa til gǫrt, enda kom ek hart niðr" (*Fornrit, 12,* 273); "Þá gekk Þórarinn fyrir konung ok mælti: 'grið mun sjá maðr skulu hafa um helgina, þótt hann hafði illa til gǫrt'" (*Óláfs saga Helga,* ed. 1849, p. 43).

phasize how delicate the comparison of manuscripts is. Ironclad conclusions can only be based on very obvious breaks.

A is itself not free of flaws. Erichsen noted the following examples:

1. A forgets to tell of the cloak which the Norwegian merchant gives Guðmundr (p. 46).

2. A omits mention of the "vingjafar" given Þórir Helgason by Þorgils Akrakarl. This makes the secreted goats a mysterious affair (p. 47). (There is no basis in the text for Sigfússon's supposition that the goats were planted.)

3. In A, Einarr proposes sworn friendship with his brother and rejects it almost in the same breath (p. 47).

Having presented his case for the primacy of A, Sigfússon lists his reasons for assuming literary dependence (quoted from his own "Summary in English"):

1. Such isolated examples [of oral variation] are always suspicious. A final conclusion must never be based on them so long as any other explanation is possible. In the present case, the simplest explanation is that there is a scribal relationship between A and C in chs. 13–18, no less than in chs. 1–4 and 19–31.

2. On consideration, the A version appears to the present author not unlike that which we should expect the original for C might have been. At the same time, it is apparent that the C version has been tampered with, whether in written or unwritten form.

3. In C some details present in A, which may at first sight appear unnecessary, are discarded. Later, however, sentences are found in C, as in A, which are incomprehensible in C because of the omissions. This is proof that C is based on A, most probably in written form.

4. In C there is a complete entr'acte in ch. 18_{16}, constructed intentionally by its author, who has merely forgotten to insert a new chapter heading at that point. The reason must be that, in the corresponding place, A has neither an entr'acte nor a new chapter heading. This discrepancy in the C version appears to be evidence of scribal relationship with A.

5. The conjunction of chs. 13–18 with ch. 19 in C is not abrupt, as if a lacuna in the MS. had been the reason why the heterogeneous chapter was composed, on the contrary, it gradually draws closer to A in similarity. This is evidence of scribal relationship.

6. Similarity of words in the two versions covers about ten

percent of the total in chs. 13–18 of A, and this must be reckoned as indisputable evidence of scribal relationship.

Point one is the common sense argument and weighs heavily. Points two to four are, as I have indicated, not adequately demonstrated. Point five imposes bookprose thinking on the freeprose interpretation. Erichsen's explanation presupposes that the writer of A knew the story well enough to avoid narrative seams. Point six provides a convenient transition to Heusler's review of the book.[61]

Heusler begins by defining Björn Sigfússon's place within the framework of the bookprose theory. His specific criticisms are threefold:

1. *Ljósvetninga saga* is not the only "öruggt dæmi" of oral variation. To it should be added many of the episodes which, though identical in content, occur in divergent forms in different sagas. Therefore the author's claim to have eliminated one of the buttresses of the freeprose theory is unwarranted.

2. Heusler maintains that it would be more satisfactory to place the point of cleavage in the oral stage. This would not preclude the recognition of flaws in C, though Heusler would judge this version less harshly than Sigfússon. A should also be subjected to a rigorous inspection.

3. Heusler questions the claim that 10 per cent of verbal congruence constitutes evidence of literary connection. "Wieviel vom Hundert dürften es sein, dass wir noch an mündlichen Zusammenhang glauben könnten?" He suggests that comparison with folktale variants or the performance of an experiment might be enlightening.

In her review of *Studia Islandica* 1–4, Anne Holtsmark gives favorable notice to Sigfússon's argument that C is a reworking of A, but adds: "Men når navneforandringene skal forklares, glipper det. Og det blir ikke klart hvorfor bare disse kapitlene blir gjennemarbeidet, dersom C-skriveren virkelig har hatt A liggende foran sig hele tiden." [62] She doubts that the author has found the ultimate solution and suggests the possibility of secondary oral tradition.

In 1956, Hallvard Magerøy published the results of a renewed inquest. His investigation is much more exhaustive, better balanced, and on the whole more convincing than Björn Sigfússon's. He propounds approximately the same thesis as his predecessor, but he provides the

---

61. *Literaturblatt für Germanische und Romanische Philologie* (1939), pp. 1–2.
62. *ANF*, 55, 139.

thesis with a partially new foundation. He too believes that A is closer to the primary version, which is consciously reformed by the writer of C. But the principle behind the reconstruction is not a rehabilitation of Guðmundr ríki (an idea which he convincingly refutes) but a general expansion of the dimensions. It is impracticable to review Magerøy's argument point by point. He adopts some of B. Sigfússon's contentions and adds new ones of his own, but despite the mass of material brought to bear he cannot deal C a really telling blow. Nor is he able to show that the increase in dimensions is really a principle rather than a quirk in C. The attempt to derive the drastic transpositions from such a principle is particularly abortive.

Magerøy summarizes his results in a chapter entitled "Grunnar til å rekna med litterær skyldskap mellom dei to sertekstene." [63] The main arguments are these:

1. The differences in C's composition can be explained as systematic alterations of A. Magerøy cites parallel alterations in *Eiríks saga rauða, Fóstbrœðra saga, Heiðreks saga* and *Bandamanna saga*.

2. Literary alteration is a less far-fetched hypothesis than the transcription of two independent oral versions.

3. The verbal correspondences must have been greater in the original manuscripts than in the gradually diverging copies with which we have to deal. Even in separate recordings of fairy tales verbal correspondences are very rare and are pure happenstance.

4. Magerøy rejects B. M. Ólsen's idea of memory lapses because the correspondences often apply to small details whereas the important items, more likely to be remembered, are frequently changed.

5. There are differences which must be due to misreadings in one or the other of the versions.

6. There are inconsistencies in C which would have been ironed out in the mind of a storyteller and which show an unthinking adherence to a written model.

My reservations are these:

1. Magerøy fails to show a dependence of C on A. The parallels are not cogent. The shorter redactions of *Eiríks saga* and *Fóstbrœðra saga* are, as Jansson has shown, the results of deliberate abbreviation, the kind of principle which Magerøy cannot put his hands on. The variants of *Bandamanna saga* are much closer especially from the point of view of sequence.

2. This point no one will dispute.

63. "Sertekstproblemet," 79–84.

3. Intervening manuscript links can be regarded as a contributing factor for a certain degree and certain types of variation. But in view of the close agreement between the manuscript groups in the remaining chapters the diversifying tendency of these links should not be overemphasized.

4. The rejection of B. M. Ólsen's hypothesis is well-founded.

5. The examples of misreading which Magerøy gives are not all convincing and it is uncertain at what point they entered the tradition. There are furthermore no reflexes of an error in the postulated model O* unthinkingly copied by both scribes.

6. The inconsistencies in C do not go beyond the normal measure reached in many sagas.

It is evident that Magerøy makes a special effort to bolster those aspects of Björn Sigfússon's argument found wanting by Anne Holtsmark, the changing of names and the extent of the remodeled passage. The name content of the versions is very different. A has seventeen proper names not in C. In turn C has eight missing in A. In addition there are the following deviations in names of persons common to both versions.

A	C
Ingjaldr	Helgi Arnsteinsson
Þorgils Akrakarl	Þórir Akraskeggr
Oddr	no name
Þorsteinn rindill	Þorbjǫrn rindill
no name	Þorgerðr

On a suggestion of S. Nordal's, Björn Sigfússon postulated that Helgi Arnsteinsson is the brother of a Hrói Arnsteinsson mentioned in *Njáls saga* and identical with the Helgi mentioned as a brother to Hrói in *Reykdœla saga*.[64] The scribe of C found his name somehow connected with Guðmundr ríki in one of those loose genealogical tables which the Icelanders have introduced into modern saga research for the purpose of explaining the presence of unknown names. The combination is a little breathtaking. The remaining deviations are accounted for either by the use of such lists or by the scribe's spirit of innovation.

Magerøy is willing to accept this explanation of the name Helgi

64. Björn Sigfússon, "Um Ljósvetninga Sögu," p. 35.

Arnsteinsson. He places it in the context of the epic tendency to re-place historical unknowns with historical knowns.[65] Elsewhere he ascribes as many deviations as possible to the written traditions. He illustrates the possibility of scribal error in the copying of names by listing nine cases of divergence found in the congruent portions of A and C.[66] It is indeed a curious fact that names were particularly vul-nerable to scribal inaccuracies, doubtlessly because of the faulty re-solution of abbreviations. As a counterpart to Magerøy's list I give the following deviations from the *Skálholtsbók* and *Hauksbók* texts of *Eiríks saga rauða* as printed by Jansson in *Sagorna om Vinland*.

S	H
gvnnladar (par. 11)	grelaðar
þorvallz (par. 34)	þorbrandz
Gudmundr (par. 84)	Gvdridr
þorbiorg (par. 127)	þorkell
þorbiorn (par. 129)	þorbiorg
Gardi (par. 213)	Gardr
snorri þorbiarnar son (par. 246)	snori þorbrandz. s.
Gudridi (par. 253)	eiriki
freydis (par. 375)	Gudrid
Snorri (par. 416)	gvðriðr

This list has in common with Magerøy's the fact that the devia-tions are obviously scribal, sporadic, and in some cases senseless. This does not hold true for the variants of *Ljósvetninga saga*. Þorgils is con-sistently Þorgils in A and just as consistently Þórir in C. This applies to Þorsteinn/Þorbjǫrn and of course to Helgi/Ingjaldr as well. The variants are not of the scribal type. Furthermore the sheer number of deviations overburdens scribal responsibility. Innovation and omission are hardly adequate to account for the thirty differences between C and A. The only alternative would be that one scribe did in fact "velja nafn út í bláinn," but even B. Sigfússon hesitates to take this step. It does not seem to me that Magerøy has come appreciably closer to a satisfactory solution of the problem.

The second question put by Anne Holtsmark was why the innovator in C limited his activity to chapters 13–18 if he had the complete manu-script before him. Magerøy gives an interesting answer. He points

65. "Sertekstproblemet," p. 30.
66. Ibid., p. 86.

out that the inserter of the three *þættir* in C and the renovator of chapters 13–18 may be one and the same person.[67] We would then observe a gradual rapprochement of the texts from interpolation to simple remodeling to restored congruency. Appealing as the thought is, I do not think that it is clearly conceived. It raises the question of the origin of the *þættir*. If they were copied from a written source, the scribe had no reason suddenly to abandon a faithful rendering when returning to the saga itself. The changes cannot be interpreted as an effort to interlock the *þættir* with the Þórir Akrakarl episode. On the other hand if the scribe inserted the *þættir* from oral tradition it would be natural to see in the freedom he allows himself in chapters 13–18 a reflex of the same source which provided the *þættir,* namely tradition. In this case we would in fact be dealing with an oral variant.

Despite the great expenditure of philological acumen on the part of Sigfússon and Magerøy the validity of Erichsen's argument has not been impaired. No adequate principle has been discovered to explain the deviations. The transpositions and name discrepancies do not fit into a pattern.

Renewed comparison of the texts leads me to propose a new solution. I too find the similarities so great that literary connection is inevitable, but a stronger case can be made for the priority of C. I begin by reviewing the course of action in both versions.

C	A
Einarr Konálsson's advice to Guðmundr.	Einarr Konálsson's advice.
Þórir Akraskeggr's transaction with Helgi Arnsteinsson.	Þorgils Akrakarl's transaction with Ingjaldr.
Helgi gives Guðmundr a cloak and prepares to depart. Þórir acquits himself of his debt at the last moment. Helgi sets sail, discovers the deception and returns. Guðmundr assumes responsibility for the case.	Ingjaldr discovers the fraud and turns the matter over to Guðmundr.
Guðmundr visits his brother, gives him a cloak and enlists his allegiance.	

67. Ibid., pp. 88–89.

C

Einarr instructs his shepherd to keep a weather eye out. The shepherd espies Guðmundr as he passes the farm at a distance on horseback. When Guðmundr returns, Einarr inquires about his errand and is told that Akra-Þórir has been summoned.

Þórir Akraskeggr enlists the aid of Þórir Helgason in return for gifts.

Þórir Helgason asks Einarr for assistance. Einarr's intercession is rejected by his brother.

Guðmundr forces Akra-Þórir's outlawing.

Guðmundr confiscates Akra-Þórir's property and summons Þórir Helgason on the charge of secreting thirty goats. Einarr Konálsson takes the confiscated money.

Þórir Helgason turns to Einarr for help. When Guðmundr again rejects mediation, Einarr abrogates their allegiance.

The childhood episode.

Þórir Helgason challenges Guðmundr to a duel at the Thing.

Vigfúss Víga-Glúmsson voices his decision to counter by challenging Einarr.

Guðmundr is unable to conceal

A

Guðmundr refuses composition and outlaws Þorgils.

The goats are discovered at the confiscation and Guðmundr names witnesses.

Guðmundr binds his brother with an oath and gives him a cloak.

The childhood episode.

Guðmundr rides to summon Þórir, is seen and questioned by Einarr.

Þórir asks for Einarr's assistance. Einarr promises to mediate and, if this is unsuccessful, to accompany Þórir.

Guðmundr rejects his brother's

C	A
his mirth and betrays his relief to Einarr, who defeats his plan by offering *sjálfdæmi*.	mediation. Einarr throws down the cloak.
Þórir Helgason is banished and spends three winters abroad.	At the Thing efforts at mediation fail and Þórir decides to challenge Guðmundr.
Guðmundr hires Þorbjǫrn rindill and sends him to spy on Þorkell hákr.	lacuna.
	Guðmundr hires Þorsteinn rindill.
	Þórir's exile.
	Þorsteinn rindill's mission.

Both Sigfússon and Magerøy tried to account for the differences in terms of an author's bias. In my opinion the solution can be found by applying purely stylistic criteria. Erichsen rearranged her columns in an effort to show matching episodes, but in so doing she obscured the main compositional divergence, namely the large blank in A (above p. 159f.). This blank contains the missing principle.

To some degree the scribe of A worked as an abridger. He saw that the point of the episode at hand was the killing of Þorkell hákr and became impatient with the lengthy prelude to the outlawing of the minor forerunner, Þórir Akrakarl. It is with a certain satisfaction that he can say after just sixty-three lines: "ok er hann ór sǫgunni." He finds it more appropriate to insert the prefatory dealings between Guð-mundr and Einarr before the more momentous outlawing of Þórir Helgason. Let us test this solution.

The first question to be answered is whether there are any other signs of abridgment in A. There are at least three good examples.

1. In C the Norwegian merchant sets sail before discovering that he has been cheated. Then he lands again and returns to put the evidence before Guðmundr. This course of action is improbable enough not to have been an innovation and its improbability led the scribe of A to economize. In his version Ingjaldr looks at the wool, sees the fraud, and leaves the matter to Guðmundr before setting sail (*Fornrit, 10,* 22–23).

2. A eliminated the curious astronomic passage from C probably because, like other editors, he failed to see its relevance. In its place he puts the brief summary: "Þetta var snimma morgins. Einarr bróðir hans var því vanr at rísa upp snimma ok hitta sauðamann sinn" (p. 30). This is plainly a combination of two sentences in C: "En Einarr skipaði sauðamanni sínum, at hann skyldi snimma upp rísa hvern morgin . . ." (p. 28) and "Einarr var sjálfr árvakr ok ósvefnugr" (p. 29).

3. In A, Guðmundr's hiring of Rindill is treated more summarily than in C. In the latter version Guðmundr speaks with him at the Thing in private and advises him to come north "ok leita þér þar margra vista, en ráð þik hvergi, fyrr en þú finnr mik" (p. 45). Rindill complies with these directions and Guðmundr offers him winter quarters as if he had never seen him before. "Hverr er sá maðr, er nef hefir í eyra hverjum manni ok falar sér misseravistir víða, en ræðr af enga?" (p. 45). A eliminates the pretense and after a short exchange at the Thing Rindill accompanies Guðmundr north.

The second question to be asked is whether the abbreviation in A left any logical flaws. I can find four cases of logical inadequacy which must be attributed to the editorial tendency in A.

1. In C we learn: "Skip kom í Eyjafjǫrð, ok átti sá maðr, er Helgi hét ok var Arnsteinsson, farmaðr mikill, ok var ávallt með Guðmundi inum ríka, er hann var út hér, mikils virðr" (pp. 21–22). It therefore comes as no surprise that Guðmundr can on a later occasion say to him: "Opt hefir þú mér hallkvæmr verit, en eigi mun nú smæstu ráða" (p. 23). According to A, however, this is the first time Guðmundr played host to Ingjaldr. When therefore he says: "Marga velgørð hefir þú mér gǫrt, en enga meiri en þessa," there is a clear inconsistency. "Marga velgørð" certainly presupposes more than a winter's acquaintance.

2. A contains the following passage after the secreted goats have been revealed to Guðmundr: "Hafrar hlaupa út, þegar þeir láta upp hurðina. Guðmundr mælti: 'Fjár mun þetta vert,'—ok ríða nú heim á bœinn, ok var Þórir úti. Guðmundr mælti: 'Seint er slíka at tryggja. Ek hugða, Þórir, at þú værir heiðvirðr maðr.' Þórir sagði: 'Eigi vissa ek þetta. En nú er ok bæði, at þú ferr at geystr, enda má vera, at eigi hafi vel verit til gǫrt'" (p. 26). According to the context Þórir can have no idea of what Guðmundr is talking about. He says "Eigi vissa ek þetta," before being told what the charge against him is. The "þetta" lacks an antecedent. C makes the connection clear with the

sentence: "Síðan reið Guðmundr aptr til Þóris ok spyrr, hverju gegndi, er þar var fé inni markat" (p. 34).

3. The third case involves the aforementioned cloak. A omits to record the merchant's gift to Guðmundr, but on page 27 states: "Ok er hestr er búinn, stígr Guðmundr á bak ok ríðr á brott einn saman ok hafði með sér skikkju þá, er Ingjaldr Austmaðr hafði gefit honum." This is the first knowledge the reader has of such a gift—unless he consults C. The last clause is furthermore an interpretation of C, which does not say in so many words that this was the same cloak that was given Guðmundr by Helgi.

4. In C, Guðmundr is able to gain his brother's confidence only because he applies to him at the very outset, before initiating his machinations. By retarding the allegiance A produces the very unlikely story that Guðmundr was still able to hoodwink his brother after he had already outlawed Þorgils Akrakarl and taken the first step in his prosecution of Þórir Helgason.

On page 152 I indicated that A had trampled the reticent pattern by making the reason for the collection of fines too obvious. The same type of indiscretion can be observed throughout the variant. C's delicately spun threads are torn so consistently that A's scribe appears in the light of a literary boor. A's champion, Björn Sigfússon, has noted the guile which is a property of the saga: "Enda er undirhyggja í tilsvörum rík í vitmönnum Ljósv. s." (*Fornrit, 10,* 20). A's failure to conform to this peculiarity betrays its intrusion. The following ten examples show the haste and lack of discrimination with which the revision was executed.

1. A's "Ok mætti þar koma um síðir, at þú þyrftir eigi meira fé at bœta Þorkel hák; ok væri þat makligt, at þeir bœtti sjálfir slíku mál sín" (p. 20), is a clumsy betrayal of a purpose concealed until after the slaying of Þorkell in C.

2. "Land hafði hann átt at Steðja ok hafra tíu, er Þórir varðveitti. Ok ætlaði hann þá ok til reka fundarins" (p. 25). A's eagerness to provide an explanation of the goats in advance of their appearance entangles him in a contradiction. Since he intended to drive the goats to the confiscation, it is doubly senseless when he says on the following page with reference to the goats: "Eigi vissa ek þetta."

3. A reads: "Einarr mælti: 'Víst væri þessa vel leitat, ef þat væri ráðit, at hugr fylgði máli'" (p. 27). "Ekki þykki mér vit þess þurfa at binda okkar á meðal, þótt vinfengi sé með okkr" (p. 28). C gives no hint that Einarr entertains suspicions about his brother's motive

in seeking friendship, but A cannot resist the temptation to share his knowledge of the consequences with the reader. In order to make doubly certain that there is no mistake about the fraternal relationship, A inserts here the childhood episode which first aroused Guðmundr's distrust. In doing so he fails to see that the passage is out of place. Instead of a parable emphasizing Einarr's guile we would expect one illustrating Guðmundr's underhandedness and the mistrust which behooved Einarr. In C the passage follows Einarr's threat to withdraw his allegiance and is less out of context. Here it serves to summarize the reserved relationship between the two brothers in general.

4. A's elimination of the circumstantial directions to the shepherd in favor of a simple "Einarr mælti, at hann skyldi víss verða þess, er þeir fœri heim aptr" (p. 30), spoils the more circumspect build-up in C, according to which the ultimate purpose of certain measures becomes apparent only with time.

5. Einarr reacts to the news of Þorgils' summoning with a "þó hefir þetta leyniliga farit." This is a flattening of C's litotes: "Einarr svarar fá" (p. 31).

6. "Guðmundi þótti Þórir hafa afráð goldit sinna orða ok kom nú í hug, at nú myndi fé œrit at bœta einn hvern mann" (p. 42). This is an example in line with my first. A again succumbs to the urge to spell out the intentions of his actors. At the same time he forgets that Þorkell hákr has already been named as the target for Guðmundr's revenge. Therefore the "einn hvern mann" loses the force of indirectness which it is supposed to carry.

7. As already mentioned Guðmundr's hiring of Rindill in A does away with the pretense that there was no previous agreement, thus sacrificing a ruse in the interests of getting on with the story.

8. "Ófimliga ferr þú at þessu verki, ok mun þér annat betr hent. Er þér vildara at ríða með mér um daga til laugar ok vinna ekki?" (p. 45). This is the most humorous boner which A's literal-mindedness leads to. C's sarcastic gibe "Eða þykki þér nǫkkut hœgra at ríða til laugar um daga?" is flattened by the tautological "ok vinna ekki." A suspicion that the taunt was misunderstood and interpreted as a straight-faced alternative to mowing is confirmed on p. 48: "Nú er þat sumar kyrrt, ok ríðr Þorsteinn með Guðmundi opt til laugarinnar."

9. The bold "Legg til ráðit, en ek mun fram fylgja" (p. 46), with which Þorsteinn receives Guðmundr's commission in A, sacrifices the comic pusillanimity of Þorbjǫrn's response in C.

10. "Ok fannsk mǫnnum mjǫk orð um þat ok þóttusk vita, at

nǫkkut myndi undir búa" (p. 48). Once again A cannot refrain from footnoting the plot.

These examples show that C preserves the more discreet version, and though a scribe may have had many talents, I doubt that one of them was to restore discretion once it was lost. A has abbreviated clumsily and become entangled not only in illogicalities but also in breaches of taste. He is an abridger in the worst sense, either bereft of any literary sense (including a sense of drama and a sense of humor) or too precipitate to take heed. His revision shows a pragmatic interest in the plot but little concern for the incidentals of presentation.

The changes in names admittedly remain unsolved. A scribe's roughshod handling of the text is not adequate to explain them. They must be attributed to a meditated plan, but what the plan was I am unable to discover.

In conclusion I feel little hesitation in discounting the idea that any of the above variants are oral. In all of them literary reworking is discernible.

Other Variants

The second group of variants consists of identical episodes or sequences which occur in more than one saga. Liestøl listed fourteen examples including both oral and literary variants. Four of them he analyzed for information about the oral form.

1. Þórdís' frustrated attempt to avenge Gísli (*Gísla saga* chap. 37, *Eyrbyggja saga* chap. 13).

2. Guðrún's protection of Gunnarr Þiðrandabani (*Laxdœla saga* chap. 69, *Gunnars saga Þið.* chap. 7).

3. Hallfreðr's *sæter* visit to Kolfinna and the subsequent lawsuit (*Hallfreðar saga* chaps. 9–10, *Vatnsdœla saga* chap. 45).

4. The slaying of the two berserkers at Haukagil (*Þorvalds þáttr ens víðfǫrla* chap. 3, *Vatnsdœla saga* chap. 46, *Kristni saga* chap. 2).

These examples suit Liestøl's purpose in so far as the variants are divergent enough to preclude literary connection. On the other hand they have certain common traits which, since they are not literary, must reflect the form of the oral prototype at the time when the variants forked. In the first example the variants share a psychological picture, certain details, and Þórdís' porridge retort. These things must then have belonged to the oral story. It is not clear how the second example serves the argument. *Laxdœla saga* shows conscious expansion of a tradition which differs from the one in *Gunnars saga* as to dialogue and the delineation of Snorri goði. In the third example dissimilarity in wording and detail is accompanied by similarity in the content of the dialogue. This indicates that a fully developed dialogue was a part of the oral pre-stage. The fourth example shows how a set of facts was subject to the bias of tradition. *Vatnsdœla saga* presents the episode artistically and emphasizes the psychological moments. The *þáttr* concentrates on the legendary aspects of the story. "So ulike desse dømi enn er, viser dei alle ein ting: dei hev so mykje sams både av hendingar, samtalor og karaktertypar, at grunnlaget for variantane må ha vore detaljrike, fyldige fråsegner." [68]

The burden of Liestøl's demonstration is twofold: some variants are old, i.e. preliterary, and these variants have, despite their dissimilarities, enough in common to prove that the preliterary stage was a detailed narrative.

Heusler probed further into the question of variants and proposed a different categorization. His rubrics are:

1. The same event is recounted in such different ways that one need not assume interdependence.

2. The accounts of an episode are so close in composition and wording that there must be a connection—either oral or written.

3. Distinct episodes receive such similar treatment that interdependence must be taken into consideration.

It is particularly the last category which interests Heusler and he wastes little commentary on the first two. Nor does he commit himself as to what is oral and what is written variation. His contribution to the problem is a recognition that the distinction is not straightforward. Liestøl implied that once a variant was established, it lived a self-sufficient existence. Heusler suggested that influences could pass between sagas even after the tradition was solidified. "Die mündlichen Vorstufen der Sagawerke lebten eben nicht als ortsgebundene, nach aussen ummauerte Hof- oder Taltraditionen." [69] Nevertheless Heusler is inclined to date this sort of influence to an early stage. He assumes literary crosscurrents between the Ingólfr/Valgerðr flirts as recorded in *Vatnsdœla saga* and *Hallfreðar saga,* "aber der Schnittpunkt liegt weit zurück." [70]

The difference in detail and wording between variants led Liestøl

---

68. *Upphavet,* p. 49.
69. Heusler, *Kleine Schriften* (Berlin, 1943), 2, 324.
70. Ibid., p. 329.

and Heusler to claim that the cleavage was old and the divergence gradual. Recent scholarship has emphasized that this conclusion is not binding. For the erosion of time it substitutes the will of the saga writer, who changed written models to fit his scheme, or the idiosyncrasies of memory and secondary oral tradition.[71] The editors of *Fornrit* have had a sharp eye for literary connections and it is interesting to note their treatment of Liestøl's variants.

1. The Helgafell episode is dealt with by Björn K. Þórólfsson (*Fornrit, 6,* xvii–xviii). Despite differences the versions are so alike that Þórólfsson reckons with literary connection. He notes that Þórdís' famous retort—"Mun eigi vel fagnat Gíslabana, ef grautr er gǫrr ok gefinn"—is in direct discourse in *Gísla saga* and in indirect discourse in *Eyrbyggja saga*. This indicates to him that it was taken from oral tradition by the author of *Gísla saga* and then flattened by the scribe who borrowed it for use in *Eyrbyggja saga*. This is borne out by the discrepancies in detail. In *Eyrbyggja saga* Snorri appears as the protector of his mother when she is struck by Bǫrkr. According to Þórólfsson these changes are dictated by *Eyrbyggja saga*'s interest in Snorri. Snorri returned from Norway the same autumn Gísli was slain, and the author assumed that he had some part in the aftermath. The blow dealt Þórdís is designed to motivate his intervention. Einar Ó. Sveinsson gives the same explanation in *Fornrit, 4,* xxi–xxii.

2. The episode common to *Laxdœla saga* and *Gunnars saga Þiðrandabana* is explained in the same way (*Fornrit, 5,* xlii). *Laxdœla saga* borrowed the scene and subjected it to epic amplification. E. Ó. Sveinsson particularly emphasizes this borrowing as indicative of the artistic freedom exercised by *Laxdœla saga*. The same opinion is expressed by Jón Jóhannesson (*Fornrit, 11,* lxxxvi–lxxxvii).

3. Sveinsson admits to a good deal of doubt about the relationship between *Vatnsdœla saga* and *Hallfreðar saga*. The former cites *Hallfreðar saga* as a source, but there are discrepancies which are difficult to account for. Sveinsson assumes that the author of *Vatnsdœla saga* either preferred another source or that a manuscript of *Hallfreðar saga* was not readily available to him (*Fornrit, 8,* xli).

4. The Haukagil episode is derived ultimately from Gunnlaugr Eiríksson (ibid.). *Þorvalds þáttr* is assumed to preserve the original most faithfully while *Kristni saga* harmonizes a number of saga sources including *Vatnsdœla saga*.

This type of explanation is bound up with the emphasis on *rittengsl*

71. Peter Hallberg, *Den Isländska Sagan,* pp. 56–57.

among modern Icelandic scholars. The problem virtually reduces itself to a reasoned opinion about the liberties which a saga writer took with a written source. For the time being neither oral variants nor *rittengsl* can be used as arguments in support of a theory. They must first be more thoroughly tested for plausibility. If *rittengsl* can be made probable in a few cases, it is perhaps permissible to generalize the principle. On the other hand it must be granted that the author's arbitrary and irrational handling of written sources is just as dangerously convenient a foundation for theory as the hasty enlistment of oral variants. The bookprosaists sometimes go to improbable lengths to defend *rittengsl* between drastically divergent texts. The purpose of the following comparison of three versions of the Helgafell episode (pp. 170–71) is to confront the reader with a selection of variants which provide a basis for weighing the alternate cases for written and oral relationship.

The Helgafell Episode

I have bracketed those verbal correspondences which *Eyrbyggja saga* shares with the shorter version of *Gísla saga* and italicized those shared with the longer version. This shows that *Eyrbyggja saga* has enough word groups common with both versions of *Gísla saga* to make literary connection probable. At the same time it shows that *Eyrbyggja saga* has one grouping found only in the shorter *Gísla saga* and four groupings found only in the longer version, thus occupying a middle ground.

The connections can be variously interpreted, but *Eyrbyggja saga* is better explained as dependent on *Gísla saga* than vice versa, as will be seen below. Were we to assume the opposite, it would be necessary to suppose that *Gísla saga* systematically plucked out all references to Snorri.

The question as to which version *Eyrbyggja saga* copied meets conflicting evidence. If it copied *Gísla saga* I, we must assume that "er svá mikla skǫmm hafði rekit af hǫndum þeim frændum," "lagði síðan upp undir borðit," "sló til Þórdísar," and "fyrir áverkann" bear a purely chance resemblance to the equivalent groupings in the longer *Gísla saga,* or that the longer version alternately consulted *Eyrbyggja saga.* If *Eyrbyggja saga* copied from *Gísla saga* II, we must assume that the "Þórdís segir, at þá var vel fagnat,—'ef grautr er gefinn Gíslabana'" is a chance resemblance to *Gísla saga* I, or that the shorter redaction alternately consulted *Eyrbyggja saga.* The uniqueness of Þórdís' retort and the extensive correspondences between the longer version and *Eyrbyggja saga* speak against fortuitous likeness. Since the shorter version of *Gísla saga* is generally conceded to be primary, it seems advisable, all things being equal, to accept an explanation already offered, namely that *Eyrbyggja saga* used the short version of *Gísla saga,* while the long version established its text with the aid of *Eyrbyggja saga.*[72] This is made doubly plausible by the fact that the longer version has a tendency to expand and borrow. We must then assume that the later redaction struck Þórdís' retort in favor of an antithetical phrase emphasizing her ambivalent position between husband and brother.

If in fact *Eyrbyggja saga* did borrow from a written *Gísla saga,* the discrepancies should be capable of rational explanation. Aside from the sections dealing with Snorri the differences are these:

1. The arrival of Eyjólfr and his men is set "einn dag ǫndverðan vetr." According to *Gísla saga* Gísli was slain "sumarnótt síðasta," after which Eyjólfr and his companions returned home to recover from their wounds. The time in *Eyrbyggja saga* therefore accords well with what the author might have known from *Gísla saga*. Likewise the mention of Otradalr as Eyjólfr's home could have been taken from the passage in *Gísla saga* immediately prior to the scene at Helgafell: "Eftir þetta fara þeir Eyjólfr í Otradal. . . ."

2. The adjective "alvápnaðir" could have been added to explain why the men placed their weapons on the floor while eating.

3. Eyjólfr reports "dráp Gísla Súrssonar ok þeira manna, er látizk hǫfðu fyrir honum, áðr hann fell." The phrasing of this report is best understood when we remember that the foregoing passage in *Gísla saga* dealt precisely with the death of Eyjólfr's men.

4. The sentence "Eigi hlutumk ek til málsverða" arises from the author's feeling that Þórdís' retort should not go unanswered, or perhaps from an otherwise concealed taste for punning.

5. The seating arrangement is mentioned in detail in order to set the stage for Snorri's intervention.

The other discrepancies involve the direct mention of Snorri's role in the scene. It remains to establish whether the author of *Eyrbyggja saga* invented Snorri's part or made use of a supplementary tradition. The first is a possibility not to be discounted. The scene is organic but not indispensable in *Eyrbyggja saga*. It is inserted into the story of how Snorri forced his uncle Bǫrkr off the farm Helgafell by a subterfuge.

---

72. Rolf Heller, "Die Literarische Darstellung der Frau in den Isländersagas," *Saga,* 2 (1958), 76–77 and note.

Nú ferr Eyjólfr heiman við enn tólfta mann suðr til fundar við Börk enn digra, ok sagði honum þessi tíðendi, ok allan atburð. [Ok varð Börkr kátr við þetta, ok biðr Þórdísi taka vel honum Eyjólfi,] – "ok mun þú ást þá ena miklu, er þú unnir Þorgrími bróður mínum, ok ger vel við Eyjólf." "Gráta mun ek Gísla bróður minn," [segir Þórdís; "en mun eigi vel fagnat Gíslabana, ef grautr er gerr ok gefinn?"] Ok um kveldit, er hon bar mat fram, fellir hon niðr spánatrogit. Eyjólfr hafði lagt sverð þat í milli stokks ok fóta sér, er Gísli hafði átt. Þórdís kennir sverðit, ok er hon lýtr niðr eftir spánunum, þreif hon meðalkaflann á sverðinu, ok leggr til Eyjólfs, ok vildi leggja á honum miðjum. Gáði hon eigi, [at hjaltit horfði upp ok nam við borðinu;] hon lagði neðar en hon hafði ætlat, ok [kom í lærit, ok var þat mikit sár.] Börkr tekr Þórdísi ok snarar af henni sverðit. Þeir hlaupa upp allir, ok [hrinda fram borðunum] ok matnum. Börkr bauð Eyjólfi sjálfdæmi fyrir þetta, ok gerði hann full manngjöld ok kveðst gert hafa mundu meira, ef Berki hefði verr í farit. Þórdís nefnir sér þá vátta ok segir skilit við Börk, ok kveðst eigi skyldu koma síðan í sömu sæng hjá honum; ok þat endi hon. – Fór hon þá at búa á Þórdísarstöðum út á Eyri. En Börkr er eftir at Helgafelli til þess er Snorri goði kom honum á brott. Ok fór Börkr þá at búa í Glerárskógum. – En Eyjólfr ferr heim, ok unir illa við sína ferð.

Þat var einn dag ǫndverðan vetr at Helgafelli, at þar gengu inn tólf menn alvápnaðir; þar var Eyjólfr inn grái, frændi Barkar, sonr Þórðar gellis; hann bjó í Otradal vestr í Arnarfirði. En er þeir váru at tíðendum spurðir, þá sǫgðu þeir dráp Gísla Súrssonar ok þeira manna, er látizk hǫfðu fyrir honum, áðr hann fell. [*Við þessi tíðendi varð Bǫrkr allgleymr ok bað Þórdísi*] ok Snorra, [*at þau skyldu fagna Eyjólfi sem bezt,*] þeim manni, *er svá mikla skǫmm hafði rekit af hǫndum þeim frændum.* Snorri lét sér fátt finnask um þessi tíðendi, en [*Þórdís segir, at þá var vel fagnat,* – "ef grautr er gefinn Gíslabana."] Bǫrkr svarar: "Eigi hlutumk ek til málsverða." Bǫrkr skipar Eyjólfi í ǫndvegi, en fǫrunautum hans útar frá honum; þeir skutu vápnum sínum á gólfit; Bǫrkr sat innar frá Eyjólfi, en þá Snorri. Þórdís bar innar grautartrygla á borð ok helt með á spánum, ok er hon setti fyrir Eyjólf, þá fell niðr spánn fyrir henni; hon laut niðr eptir ok tók sverð hans Eyjólfs ok brá skjótt ok *lagði síðan upp undir borðit,* [*ok kom í lær Eyjólfi, en hjaltit nam við borðinu, ok varð þó sárit mikit.*] Bǫrkr [*hratt fram borðinu*] *ok sló til Þórdísar.* Snorri hratt Berki, svá at hann fell við, en tók til móður sinnar ok setti hana niðr hjá sér ok kvað œrnar skapraunir hennar, þótt hon væri óbarin. Eyjólfr hljóp upp ok hans menn, ok helt þar maðr á manni. Þar urðu þær málalykðir, at Bǫrkr seldi Eyjólfi sjálfdœmi, ok gerði hann mikit fé sér til handa *fyrir áverkann;* fór hann við þat í brott. Af þessu óx mjǫk óþokki með þeim Berki ok Snorra.

Ok þegar Eyjólfr þykkist til færr, ferr hann
heiman við tólfta mann, ok suðr yfir Breiðafjörð
til fundar við Börk, ok segir honum tíðendi þessi
ok allan atburð þessa máls, ok þykkist hafa illt
af fengit. *Börkr verðr glaðr við þessa sögu, ok
biðr nú Þórdísi, at henni takist vel til ok fagni vel
Eyjólfi*– "því at *hann hefir rekit af höndum oss
skömm* ok svívirðing; ok lát þér nú í hug koma
ást þá, er þú hafðir á Þorgrími bróður mínum
ok tak nú við þeim vel ok ger beint við þá."
Þórdís segir: "Gráta mun ek Gísla bróður minn;
en fagna ek dauða hans." Ok um kveldit var set
borð fyrir þá Eyjólf ok Börk. Þeir tala nú margt
um kveldit ok váru allkátir. Síðan váru borð
tekin, ok bar Þórdís mat á borð. Eyjólfr hafði
sverð þat í hendi, er átt hafði Gísli bróðir hennar.
Hon slær þá niðr spánunum, er hon ætlaði áðr at fá
mönnum, ór keraldi því, er hon helt á, ok lýtr
hon niðr, ok lætr hon sem hon vili samna saman
spánunum; hon þrífr um meðalkafla sverðinu ok
bregðr því skjótt; *hon leggr þá neðan undir borðit,*
ok ætlar at leggja neðan í smáþarma Eyjólfs; en
gaddhjalt var á sverðinu, ok gáði hon eigi þess, ok
nam gaddrinn við borðinu, ok berr lagit neðar,
en hon hugði, ok *kom í lærit, ok var þat svöðusár
mjök mikit.* Þeir Eyjólfr hlaupa nú upp skjótt, ok
förunautar hans, ok *hrinda fram borðunum,* ok
steypist niðr matrinn allr. Börkr tekr Þórdísi
höndum, ok tekr af henni sverðit, ok kvað hana
vera vitlausa, ok *lýstr hana kinnhest.* Börkr býðr
Eyjólfi eindæmi fyrir þenna atburð, ok gerir Eyjólfr
þegar í stað full manngjöld *fyrir áverkann;* en
kveðst gera mundu meira miklu, ef Berki hefði
eigi farit svá vel. Eftir þetta nefnir Þórdís sér vátta,
ok segir skilit við Börk bónda sinn, ok kveðst eigi
mundu koma í sama rekkju honum síðan; ok þat
efndi hon. Fór hon þá út á Eyri, á Þórdísarstaði,
ok bjó hon þar nökkura vetr síðan. En Börkr var
þá eftir á Helgafelli, þar til er Snorri goði kom
honum í brott þaðan; ok fór hann þá at búa í
Glerárskógi í Hvammsfirði. Eyjólfr fór heim vestr
í Otradal, ok undi illa við sína ferð.

The function is to explain the bad feelings between Bǫrkr and Snorri. "Af þessu óx mjǫk óþokki með þeim Berki ok Snorra." The thread is picked up in chapter 14 when Bǫrkr says: ". . . vil ek nú, at vér gefim upp óþokka þann, er millum hefir farit. . . ." On the other hand the motivation is not strictly necessary since Snorri's feigned squandering of his uncle's money was cause enough for a falling out. It is therefore conceivable that the author of *Eyrbyggja saga* simply borrowed the Helgafell scene and inserted Snorri, whom he knew to have stayed at Helgafell at the time of Gísli's death (cf. *Ævi Snorra Goða*), in order to add fuel to the flames.

I do not believe that this is the case. There are two items in *Eyrbyggja saga* which suggest strongly that the author had access to supplementary oral sources.

1. According to *Gísla saga*, Þórdís announced her divorce immediately. In *Eyrbyggja saga* she waits until Snorri has wrested Helgafell from Bǫrkr before initiating legal action. If *Eyrbyggja saga* were completely dependent on *Gísla saga*, it would presumably have followed its model on this point as well. That it did not do so indicates that independent sources were tapped.

2. *Gísla saga* states: "Ok fór Bǫrkr þá at búa í Glerárskógum." At the end of chapter 14 *Eyrbyggja saga* reads: "Eptir þat fór Bǫrkr í brott frá Helgafelli ok vestr á Meðalfellsstrǫnd ok bjó fyrst á Barkarstǫðum milli Orrahváls ok Tungu. Síðan fór hann í Glerárskóga ok bjó þar til elli." This account plainly rests on a different and fuller tradition.

The balance of evidence shows that the author of *Eyrbyggja saga* probably knew the story of Þórdís' frustrated vengeance, but he chose to base his account on a written *Gísla saga* subject to the changes dictated by his own tradition. The variants as we have them are literary, but they ultimately reflect two oral traditions: in one of them Snorri was present at Helgafell, in the other he was not.

Þorgeirr Hávarsson's Death

I turn next to the different accounts of Þorgeirr Hávarsson's death in *Fóstbrœðra saga* (chaps. 16–18) and *Ljósvetninga saga* ("Þórarins þáttr ofsa"). In these variants there are no verbal correspondences to suggest literary borrowing and neither text can be rationally derived from the other.[73] But despite the relative brevity of *Ljósvetninga saga* there are a number of striking similarities in the battle description.

73. See *Fornrit, 10*, lvi, and Kroesen, *Over de Compositie der Fóstbrœðra Saga*, pp. 14–15.

1. There are forty attackers.
2. Þorgeirr fights against great odds.
3. Þorgeirr's final defense takes place in the ship's stem.
4. Þorgeirr slays two men named Ívarr (Már in *Fóstbrœðra saga*) and Þórir.
5. In all Þorgeirr kills fourteen (thirteen in *Fóstbrœðra saga*) before succumbing.

The explanation is near at hand. The similarities can all be retraced to Þormóðr Kolbrúnarskáld's "Þorgeirsdrápa." Items 1–3 are contained in the first *helming* of stanza 12 (*Skjaldedigtning* IB):

> Stirðr réð stafn at verja
> strenghreins tøgum drengja,
> ítr þvít, ǫrr, vas heitinn
> auðstjóri þrek, fjórum;

Item four is contained in the second *helming* of stanza 14:

> Már hét maðr ok Þórir
> málsnjallr es lét falla
> (áðr frǫgum) þá (þeira)
> Þórgeirr (lokit eirum).

Item five recurs in the first *helming* of stanza 15:

> Olli fjǫrr áðr felli
> (flugtrauðr) hjarar dauða
> (sá vas rœkjandi enn ríki
> reggs) þrétían seggja.

It is fairly clear that the author of *Ljósvetninga saga*'s account had no oral tradition about Þorgeirr's last stand but took all his details from Þormóðr's stanzas. That he based his story on written stanzas is indicated by the unmetrical Ívarr for Már, though this error may belong to the scribal tradition. Benedikt Sveinsson regarded Hrútafjǫrðr in *Ljósvetninga saga* as a misreading of Hraunhǫfn, but this is less certain.[74] The variation in the number of slain could be either oral or written. One manuscript reads thirteen and another (142) reads sixteen.

After the battle the detailed similarities between the versions cease. There is a great discrepancy in the account of Þórarinn's treatment of the severed head. *Ljósvetninga saga* states that Þórarinn took it with

74. *Fóstbrœðra Saga*, ed. Benedikt Sveinsson (Reykjavík, 1925), p. xii.

him to Eyjafjǫrðr, laid it in salt, exhibited it at the Thing, and then buried it at Vaðilshorn. According to *Fóstbrœðra saga* he carried it off in a pouch fastened to his horse's cruppers. He and his men made sport of it until it began to take on an uncanny aspect. Then they buried it. Since it is unlikely that Þormóðr's eulogy expatiated on the indignities to which his friend's skull was subjected, we are probably dealing with genuine oral variants.

The passage provides us with a showcase example of the preservative power of scaldic stanzas. Those details which were entrusted to a metrical form survived unimpaired, while that part of the tradition left to unformed oral transmission became distorted to a point where only the general idea behind Þórarinn's behavior was retained. The variants are clearly oral, but they are decidedly inimical to the concept of a petrified tradition.

Ingólfr and Valgerðr

A relationship similar to the one between the preceding variants can be made probable for the two accounts of Ingólfr Þorsteinsson's flirt with Valgerðr Óttarsdóttir.

Hallfreðar saga	*Vatnsdœla saga*
chapters 2–3	chapter 37

Óláfr hét maðr, er *bjó at Hauka-gili;* hann var auðigr maðr ok átti þá konu, er Þórhalla hét ok var dóttir Ævars ins gamla. Aldís hét dóttir þeira ok var skǫrulig kona; hennar bað Óttarr ok fekk með miklu fé; sonr þeira hét Hallfreðr, en annarr Galti; dóttir þeira hét Valgerðr ok var allra kvenna fríðust. Óláfr at Haukagili fóstraði Hallfreð, ok var hann vel haldinn þar. Hann var snimma mikill ok sterkr, karlmannligr ok skolbrúnn nǫkkut ok heldr nefljótr, jarpr á hár, ok fór vel; skáld var hann gott ok heldr níðskár ok

Óláfr *bjó at Haukagili,* en Óttarr í Grímstungum; hann átti Ásdísi, dóttur Óláfs, ok á lǫgfundum áttu þeir eina búð. Synir Þorsteins óxu upp ok váru gǫrviligir menn. Guðbrandr var mikill maðr ok sterkr. Ingólfr var manna fríðastr ok þó mikill; hann hafði ok atgǫrvi yfir flesta menn. Ok á einu haustþingi kómu þar margir menn saman, ok var leikr stofnaðr. Ingólfr var í leiknum ok sýndi þá enn atgǫrvi sína, ok eitt sinn, er hann

Hallfreðar saga

margbreytinn; ekki var hann vinsæll.

Þorsteinn Ingimundarson var þá hǫfðingi í Vatnsdal. Hann bjó at Hofi ok þótti mestr maðr þar í sveitum; hann var vinsæll ok mannheillamaðr mikill. Ingólfr ok Guðbrandr váru synir hans. Ingólfr var vænstr maðr norðan lands; um hann var þetta kveðit:

Allar vildu meyjar
með Ingólfi ganga,
þær es vaxnar váru;
vesǫl kvazk æ til lítil.
"Ek skal ok," kvað kerling,
"með Ingólfi ganga,
meðan mér tvær of tolla
tennr í efra gómi."

Haustboð var efnat í Grímstungum ok knattleikar. Ingólfr kom til leiks ok mart manna með honum neðan ór dalnum. Veðr var gott, ok sátu konur úti ok horfðu á leikinn. Valgerðr Óttarsdóttir sat upp í brekkuna frá ok konur hjá henni. Ingólfr var at leiknum, ok fló knǫttrinn upp þangat. Valgerðr tók knǫttinn ok lét koma undir skikkju sína ok bað þann sœkja, er kastat hafði. Ingólfr hafði þá kastat; hann bað þá leika, en hann settisk niðr hjá Valgerði ok talaði við hana allan þann dag.

chapter 3

Nú var slitit leiknum, ok fóru menn heim, þeir er eigi váru í boði. Síðan vanði Ingólfr *kvámur sínar*

Vatnsdœla saga

sótti eptir knetti sínum, bar svá til, at hann fló til Valgerðar Óttarsdóttur; hon svipti at mǫttli sínum, ok tǫluðusk þau við um hríð. Honum sýndisk konan forkunnliga fríð; ok hvern dag, þann er eptir þingsins var, kom hann til tals við hana. Eptir þat gerir hann þangat *kvámur sínar* jafnan. Óttari var þetta í móti skapi, ok *kom á rœðu við Ingólf* ok bað hann eigi þat gera, er báðum þeim var til ósœmðar, ok kvazk heldr vilja gefa honum konuna með sœmð en hann fífldi hana með vanvirðu. Ingólfr kvazk gera mundu um kvámur sem honum sýndisk ok kvað honum enga ósœmð at því. *Óttarr hitti nú Þorstein ok bað hann* eiga hlut í með Ingólfi, at hann gerði at. Hann kvað svá vera skyldu. Þorsteinn mælti til Ingólfs: "Hví verðr þér þat fyrir, at gera Óttari sneypu eða svívirða dóttur hans; hefir þú illt ráð upp tekit, ok mun okkr verða at sundrþykki, ef þú gerir eigi at." *Lét Ingólfr þá af kvámum,* en *orti mansǫngsvísur nǫkkurar um Valgerði* ok kvað síðan. Óttarr fór enn á fund Þorsteins ok kvazk illa una við kveðskapinn Ingólfs,—"þykkir mér þú skyldr til at leggja nǫkkut ráð á." Þorsteinn kvað eigi at sínu skapi gǫrt,—

Hallfreðar saga

í Grímstungur til tals við Valgerði.
Óttarr *kom at máli við Ingólf* ok
mælti: "Eigi gezk mér at kvámum
þínum, ok spurt muntu þat hafa, at
vér hǫfum eigi setit um skapraunir
eða skammir; muntu komask at
ráðahag við hana, ef þú vill." Hann
kvazk mundu vera sjálfráði ferða
sinna, hvat sem Óttarr segði, lét svá
at eins skipaðan dalinn, at hann
kvazk engis manns nauðarmaðr vera
skulu. *Síðan hitti Óttarr Þorstein ok
bað hann* halda svá son sinn, at hann
fengi enga ósœmð af honum,—"því
at þú ert vitr maðr ok góðgjarn."
Þorsteinn segir: "Víst gerir hann
slíkt í móti mínum vilja, ok heita vil
ek þér mínu umtali." Ok skilja þeir
við þat. Þorsteinn mælti til Ingólfs:
"Annan hátt hafi þér en vér hǫfðum
á unga aldri, gerið yðr at ginnun-
gum, er hǫfðingja efni eruð; lát af
tali við dóttur Óttars bónda." Ingólfr
kvað við hans umtal batna skyldu ok
lét þá af kvámum fyrst í stað. *Síðan
orti Ingólfr mansǫngsdrápu um Valgerði.* Óttarr reiddisk því mjǫk; ferr
enn at hitta Þorstein ok kvað sér nú
leitat mikillar skapraunar;—"nú bið
ek, at þú lofir mér at stefna syni þínum, því at ek nenni eigi, at kyrrt
sé." Þorsteinn segir: "Meðallagi er
þat ráðligt, en eigi vil ek banna þér."
Þá mælti Jǫkull, bróðir Þorsteins,
því at hann var þar hjá: *"Heyr á
endemi.* Þú myndir stefna oss frændum hér í sveit; skaltu fá ófagnað."
Jǫkull bjó uppi í Tungu í Vatnsdal.

Vatnsdœla saga

"ok hefi ek um talat, ok tjóar
eigi." Óttarr mælti: "Bœta
máttu fé fyrir Ingólf eða leggja
leyfi til, at vér sœkim hann til
laga." "Fýsa vil ek þik," kvað
Þorsteinn, "at þú gefir at engan
gaum, ok máttu at lǫgum gera
þat." Óttarr fór stefnufǫr til
Hofs ok stefndi Ingólfi til
Húnavatnsþings ok bjó mál til
sóknar. Ok er Jǫkull spyrr
þetta, gerði hann sik óðan um
ok *kvað slíkt mikil endemi,* ef
þeir frændr skyldi þar sekir
gǫrvir í átthaga sínum, ok kvað
Þorstein mjǫk eldask;—"ok
þótt vér sém eigi lǫgmenn, þá
munu vér eyða málit með ǫx-
arhǫmrum." Ok er várþing
kom, bað Ingólfr Þorstein leggja ráð til um málit, ella kvazk
hann mundu fœra øxi í hǫfuð
Óttari. Þorsteinn mælti: "Nú
vil ek, at þú neytir goðorðsins
ok takir við;"—ok svá var
gǫrt. Ok er í dóm kom málit,
gengu þeir Ingólfr ok Jǫkull
at dóminum ok hleypðu upp
með hǫggum, ok fell niðr
málit. Litlu eptir þingit segir
Óttarr Óláfi, mági sínum, at
hann myndi eigi við vera ok
selja land sitt. Hann gerði svá,
fœrði bú sitt suðr um heiði.

Hallfreðar saga	*Vatnsdœla saga*

Þorsteinn sýndi enn góðvild sína ok setti menn til með þeim á Húnavatnsþingi, en bauð handsǫl fyrir son sinn. Þorsteinn bað þess, at Óttarr ynði því, at hann dœmði um drápumálit ok þat, er milli þeira var; þessa fýstu menn Óttar, ok varð þat at sættum, at Þorsteinn skyldi einn gera. Síðan mælti Þorsteinn: "Skjót eru hér mín ummæli; mun ek sjá fyrir hvárumtveggjum, hversu sem ykkr líkar; ek geri hálft hundrað silfrs til handa Óttari, en hann skal selja jarðir sínar ok ráðask í brott ór þessi sveit." Óttarr kvazk eigi vara, at honum myndi slíkr ójafnaðr gǫrr vera. Þorsteinn kvazk eigi síðr fyrir hans hlut sét hafa við skaplyndi hvárratveggju. Ok eptir þat rézk Óttarr suðr í Norðrárdal ok bjó fyrst á Óttarsstǫðum.

As the italicizing shows, there are only scattered and very approximate verbal correspondences. Combined with the differences in content they are not considerable enough to warrant the supposition of scribal editing.[75]

The correspondences are greatest at the beginning and gradually diverge into complete disagreement toward the end. The picturesque meeting, Ingólfr's visits, Óttarr's protests, Þorsteinn's reproaches, and Óttarr's request for permission to prosecute are contentually identical. But within the framework the differences are great. In *Hallfreðar saga* the meeting takes place during a feast at Grímstunga, in *Vatnsdœla saga* during an autumn Thing meeting. In *Hallfreðar saga* the visits take place after the guests have returned home, in *Vatnsdœla saga* during the remaining days of the Thing. Again, the series of protests and replies make use of different stereotypes.

75. See Bjarni Einarsson, *Skáldasögur*, pp. 176–80 and the literature cited there.

It would seem on the face of it that the two versions had expanded a basic nucleus of information in a contradictory manner. By analogy to the *Fóstbrœðra saga/Ljósvetninga saga* variants and on the grounds of internal probability I suggest that the basic nucleus was found in scaldic tradition. The hypothesis would be bolder were it not for the fact that the stanzas on which the variants are based are mentioned in both passages. What is more likely than that the circumstances of the first meeting were included in Ingólfr's *mansǫngsvísur?* Kormákr captured a rather similar situation in the stanzas which are first recorded in his saga. The substance of the stanzas in question must have been that Ingólfr saw and spoke with Valgerðr at an autumn match, in the course of which she hid his ball under her cloak. Since the exact occasion was not specified, the author of *Vatnsdœla saga* supposed that it was an autumn Thing while the author of *Hallfreðar saga* guessed at an autumn feast at Grímstunga. How much of the ensuing conflict was alluded to in the *mansǫngsvísur* is hard to tell, but I am inclined to think that some of the preliminaries were mentioned.

As in the *Fóstbrœðra saga/Ljósvetninga saga* variants agreement is abruptly terminated. The break comes during the litigation at the Húnavatnsþing. In *Vatnsdœla saga* Ingólfr and Jǫkull forcefully abridge the prosecution. In *Hallfreðar saga* Þorsteinn wangles the role of mediator and exiles Óttarr from the district. The discrepancy is certainly not scribal; nor can the oral prototype have been in fixed form.

If I am right in thinking that the beginning of the story has scaldic support while the latter part is based on *munnmæli,* we have another example of a rather mutable prose tradition.

The Slaying of Galti Óttarsson

Vatnsdœla saga	*Hallfreðar saga*
chapter 45	chapter 10
Lið Óttars dreifðisk norðr til sveita, ok var eigi at því gaumr gefinn. Hallfreðr ok Galti, synir Óttars, fóru norðr ok enn fleira barna hans. Opt kom Hallfreðr til Skegg-Ávalda	Nú koma menn til þings, ok á þinginu gengu þeir Hallfreðr ok Galti til búðar Þorkels ok fréttu, hvar koma skyldi. Hann segir: "Ek mun bjóðask til

Vatnsdœla saga

ok talaði við dóttur hans, er Kolfinna hét. Þeirar konu fekk Gríss Sæmingsson, en þó lék it sama orð á með þeim Hallfreði, sem segir í sǫgu hans. Ok eitt sinn, er hann kom út, því at hann var farmaðr, en Gríss var á þingi, þá kom Hallfreðr þar, sem Kolfinna var í seli, ok lá þar hjá henni. Ok er Gríss vissi þetta, líkar honum stórilla, en Hallfreðr fór útan þegar samsumars. Á leiðmóti í Vatnsdal var fjǫlmenni mikit, ok tjǫlduðu menn búðir, því at vera skyldi tveggja nátta leið. Þorkell átti búð mesta ok fjǫlmennasta. Skegg-Ávaldi átti búð saman ok Hermundr, sonr hans. Ok er Galti Óttarsson var genginn ørenda sinna, mætti hann Hermundi, en hann minntisk á sakar þær, er Hallfreðr hafði gǫrt við þá, ok hljóp at Galta ok drap hann ok fór síðan í búð til fǫður síns. Ok er Þorkell spyrr vígit, spratt hann upp með sveit sína ok vill hefna. Hildr stóð í durum, móðir Hermundar, ok mælti: "Hitt er nú, Þorkell, betra ráð, at hlaupa eigi svá skjótt, *ok var þér þat í hug eitt sinn,* þá er vit fundumsk, *at þú myndir eigi drepa son minn* fyrir augum mér." Þorkell [svarar]: "Nú er fleira í komit en þá vissu vit ván; *gakk nú út ór búðinni,*" kvað Þorkell, "því at þá muntu eigi sjá son þinn hǫggvinn fyrir augum þér, ef þú gerir svá."

Hon skilði þó raunar, hvat hann mælti til hjálpar manninum, ok þótti

Hallfreðar saga

gørðar, ef þér vilið þat hvárirtveggju, ok mun ek þá leita um sættir." Ganga þeir nú út ór búðinni, en Brandr Ávaldason, bróðir Kolfinnu, lá á búðarveggnum. Hann hjó Galta banahǫgg, í því er hann gekk út. Hallfreðr sagði Þorkatli vígit. Þorkell gekk með honum til búðar Gríss ok bað hann fram selja manninn,—"ella munu vér brjóta upp búðina." Þá hljóp Hildr, móðir Brands, í dyrrnar ok spyrr, hvat Þorkell vildi. Hann segir ørendit. Hildr mælti: *"Eigi mundi þér þat í hug, at drepa son minn,* þá er ek skaut þér undan skikkjuskauti mínu ok firrða þik bana eptir víg Glœðis, þá er þeir Þorgils ok Þorvaldr vildu drepa þik." Þorkell mælti: "Liðit er nú þat. *Gangi konur út ór búðinni,* ok vilju vér leita mannsins." Brandr var faldinn, ok komsk hann svá út, ok hittisk hann eigi. Þorkell kvað hann farinn mundu til búðar Húnrøðar. Hallfreðr mælti þá: "Grunr er mér nú á um liðveizlu, ok býð ek nú Grísi hólmgǫngu." Gríss kvað hann þat boðit hafa fyrr, sem hann ætti at beiða. Þá kvað Hallfreðr vísu:

[stanza

Hallfreðr learns of the death of King Olaf and is advised in

Vatnsdœla saga

bæði skjótt ok skǫruligt hans órræði, ok tók hon síðan búnaðinn af hǫfði sér ok bjó hann með, en settisk í rúm hans, at eigi gengi fleiri konur út en ván var. Þorkell bað þær skynda ok þrøngðisk at þeim ok mælti: "Standi þér eigi svá, því at œrin er þó raun konunnar, at hon sjái eigi manninn hǫggvinn eða heyri til." Þeir vildu þegar inn hlaupa ok drepa Hermund. Þorkell fór þá í búðardyrrnar ok mælti: "Sjám hvat oss hœfir, at drepa eigi heraðsmenn vára sjálfra ok þingmenn, ok sættumsk heldr." Var þá leitat um sættir milli þeira, ok var svá til þuklat, at hvárirtveggju unðu vel við, ok gǫrvar bœtr svá miklar, at þeir váru vel sœmðir, er taka áttu. Leysti Þorkell svá þetta mál sér af hendi með drengskap, ok allir unðu vel við. Ǫllum málum var til hans skotit um heraðit, því at hann þótti mestrar náttúru í Vatnsdœla kyni annarr en Þorsteinn Ingimundarson.

Hallfreðar saga

a dream not to fight. Þorkell mediates the feud.]

These variants are strikingly different. In the first place two names fail to coincide:

Hallfreðar saga	Vatnsdœla saga
Ávaldi	Skegg-Ávaldi
Brandr	Hermundr

The remaining differences can be shown by a summary in parallel columns.

Hallfreðar saga	*Vatnsdœla saga*
Hallfreðr and Galti ask for and receive a promise of assistance from Þorkell. Galti is killed as he leaves the booth.	Þorkell is not mentioned. Galti is killed while going to relieve himself.
Hallfreðr tells Þorkell what has happened and they go together to Gríss's booth.	Þorkell learns of the killing and goes to Ávaldi's booth.
Hallfreðar saga explains Þorkell's obligation to Hildr and records Þorkell's curt retort: "Liðit er nú þat."	*Vatnsdœla saga* gives only a reference to Þorkell's obligation and attributes to him a more detailed reply. Hildr is to leave the booth so as not to see her son slain.
Þorkell orders the women out of the booth.	same.
Brandr is disguised as a woman and escapes.	Hermundr is disguised. Hildr takes his place in the booth so that only the proper number of women leaves.
Þorkell is unable to find Brandr and suggests that he went to Húnrøðr's booth.	Having gained time, Þorkell prevails on his men to compose the matter peaceably.
Hallfreðr becomes suspicious of Þorkell's sincerity and challenges Gríss to a duel.	Þorkell mediates the quarrel to the satisfaction of everyone.

The only point of real convergence is, as Liestøl pointed out, the content of the dialogue between Þorkell and Hildr, or, more narrowly, the allusion to Hildr's saving of Þorkell's life. The differences are otherwise so great that this cannot be a case of written variants. The question is whether they are so great as to preclude the possibility of secondary oral tradition. Despite the allusion to *Hallfreðar saga* the complete elimination of Hallfreðr and Gríss from the episode and the entirely different upshot of the story indicate that *Vatnsdœla saga* cannot be very directly dependent on the account in *Hallfreðar saga*. All that can be said is that both sagas tell the same story.

The variants are perhaps instructive in an oblique way. If the reference to *Hallfreðar saga* is not a later interpolation and really stems from the author, then the author knew *Hallfreðar saga* (presumably in written form) and knew that it contained the account in which he was interested. Since he knew of the saga, he must have known where it could be found. Yet he did not feel impelled to look it up. He is therefore not trammeled by a written tradition; he must be regarded as a storyteller and not as a compiler. His variant provides further evidence of labile tradition, curiously coupled with a firm trust in his own knowledge of it.

I conclude that the above variants of both categories afford no basis for the old doctrine of fixed oral form. On the contrary, they show that the traditions were subject to extensive and probably rapid mutations. Nonetheless they do support Liestøl's contention that the tradition was scenically fully developed. They show that a saga writer was not bound by the written word; he did not have to compose by compiling written sources. Had he done so, the last three sets of variants would show far greater affinities. He composed rather from his stock of lore and recollections. Even if the details were fluid, the tradition was narratively firm, that is to say, the gist of the story was constant.

Select Bibliography

Bååth, A.U., *Studier öfver Kompositionen i Några Isländska Ätt-sagor*, Lund, 1885.

Baetke, Walter, "Über die Entstehung der Isländersagas," *Berichte über die Verhandl. der Sächs. Akademie der Wiss. zu Leipzig, Philol.-Hist. Klasse, 102*, Part v (1956), 1–108.

Beyschlag, Siegfried, "Erzählform der Isländersaga," *Wirkendes Wort, 1* (1950–51), 223–29.

——, "Konungasögur," *Bibliotheca Arnamagnæana, 8*, Hafniæ, 1950.

——, "Möglichkeiten Mündlicher Überlieferung in der Königssaga," *Arkiv för Nordisk Filologi, 68* (1953), 109–39.

Bugge, Alexander, "Die Entstehung der Isländischen Saga," *ZfDA, 51* (1909), 23–38.

Bugge, Sophus, *Norsk Sagaskrivning og Sagafortælling i Irland*, Kristiania, 1908.

Einarsson, Bjarni, *Skáldasögur*, Reykjavík, 1961.

Gödel, Vilhelm, *Fornnorsk-Isländsk Litteratur i Sverige*, Stockholm, 1897.

Guðmundsson, Barði, *Höfundur Njálu*, Reykjavík, 1958.

Hallberg, Peter, *Den Isländska Sagan*, Stockholm, 1956; Eng. trans. Paul Schach, *The Icelandic Saga*, Lincoln, Nebraska, 1962.

——, "Njálas Författare och Hans Samtid," *Nordisk Tidskrift, 35* (1959), 524–35.

——, "Nyare Studier i den Isländska Sagan," *Edda, 53* (1953), 219–47.

Hamre, Håkon, "Moderne Islandsk Sagagranskning," *Syn og Segn, 50* (1944), 97–106.

Heinzel, Richard, "Beschreibung der Isländischen Saga," *Sitzungs-berichte der K. Akademie der Wiss. Wien, Phil.-Hist. Classe, 97,* Part i (1880), 1–204.

Helgason, Jón, *Norrøn Litteraturhistorie,* København, 1934.

Heller, Rolf, "Die Literarische Darstellung der Frau in den Isländer-sagas," *Saga, 2* (1958).

Heusler, Andreas, *Die Altgermanische Dichtung,* 2d ed., Potsdam, 1945.

——, "Die Anfänge der Isländischen Saga," *Abhandlungen der K. Preuss. Akad. d. Wiss., Phil.-Hist. Classe* (1913), 1–87.

——, *Das Strafrecht der Isländersagas,* Leipzig, 1911.

——, "Zum Isländischen Fehdewesen in der Sturlungazeit," *Abhand-lungen der K. Preuss. Akad. d. Wiss., Phil.-Hist. Classe* (1912), 1–102.

Hofmann, Dietrich, "Die Mündliche Vorstufe der Altnordischen Prosaerzählkunst," *Annales Universitatis Saraviensis, 10* (1961), 163–78.

Holtsmark, Anne, "Det Nye Syn på Sagaene," *Nordisk Tidskrift, 35* (1959), 511–23.

Íslenzk Fornrit, various editors, 16 vols. Reykjavík, 1933–.

Jóhannesson, Jón, *Gerðir Landnámabókar,* Reykjavík, 1941.

Jónsson, Finnur, "Norsk-Islandske Kultur- og Sprogforhold i 9. og 10. Århundrede," *D. Kgl. Danske Vidensk. Selsk. Hist. og Fil. Medde-lelser, 3,* Part ii (1921).

——, *Den Oldnorske og Oldislandske Litteraturs Historie,* 1st ed. 3 vols. København, 1894–1902; 2d ed. 3 vols. København, 1920–24.

——, *Udsigt over den Norsk-Islandske Filologis Historie,* Køben-havn, 1918.

Ker, William Paton, *Epic and Romance,* London, 1896. Paperback, New York, 1957.

Kersbergen, Anna, *Litteraire Motieven in de Njála,* Rotterdam, 1927.

Koht, Halvdan, *The Old Norse Sagas,* New York, 1931.

Lehmann, Karl, and Hans Schnorr von Carolsfeld, *Die Njálssage Insbesondere in Ihren Juristischen Bestandtheilen,* Berlin, 1883.

Lie, Hallvard, "Noen Metodologiske Overveielser i Anl. av et Bind av Islenzk Fornrit," *Maal og Minne* (1939), 97–138.

Liestøl, Knut, "Tradisjon og Forfattar i den Islendske Ættesaga," *Maal og Minne* (1936), 1–16.

——, "Tradisjonen i Hrafnkels saga Freysgoða," *Arv, 2* (1946), 94–110.

——, *Upphavet til den Islendske Ættesaga*, Oslo, 1929; Eng. trans. *The Origin of the Icelandic Family Sagas*, Oslo, 1930.

Maurer, Konrad, "Ueber die Hœnsa-Þóris Saga," *K. Bayer. Akad. d. Wiss., München, Philos.-Philol. Classe, Abhandl., 12*, Part ii (1871), 157–216.

Meissner, Rudolf, *Die Strengleikar*, Halle, 1902.

Müller, Peter E., *Ueber den Ursprung und Verfall der Isländischen Historiographie*, Kopenhagen, 1813.

Nordal, Sigurður, *The Historical Element in the Icelandic Family Sagas*, Glasgow, 1957.

——, "Hrafnkatla," *Studia Islandica, 7* (1940); Eng. trans. R. G. Thomas, *Hrafnkels Saga Freysgoða*, Cardiff, 1958.

——, "Sagalitteraturen," *Nordisk Kultur, 8*, Part B (1953), 180–273.

——, *Snorri Sturluson*, Reykjavík, 1920.

Ólsen, Björn M., "Om Gunnlaugs Saga Ormstungu," *D. Kgl. Danske Vidensk. Selsk. Skrifter, 7.R., Hist. og Fil. Afd., 2*, Part i (1911), 1–54.

——, "Um Íslendingasögur," *Safn til Sögu Íslands, 6*, Parts v–vii (1937–39), 1–427.

Olson, Emil, "Den Isländska Sagans Ursprung," *Nordisk Tidskrift* (1918), pp. 411–29.

Paasche, Fredrik, *Norges og Islands Litteratur indtil Utgangen av Middelalderen*, Kristiania, 1924 (2d ed. 1957).

Scovazzi, Marco, *La Saga di Hrafnkell e il Problema delle Saghe Islandesi*, n.p., 1960.

Sveinsson, Einar Ó., *Sturlungaöld. Drög um Íslenzka Menningu á Þrettándu Öld*, Reykjavík, 1940; Eng. trans. Jóhann S. Hannesson, *The Age of the Sturlungs. Icelandic Civilization in the Thirteenth Century*, Ithaca, 1953 (*Islandica, 36*).

——, *Dating the Icelandic Sagas*, London, 1958.

——, "The Icelandic Family Sagas and the Period in Which Their Authors Lived," *Acta Philologica Scandinavica, 12* (1937–38), 71–90.

——, "Les Sagas Islandaises," *Archives des Lettres Modernes, 36* (1961).

——, *Um Njálu*, Reykjavík, 1933.

Thomas, R. George, "Studia Islandica," *Modern Language Quarterly, 11* (1950), 281–97, 391–403.

Turville-Petre, Gabriel, *Origins of Icelandic Literature*, Oxford, 1953.

Vogt, Walter H., "Frásagnir der Landnámabók," *ZfDA, 58* (1920), 161–204.

Vries, Jan de, *Altnordische Literaturgeschichte*. 2 vols. Berlin, 1941–42.

Walter, Ernst, "Studien zur Vápnfirðinga Saga," *Saga, 1* (1956).

Index

The index is intended chiefly as a guide to the secondary literature. The italicized numbers after each author refer to the first full citation of a work by that author. In this way the italicized page references comprise a complete bibliography of the works cited, excluding only the introductions to the *Fornrit* volumes. Icelandic words beginning with letters not in the English alphabet are indexed following Z.